WORLDS APART

Race in the Modern Period

O. R. Dathorne

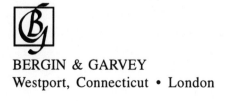

BERGIN & GARVEY
Westport, Connecticut • London

Library
University of Texas
at San Antonio

Library of Congress Cataloging-in-Publication Data

Dathorne, O. R., 1934–
    Worlds apart : race in the modern period / O. R. Dathorne.
      p. cm.
    Includes bibliographical references and index.
    ISBN 0–89789–722–6 (alk. paper)
    1. Race in literature.   2. Blacks in literature.   3. Literature, Modern—History and criticism. I. Title.
    PN56.R16D38   2001
    813′.54093520396—dc21   00–041447

British Library Cataloguing in Publication Data is available.

Library of Congress Catalog Card Number: 00–041447
ISBN: 0–89789–722–6

First published in 2001

Bergin & Garvey, 88 Post Road West, Westport, CT 06881
An imprint of Greenwood Publishing Group, Inc.
www.greenwood.com

Printed in the United States of America

The paper used in this book complies with the Permanent Paper Standard issued by the National Information Standards Organization (Z39.48–1984).

10 9 8 7 6 5 4 3 2 1

For
Hilde Ostermaier Dathorne

Contents

Introduction

This study is an attempt at exploring the extent to which textuality—the actual compilation of a text in the West—is a way of owning and naming alien lands and places, peoples and property. I want to argue from the onset that written signifiers of the earlier "travelers" to the East, of "explorers" to Africa like Vasco de Gama, and of "discovers" like Christopher Columbus and Amerigo Vespucci authenticated and validated people and territory for the West. And I am suggesting that only in this way was the West able to establish a hegemony that was willingly accepted even by people who lived on the margins of the Western world, and who themselves became firm believers in these predispositionings of the West, its beliefs, fears, contentions, even its skewered views of the selfsame others.

My first chapter is a way of flipping the argument around. I try to look at the signs of these very "others," specifically the three Nobel laureates, Toni Morrison, Wole Soyinka, and Derek Walcott, and I ask a basic question—what makes them similar? Perhaps any likeness is merely an essentialist delusion shared by the Nobel Committee and Minority Studies departments. Or perhaps there is a degree of verisimilitude derived from the orality of an African culture they all share. Therefore, in the first chapter I examine two motifs that run through Morrison's work, the African in flight (running away and flying away), and the reborn person in *Beloved* also celebrated as an *abiku* by Soyinka. I also discuss how Walcott attempts to compose an "english," arguing that this is a Caribbean language. Hence, even in their very "orality," these three writers are products of the West.

Hopefully, I demonstrate that whether the writer wants it or not, orality will stick out like the provisional sore thumb. It becomes important to balance the oral signs of those who are the colonized-in-the-making with the verbal images of the colonizer. In chapter 2, I contend, despite Jacques Derrida to the contrary, it is actually the written symbol that acquires prestige, for no reason other than that the powerful purveyor of the written attaches supreme importance to script, indeed soon begins to classify otherness in terms of "pre-literate," "illiterate," and "literate." Interestingly, as Homi Bhabha asserts elsewhere, it is as the legendary inventor of the "Book" that the West is even able to claim an originary monopolilization of religion itself.

In a way, what occurs is that the speech act is downgraded and the writing act upgraded, so that since "truth" may only exist between the leaves of a Western book, then this is indeed what the "educated" other will learn, accept, and cherish. Colonialism needs, therefore, few muskets; the twirl of a baton and the fanfare of the flag will be enough to convince willing populaces that they are unredeemably apart from, and yet part of, the Center.

In chapter 3, I attempt to show the origins of a physical presence in early modern Britain, with Queen Elizabeth's clarion call expelling Blackamoors, even as their images were retained on the London stage as little more than beasts of burden. Seemingly then both the Elizabethan and Jacobean center of power, the palace itself, were quite content to make do with make-believe Blacks constructed in their own image. Such images were partly derived from travelers' tales.[1] Indeed Anthony Gerard Barthelemy is most concerned with demonstrating the role of the English who blacked up to play Moors, so that the racial construct could be anything that the English imagined.

I show that long before Blacks enter English consciousness in a capacity, for instance, as servants who decorate the portraits of ladies of fashion, as Kim F. Hall so ably demonstrates. Black men and women were constructed in the English imagination as their polar opposites. Interestingly, this was at a time when the language itself was being formed, so no wonder a word like "fair" passed through various associations connected with color, aesthetic approval, and race: Fair was good; black was bad. I spend some time on Ben Jonson showing how the *Masque of Blackness*, like his other plays concerned with working-class women, depict not mere trivia to entertain the court, but well learned lessons in avoiding the unfortunate coloration of the "Ethiope" at all costs. Indeed, Queen Anne of Denmark, James's wife, was frowned upon for daring to play a Blackamoor, and for the high jinks of blacking up as well as other infringements. Lady Mary Wroth was dispatched posthaste from the palace. I therefore do not contend, as so many others do, that the Jacobean period was a merry time of unbridled diversity. The British people all lived then, as they still do now, in a tiny kingdom, and knew very little of the world beyond. What was a little unusual with James I was that he was bisexual, and that he had come from Scotland and his bride from Denmark. There the "difference" ends.

Black people, however, do not begin in English culture only as exotic

Blackamoors. They are also "Noble Savages," and as such confused with both Indians from India and "Indians" from the Americas. Edmund Spenser is heavily indebted to two ur-texts in Italian, Matteomaria Boiardo's *Innamorato* (1487) and Ludovico Ariosto's *Orlando Furioso* (1532).[2] In both cases we see the manner in which a very human world interacts almost on terms of equality. Of course the king of Tartary or king of the Moors in the former instance, and the king of Africa in the latter will lose out in war, much as they lose in love, but at least there is the illusion of an equal playing field. In Spenser's case, the fifth of the sixth books of the poem rails against Spaniards and French, and the Catholicism of Mary Queen of Scots. The ultimate other is manufactured in the recalcitrant Irish, who for some reason, did not take too kindly to British control. The direct British archetype of the Noble Savage is actually Aphra Behn's *Oroonoko* (circa 1688), not the later Jean-Jacques Rousseau. There the confusion is much evident among the Indian from India, the New World Indian, and the African, both in the Old and New World. In chapter 4, it seemed important to discuss who and what this "Indian" construct meant, if only because Native Americans were put upon as harshly as the Africans, and in the New World space formed both an alliance and an animosity.

However, the world is European-made, as I try to show in chapter 5. And the most basic and obvious application of Gayatri Chakravorty Spivak's "worlding" is to be found in the Enlightenment sciences that named all flora and fauna, as Carl Linnaeus and his disciples designated, and further proceeded to invent a thing called "race" that could be suitably appended to the old pseudo-theological Chain of Being and the new pseudoscientific Tree of Life. Whatever the theory, so long as it was not invented by the other, it carried with it the old allusions of negativity, the "floating signifiers" that Stuart Hall has spoken about, and which meant that something such as "race"could have no real, fixed meaning.

Eurocentrism was bogged down in a narrow Christian perspective; hence, as I mention, Bartolomé de Las Casas and Juan Ginés de Sepúlveda were certainly not "enlightened" even by the standards of their time. The famous debate in Valladolid, Spain, in 1550 concerned itself with whether Native Americans were humans or beasts, and the extent to which their enslavement could be justified. If the Native Americans were not of a lower order, then the Africans certainly were; thus, in a way, the rhetoric of Valladolid justified the African slave trade.

I begin to show in chapter 5 how the kidnapping and circus parades of Native Americans and Africans begin a cultural misunderstanding. Albrecht Dürer, for instance, does exult over what he sees, but seriously mistranslates Aztec ornamentation into familiar European objects. Indeed, after a while the odder human Others are themselves objectified, put on exhibition and displayed as curiosities. At the height of the

Enlightenment, James Cook and William Dampier bear back human specimens as souvenirs from the South Seas. The sexual organs of the South African San woman, Saartjie Bartmann, become an object of great curiosity.

Interaction between an All-Knowing One and a Non-knowing Other had many serious implications. The most important was the invention of what Spivak addresses as the Native Informant, much beloved by participant anthropologists, sociologists, and all of the field researchers in academe who sought to give an element of verisimilitude to their conclusions. The Native Informant was indigenous and thus held to be knowledgeable, but such knowledge could not be transposed to a reading public in the West without the active intervention of what I shall term the Alien Expert. The main reason for this I allege is that the Native Informant possessed only a "half-sign"—perhaps a mental concept that had not been written, perhaps a written sign that bore no relevance to the mental idea.

From here I deal with three chapters on Africa proper, where apart from restricted signs such as those used in Vai, Nsibidi, and Bamum, the signification for textmaking is borrowed from European and Arabic signifiers. I begin chapter 6 with how Africa is invented, imagined, and romanticized, and how Africans grafted themselves on to the implanted constructs of who and what they supposedly were. Therefore, whether we lived in Africa proper or in the African diaspora, it was extremely difficult to form any picture of the real, erased as it had been, but still left with "traces" of what the inscribing "worlding" master narrative of the West had designed.

In the same way that the continent of Africa is imagined (I usually suggest somewhat like a small village), the diaspora is also conjured up as a small, happy family directly related to the continent. Therefore, the chapter I have termed "inventing Diaspora" is just that—borrowing a word usually used for another ethnic group, and applying it to a different variety of people who live in the New World, speak different European languages and Creoles, and come from assorted African tribal groups. I argue that there are pockets of cultural presence, despite the nature of the master text and the colonial stricture. Up to the present, for instance, in Venezuela (Barlovento), Cuba (Santiago de Cuba), Brazil (Salvador de Bahia), and Haiti, as well as places of resistance in the Caribbean, Africa exists, but in a somewhat altered form, syncretized with Europe.

In chapter 8, I did not want to merely describe the presence and activities of Afro-Europeans, especially well-known intellectuals who lived in Spain, Holland, England, and what is now the United States and now Germany. I wanted to show that they were very Europeanized, and had loyal feelings for their countries of adoption. I should stress that "experiments" in the civilizing process were no more praiseworthy when undertaken by the Duke of Montagu or some other royal personage. Indeed the results were disastrous, as many of the new arrivals seemed to have been considered on the level of the horse and other personal possessions, if we are to judge from contemporary portraits. Indeed, in viewing these people, there is an invisibility about them, as their dark figures contrast with milady's whiteness, and as they blend with the background scenery they become almost insubstantial.

With chapter 9, I use Gilles Deleuze and Félix Guattari to show their preference of their model of the rhizome rather than the tree. They assert that the nomad rather than the settler is a preferred lifestyle, not in the way it is sometimes falsely interpreted as a clarion call for wanderlust. Instead, they seek new ways of getting rid of the troublesome hierarchy that is at the center of Western thought. Particularly, they were concerned with showing that the so-called "Oedipus complex" should certainly not be restricted to the family. Therefore, because Deleuze and Guattari include a denunciation of the entire (capitalist) world, the issue of race with which I am concerned is omitted perforce. Indeed, they note an element of both racism and incestuousness about the proximity of the main players in the Oedipal legend.

I conclude by arguing that it is a little difficult to separate gender from race from class. As Spivak pointed out, this is the main reason why no one can defend this construct called the "subaltern," since it is/may well be woman, lower caste, perhaps even non-Indo European (if "race" exists). In part, I use the England of Shakespeare, Charles Dickens and Joseph Conrad because it is a society that I know well, and I pinpoint Hannah Cullwick, a Victorian maid of all work, as an interesting example of a woman who was prepared to dress as a man, a gentleman, or an upper-class lady, and blacken her face with soot in order to please the man she dubbed "Massa," Arthur Munby.

Through these chapters I have attempted to show that the people who purport to represent race, gender, and class are indeed "worlds apart," and that race was "invented" quite early in the Modern period, irrespective of the fact that there were few people who lived in England who could be dubbed "blackamoors" or "negars" (the words of Queen Elizabeth I). This is a particularly intriguing thought since the negative attitude marked the English language from its inception, and passed it on, warts and all, for us natives to mimic.

NOTES

1. Alden T. Vaughan and Virginia Mason Vaughan, "Before *Othello*: Elizabethan Representations of Sub-Saharan Africans," *The William and Mary Quarterly* 3d ser. 54.1 (Jan. 1997): 19; and Anthony Gerard Barthelemy, *Black Face Maligned Race: The Representation of Blacks in English Drama* (Baton Rouge: Louisiana State UP, 1987) 182 ff.

2. I am thinking here specifically about Edmund Spenser's *The Fairie Queene* [1590 and 1596] (New Haven: Yale UP, 1981). See also the following: Matteomaria Boiardo, *Orlando Enammorato* (1487), and Ludovico Ariosto, *Orlando Furioso* (1532), particularly as treated in Peter V. Marinelli, *Ariosto and Boiardo: The Origins of Orlando Furioso* (Columbia: U of Missouri P, 1987).

Chapter 1

The "Trace" of Orality

We had to wait until the nineteenth century before we began to understand the nature of exploitation, and to this day, we have yet to fully comprehend the nature of power. (Michel Foucault, *Language, Counter-Memory, Practice* [1977], 213)

... think of how these [Black] cultures have used the body—as if it was, and it often was, the only cultural capital we had. We have worked on ourselves as the canvases of representation. (David Morley and Kuan-Hsing Chen, eds., *Stuart Hall: Critical Dialogues* [1996], 470)

Traditions, if they are traditions, cannot be invented, for they are not arbitrarily created, referring, as they do, to practices actually lived, or ideas and beliefs known to have been actually held, for long time. (Kwame Gyekye, *Tradition and Modernity: Philosophical Reflections on the African Experience* [1997], 232)

Kwanzaa ... was created in 1966 by Maulana Karenga. . . .(*Jet*, Vol 92. 20 [Nov. 17, 1997], 6)

Textuality does not merely relate conditions of coloniality and postcoloniality, but may very often be seen as dictating them. The text then does not merely inform, I will contend, but it actually deforms, forms, and reforms. The process by which this occurs may well be one in which the metropolitan center inscribes its dictates on the land, its people and their customs, and in the process of textualizing them, reduces them to concepts that are made more easily understood at "home," far from the complications of the margin.

One ought not to be be too overconcerned by this, seeking to label it, and, additionally, either to attack or to explain it. The construction of people and place abroad for home consumption goes both ways. Certainly power may have the authority of naming the sound image in the signification game, but the very real signified is no mere agreed and essentialized mental conjuration, common to both the mindset and the set minds of colonizer and colonized. Often, very different concepts are implied by both, not merely in the words and pictures and the signs of the signifier, but also in the initial signified that lies dormant within the deep recesses of indigenous societal belief and norm.

IDEA OF THE TEXT

We could begin first by looking at the idea of the text, not the piece of work published in Paris and London, but the unformed idea of what it is and what it represents. First and foremost, within the similar societies of sub-Saharan Africa. In India and the Caribbean (where the former two come together), the production of a text carried enormous prestige. It was not merely intended to be an exercise in being clever, but instead a demonstration, real and concrete, that (a) the colonized had mastered what had been imbibed and (b) was now ready to take on the colonizer in the language of the colonizer, using the tools and the equipment of the colonizer. It goes without saying that farmers and laborers, the sweaty, tramping/trampling masses of the proletariat, do not compose poetry, write novels, and paint pictures. What we do find in the three areas I am discussing—Africa, India, and the Caribbean—is that the so-called "subaltern"[1] is the resource and speaker for the many oral occasions that require speech, dance, and music. And this performer is not a Johnny-come-lately who awakens one day, suitably inspired, and composes a dirge. Needless to stress, the entire corpus has been passed down from ancestral times.

"Orators" and "writers" have to agree on specific commonalities or there can be no communication. Without orality, there is no indigenous speech or custom, no creolity, no dirge, no praise poem, no *obeah*, *santería, vodún*. Without the sound of the voice, and the gesture of the body bearing witness to what it has learnt over a period of time, there is no orality, because none of this was seen with the aestheticism that the indigenous been-tos (so called ironically because they had *been to* Europe) vouchsafed to give it. But without this academic blessing, I suspect that the world of what W.E.B. Du Bois and his friends[2] used to term the "folk negro" would have still survived for one major reason—namely, it was needed to act, perform, take part in the business of living and dying, being born and becoming ill, being initiated and marrying. So the scholars did not have to bless this material; it was there, whole and in demand; it was always being called upon to remedy or rectify, so it self-prolonged itself.

Obviously, the "writerly" (in Henry Louis Gates's not in Roland Barthes's sense) is different. The non-oral writerly is the way in which a certain preciosity takes the place of a former prescience. The writerly engages the individual not the group in an unusual tongue, for no actual event. Within the context of orality, one called upon the dirge singer at moments of death, and even New World people like ourselves, realizing that we had forgotten the African and Indian languages and the airs, made up new dirges to accompany us during the weary/wary hours of our wakes; made up from simple songs the sound of the *que-que* to describe the fun of two young people getting married. Granted then that there is a certain appropriation by a New World individual (Indian and African) who does not perhaps see as acute the need to have the Old World labor division. But I will stress this: The art is still functional, necessary, and dictated by occasion.

With the push toward literacy (equated with civilizing us), we first began to unlearn, and then later to despise our orality. But there was the catch that, when we finally began to write, we reproduced the heard sounds of the nation's childhood, since most of us sought to free ourselves from the very encumbrances that had made us into creators of the writerly, and ignorers of the heard "readerly," what Gates calls the "talking book." In a way, therefore, so-called creativity in Third World peripheries has meant a rupture with the past, a complete break with what art was expected, indeed demanded, to do, and how it was required to act out its essential and basic significance. Now Art (capitalized) was owned and commodified, and became the expression of educated?/Westernized people, showing how they saw the world.

Pretending that it was different scarcely mattered, since all we could reasonably be certain of was that a certain decentering was taking place, which was reappropriating responsibility, indeed creating a new author (ity) in the space left vacant by the imposition of Western custom, law and culture. Additionally, there were tangible gains to be had from the proper acquisition of Western values, among them the certainty of employment within the new economy, and the likelihood of a place in the new hierarchy established by the new colonial order. And the order was worldwide, so that skills learned in Senegal or Bombay or Guyana could be transferred to the associated metropolitan capitals for profit and gain. Thus it made sense to embrace the new system, since it was "universal"—it said as much—and since it worked. The old way of life, with its emphasis on a perishable orality was bound to go, because the old people (the current wisdom went) would die out and, in the absence of written signs to extend cultural longevity, the people would perish. No one bothered to acquaint the seers with the dire straits of their predicament, so they kept up their amiable chat and loquacious babbling.

TALKING WRITERS/TALKING TEXTS

Orality is at the basis of the reappropriation of roles performed by
Wole Soyinka, Toni Morrison, and Derek Walcott. I name them for the
very obvious reason that a Western-approved canonicity implicit in the
award of the Nobel Prize has conferred on each presumably something
that the West recognizes, and yet not quite. So that even though they
write in English, they (a) describe a non-Western situation and (b) relate
it in an un-Western language ("english,"[3] according to Bill Ashcroft, Gareth Griffiths, and Helen Tiffin in *The Empire Writes Back* [1989]) while (c)
reaching back to the inarticulate "folk" to retrieve their "prattle"—rather
like Brendan Behan who, on his nightly pub-crawls, kept his ear literally
to the floor of the pub to detect authentic Irish sounds.

To go back for a moment to the severance, what I called the rupture,
this much is evident quite early in all of the writers mentioned. Now I do
not want to conflate the writing with the writer, but I will add that in all
our cases we are dealing with very Westernized individuals, who choose
to go to university—Wole Soyinka to Leeds, Toni Morrison to Howard,
and Derek Walcott to the University of the West Indies at Mona. Soyinka
became a university teacher; Morrison worked for Random House; and
Walcott, having opted not to take his Diploma in Education by stalking
out of the examination room, went back to Trinidad, where (with
Government help) he ran workshops. Of course, it says much about the
hegemonic claims of academy that they all, today, despite their Nobel
Prize wealth, have drifted back to the "teaching machine,"[4] because it
carries its own peculiar sort of authority and prestige. Additionally, it
doesn't hurt that academia pays you to talk.

Frantz Fanon readily recognized and castigated this "education" away
from local sources, commenting quite critically that:

The native intellectual who comes back to his people by way of cultural
achievements behaves in fact like a foreigner. Sometimes he has no hesitation in
using a dialect in order to show his will to be as near as possible to the people;
but the ideas that he expresses and the preoccupations he is taken up with have
no common yardstick to measure the real situation which the men and the
women of his country know. The culture that the intellectual leans towards is
often no more than a stock of particularisms. He wishes to attach himself to the
people; but instead he only catches hold of their outer garments.[5]

In other words the subaltern/folk Negro recognizes not only that the
emperor is naked, but that, in all likelihood, he cannot really aid them.
Actually, it was particularly honest of Fanon to admit to this, since he
must have seen aspects of himself—condemned to fight another man's
war in Algeria—on a permanent exile from Martinique. Perhaps it is this
fear of their nakedness that keeps the Third World intellectuals forever at
the edges of a still another periphery, never venturing back to their own

community for too long periods, since someone might reveal their nakedness. Two ready examples come to mind: like Fanon in Algeria, Walter Rodney in Tanzania, and Sylvester Williams in Ghana, among others, could much more easily act out the revolution. Even CLR James was relatively content to theorize from London and later Washington, after Eric Williams made his own displeasure very clear to James.

Having said that Soyinka, Morrison, and Walcott have much in common, let us note that they are miles apart from any one political line of thinking. Soyinka is more conservative than is at first apparent, in that he has chosen his battles carefully. Usually they have tended to deal with homefront issues of Nigerian democracy or lack thereof. Morrison has positioned herself very nicely as a kind of arch-Sphinx, forever given to articulation in riddles, a kind of cultural guru on a grand global scale. And Walcott spent half a lifetime inventing a persona of a man divided between Europe and the Caribbean—a peculiar posture, since nobody from where we both come ever harbors these delusions. Soyinka and Morrison remained constant. Walcott tried to go radical in *Midsummer* (1993)—a madness that did not succeed however satisfactory the meetings with Joseph Brodski. He ain't no Brodski, and St. Lucia is neither Eastern Europe nor Greece, which is something one of his admirers must tell him one day, before we both pass away.[6]

SOYINKA, NGUGI, AND WESTERN SCHOOLING

In one of Soyinka's early plays, "The Lion and the Jewel," the core of the issue of orality is apparent. The village schoolmaster, Lakunle, rivalled by the elderly traditional chief, Baroka, is courting Sidi. We are not left too long in doubt about who will win Sidi's hands, particularly after the schoolmaster, with his smattering of, but nevertheless zeal for, Western education roundly berates the "savage custom, barbaric, out-dated" of brideprice. Then Soyinka the dramatist writes:

Sidi: Is the bag empty? Why did you stop?
Lakunle: I own only the Shorter Companion
             Dictionary, but I have ordered
             The Longer One—you wait![7]

The main point is that these can be neither Sidi's words nor Lakunle's response. First, people don't speak like that to each other—there must be the assumption that there is a third set of ears listening for certain nuances. Second, presumably this type of conversation would have taken place in Yoruba, and so the Western references, indeed the schoolmaster himself, would have all been rather ridiculous. Third, Sidi herself would have been part of the colonial endeavor and would have shown a great deal of respect for the schoolmaster and his longwindedness. Even at that pre-1960s time period, before coups reduced the "big man" to jail fodder, she would have had little or no regard for the chief, since he had merely sought her as an addition to his compound of wives. What then is happening here?

Beneath the satire of the text is the nostalgia of the been-to, the longing for nativeness, the very concept Soyinka had decried as the self-serving romanticism of Léopold Sédar Senghor's *négritude*. But this is exactly what is occurring—the tiger is proclaiming its tigritude—the chief is asserting the superiority of his traditionality by having the audience at the play—solid, professional classes who first saw it at Mbari Club in Ibadan—ostensibly laugh at themselves, and support the oral and the traditional. However, all of this was a mere reaction from the earlier writers, who in Africa, the Caribbean, and India had sided the other way. Previously, the chief would have been seen as ignorant, sorely lacking in charm, and undeserving of Sidi. Now Soyinka, like many other writers, was inverting the process.

Note that I am neither suggesting that this was necessarily good or bad, nor intimating in any way that Soyinka invented the process. I am only contending that, if anything, this was the same sharp reflex that dictated the much-maligned *négritude* poets to turn away from praise of the West to adoration of the mosque and the marketplace; intoning, in an elegant French, written from the center, just how aesthetically purifying native life could be. For Soyinka and a host of other writers in Africa, the Caribbean, and the Third World, like the *négritude* threesome, it was also a way of advancing a degree of self-significance.

The old Longmans *West Indian Readers* culled by one Captain J. O. Cutteridge had inscribed in one of its six volumes these immortal lines, if I correctly recall from memory: "My father is a blacksmith. When I grow older I wish to be a carpenter." Note the total lack of ambition that Cutteridge ascribed to his young English-speaking charges. The same, by the way, should be said for the West African school series, edited by D. W. Grieve, with which Nelson, the British publisher, flooded the West African school market. These were the mirrors into which we were told to look to find out about who we truly were, as we made our way to everlasting fame and fortune within the circumscribed parameters of the British Empire.[8]

Such a colonial education makes Ngugi wa Thiong'o particularly agitated. Its language was an intentional attempt to silence him, deprive him of his own language, and reward him for speaking in another. As he puts it:

The attitude to English was the exact opposite: any achievement in spoken or written English was highly rewarded; prizes, prestige, applause; the ticket to higher realms. English became *the* measure of intelligence and ability in the arts, the sciences, and all the other branches of learning. English became the main determinant of a child's progress up the ladder of formal education. . . . Literary education was now determined by the dominant language while also reinforcing that dominance. Orature (oral literature) in Kenyan languages stopped. . . . Thus language and literature were taking us further and further from ourselves to other selves, from our world to other worlds.[9]

Ngugi is categorically contending that this was no idle power ploy but one designed to rob the next generation of its speech, its orality, its accustomed customs.[10] Thus African, Indian, and Caribbean children would share the same predicament. Remodelled in the Name of the White Father, they could do little to lay claim to the indigenous matrilineality of their societies. Homi Bhabha makes the equally telling point of the Bible in English being pedalled by missionaries in India as God's word.[11]

In general then, for Soyinka and Walcott, this was what colonialism meant. While proffering the West, it denied you yourself, asserting categorically not only that there was something wrong with you and your country and its vegetation and its people, but also that the only possibility of cure was instant migration. Hence the so-called nomad, actually the vagrant, is not at all a romantic figure, but one caught up in the delusion of the perfection of the center as Utopia, and whose life has been a quest for it. And if most of us ended up in the United States, or reverted to becoming Atlanticists of the eighteenth century, always and forever coming or going over vast stretches of water but never arriving, it is sad but true that we were educated away from any basic, even simplistic, understanding of an indigenous "home."

BRATHWAITE'S NOMADISM: THE ACQUISITION OF ORALITY

The problem of so-called nomadism impacts directly on the writer.[12] Edward Brathwaite has pointed out that:

The problem of and for West Indian artists and intellectuals is that having been born and educated within this fragmented culture, they start out in the   world without a sense of "wholeness." Identification with any one of these orientations can only consolidate the concept of a plural society, a plural vision. Disillusionment with the fragmentation leads to a sense of rootlessness. The ideal does not and cannot correspond to inherited reality. The result: disassociation of the sensibility.[13]

This is partly true, yet more than a little ironical for Brathwaite to make this remark, as he himself realized. He too had sought fame and fortune abroad, at first spending several years of his life teaching in Ghana, then on to the mother country. He deals with this at some length later on in his essay "Timeheri" where he described himself as "rootless." But the overall suggestion, quite counter to Walcott, is a little like a confessional. After Ghana he found hope—he put on Rasta gear and went back to the University of the West Indies in Jamaica, where the nomad has been for the last twenty years or so.

The poetry he wrote then, some of which seeped into his earlier published material, is directly from J. H. Kwabena Nketia's translations of Akan dirges—nothing very Barbadian about this. Particularly relevant is the whole of the "Tano" series of poems in Part VI, "Arrival," the last section of *Masks*. The curious should also contrast this with Kofi Awoonor (the Ghanaian poet then known as George Awoonor-Williams and "ward" of the late Neville Dawes) and the relevant sections in Nketia's *Funeral Dirges of the Akan People* (1955) and his later, more publicized, *Folksongs of Ghana* (1963). Brathwaite mentions Nketia's work in *Roots*, a book of essays published in 1986.[14]

I want to go back to the idea of the pretend-nomad. At a later stage, when Brathwaite did start publishing his poetry, he was, for all practical purposes, "exiled," that is living on a university sabbatical in London with his family, and attempting to finish his doctorate. Yet today Brathwaite would (beard, garb and all) consider himself pretty close to the roots of Jamaican Rastafari. But he is certainly not the homebody suggested in the piece I quoted, and more than likely still sees himself as the romanticized nomadic figure he calls half-mockingly "Old Tom" who asks in a poem, "Where then is the nigger's / home?,"[15] and flatly asserts in another poem the Wanderlust of the happy camper, or as Brathwaite puts it, this is the saga of a "path- / less harbour- / less spade."[16]

The oral language (Brathwaite would prefer "nation language") of derision and posturing must not lull us into an authentic swoon of compassion. Here the words are borrowed from Ghana, and the posture from the United Kingdom. There was even something a trifle "romantic" in the the natural outsiderness of the "spade"—after all Colin MacInnes had written *City of Spades* (1957) thus lending word and concept a degree of fuzzy warmth, and even Sam Selvon gave a brand of humorous currency to the word.[17] But what "poor old Tom" did not recognize in his ever-so-short lines was that London was on the brink of change; new people were moving in from the fringes of the empire, and if not radically changing it (as Homi Bhabha would assuredly later confirm) at least changing themselves in the process.

Let me say that I do realize how true this wandering was/is, even for the tribally bound, language-owning African, as it was for the tribeless, no-tongued New Worlder. We were all in the bind of never knowing our true home, and I stress it began with Cutteridge and Grieve, those Englishmen in faraway places at the center of power, who wrote mighty little books that fixed peculiar notions in our sorry little heads. They even challenged us with the upsidedown task of inventing the signified, once we had mastered the unconnected sound-image of the signifier. "Snow" readily springs to mind as something about which we were most eloquent, prepared by the hegemonic system, despite our 80 degrees Fahrenheit, to churn out reams on the subject for examination purposes. Fanon has truthfully commented on the equally unreal concept of children in Martinique having to invent stories about vacations they never took, like good French children, when school was not in session.[18]

URBAN ORALITY AND TONI MORRISON

I would contend that Toni Morrison's situation was no different from any other New World colonial. She is colonized in the very real sense of living in a country whose resources she neither owns nor controls, and also having inherited a logic that said all successful persons must leave home/the South/the ghetto/the "colonial" periphery and head for New York. This is the point at which we all meet, the extent of disingenuousness whereby we, with our precious degrees from the West, constantly battle against the West, putting forward tradition as an artificial foil to modernity, and showing how every time tradition wins.[19] It is a sad commentary and a serious lack of honesty about the Western world we all inhabit.[20] I met Toni Morrison in New York in 1969. She worked for Random House; Yale had invited me to give a lecture. Neither Random House nor Yale cared a great deal about her orality or mine.

Even as Soyinka, Brathwaite, Morrison and, to a greater extent, Walcott, were all wrapped up in this construct of a traditional and invented Africa, the thing changed on us all. The African continent never promised to be still, unmoving and stagnant, and in a way (as those stalwarts of nineteenth-century Black imperialism discovered[21]), "Africa" didn't guarantee that it would live up to our alien expectations. So what we all thought we knew—orality, tradition, the nostalgic past, and the village—suddenly got up one day and moved to town—in this case New York.[22]

Alessandro Triulzi recognized it in this way, writing about the new orality:

It was the pavements, the squares, the village neighbourhoods and the rundown fringes of the city that elaborated and transmitted this new form of orality that I shall term "urban" the word inscribed, drawn, on the walls of Mogadisho, the word spread by pavement radio in Kinshasa, the satirical word, traded like goods, in the market place of Lomé. This return of orality and its shift from the country to the city is one of the new signs of contemporary Africa and its strategies of identity. It is no longer the fixed, ennobled word of oral tradition, passed on by the *griots* and dynastic narrative-charters in the political power-centres of Africa, old and new. Rather, it is the living word, profane and multiform, of the new, urban generations of independent Africa.[23]

This is a newer, more dangerous orality that saw Nelson Mandela walk out of prison, and witnessed the fall of Mobutu. In a way, it was always there, but nascent in the barber shop signs, bus mottos, proverbial wisdom in the new street pidgins, and above all, in the sound of the West African highlife, Congolese *soukous*, and South African township music.[24] Orality had gotten a new voice, and indeed it was partly New World rhythms returning to the Congo and South Africa.

Curiously then, in a way, the orality that Morrison preserved in her work has a kind of quaint, antiquarian flavor. Let me give two examples: the trope of flying/flight in *Song of Solomon*, and the child returning-from-the-dead in *Beloved*. In the former instance, the idea of the flight back is intrinsic to African American, indeed New World mythologizing. But what makes it oral is that it was never treated as anything other than a desperate verbal, folk yearning for the return. Morrison would have heard this account as a youngster and as an adult,[25] but incorporating it into her novel was a way of denying flight while affirming freedom. Flight then, both flying away to the North, to Jesus, and so on, and flight in the sense of "escape" both became in *Song of Solomon* an extravagant way of reviving the African presence, as created myth, not as lived reality. Surely you will agree with me that Morrison is a bright woman—she won the Nobel Prize—and she knows that people of any complexion *do not fly*. She is incorporating a New World invention into the text. Note it is like Kwanzaa, homemade; it would hardly be necessary to flee from the African base.

The other instance in *Beloved* belongs much more closely and obviously to the African oral tradition. Beloved is the same *abiku* of whom J. P. Clark and Soyinka write in the poems of the same name.[26] In West Africa the term is used to explain infant mortality; Clark sees in it the possibility of prayer that would stem its purpose; Soyinka, on the other hand, accepts with a degree of fatalism, the irredeemable course of the *abiku* that must constantly and forever pass through the cycles of death and birth and death and birth, forever. This, let me stress, is not reincarnation, but a body (not just a spirit) caught up in the inevitability of its own fate.

Morrison of course creates a different grounding for Beloved, in that she provides the returning dead with a different, non-phantom space. In a way, she does not repeat our New World vulgarization by making Beloved part jumbie/jombie;[27] in another way, she does trivialize the undead, since orality is a mere base for her to blend the very modern idea of European homoeroticism and an African mother-daughter link. She is very much outside, observing the symbol of breastfeeding, a little like a voyeur from *National Geographic*, and yet still involved enough in the passionate relationship between the two, to lay claim to the blending of their bodies, and the unity of their thoughts. Very powerful sentences help construct this union, so that in reading, especially aloud, there is no one, no other, but both merging together in a rich univocality of desire and love.

I would be hard put to argue that, because I like this, it is in all ways authentic to an experience we can dub "African." I hope that I have shown that both in the case of the New World conceptualization of the flight away from here to there, and in the African re-creation of the ghost daughter, these aspects of textuality are more to do with learned experiences from orality, and individual, creative impulses, rather than some exotic version of racial osmosis. At the end, therefore, we don't have here an African, African American, or Caribbean version of orality, but an individual stamp on the material. This is not orality, but the molding of orality. This is not tradition, but the individual acquisitioning and utilizing of tradition.

I am being very careful to imply, but not argue that individuality is Western, and that it has come to be associated with the West, like capitalism, democracy, and military invasions. Indeed Peter Stallybrass has shown that the word and concept are relatively new to the thought and vocabulary of the English language, and lacking the signifier, I would argue that the signified was either absent or, at most, vague in early modern Britain. As Stallybrass puts it:

Perhaps the first point to note is the absence of the word "individual," even as meaning indivisible, until relatively late. Despite the variety of words in medieval Latin suggestive of "society" (*societas, communitas, corpus, universitas, multitudo, congregatio, collectio, coetus, collegium*), there was no word equivalent to "individual." The nearest term was probably *persona singularis* although this was pretty much a technical scholastic term. A person was *civis*, a member of the *civitas*, one was *fidelis*, a member of the church; one was not an individual.[28]

The European One/Self, of which so much has been made, is therefore found to be nonexistent as late as the early fifteenth century. Thus it seems quite reasonable to say that the other can be One/Self and individual, and above all, the writer need not be beckoned by any cause merely because he happens to be born within the confining limits of a colonial/postcolonial environment. I have to say all this before I roundly upbraid Walcott.

BADMOUTHING WALCOTT BADMOUTHING

This must be stated in Walcott's defence—for he needs defending and more defending. The problem is that I feel great concern about the condition of the man's mind, given all that he has written and said. If you, dear reader, are not a minority in the United States, it is difficult to explain to you how, indeed why, you feel a sense of responsibility for your brother's and sister's follies. There is the unconscious and inevitable twinge of embarrassment and pain when you see or read something painful, or see somebody looking like he's making an ass of himself in public. Some of my concerns are:

Item: The chief character in *Dream on Monkey Mountain and Other Plays* (1970) is called Macak. I am embarrassed because he dreams of a White Goddess, and because his dream of the return to Africa is presented as folly; because he is mocked at; because the Corporal has seemingly imbibed Count Gobineau's teachings; and because the only orality the Corporal can sputter is to do with the backwardness of his race: "[S]ome of the apes had straighten their backbone, and start walking upright, but there was one tribe unfortunately that lingered behind, and that was the nigger."[29]

Item: I am angry that it is the White Goddess who brings the assurances to Macak that he is not as ugly as he thinks, that he can leave the forest and rejoin human society. And Macak adds, "she say if I want her, she will come and live with me, and I take her in my arms and bring her here."[30] I am concerned because the White Goddess keeps reappearing, embarrassingly so in Walcott's personal voice, at the end of "What the Twilight Says" as "white . . . one of a small army of his dream . . . among the sentries who had watched till dawn."[31]

Item: I am saddened by the fact that he could possibly have written, "My generation had looked at life with black skins and blue eyes."[32] I took this very personally, since we are of the same generation.

Item: That even rereading *Drums and Colors* (performed in 1958) after all these years was most distressing. I am aggrieved by the fact that Pompey and Mano are just clowns; by references to Jews and Blacks who are nameless; by the wholesale adoption and usage of the racialized myths of Christopher Columbus and Sir Walter Raleigh; and by the presentation of Henri Christophe, Toussaint L'Ouverture, and Jean-Jacques Dessalines as happy fools and hearty laughers, intent only on the slaughter of children.[33] I know that this is the Western oral version of the Haitian revolution, but Walcott could have stayed with CLR James's version, especially as James professed the highest regard for him.

Item: I am particularly concerned that after A. J. Seymour (now deceased, former editor of *Kyk-over-al)* and Frank Collymore (also deceased, former editor of *Bim)* both gave Walcott's early work the initial exposure it needed, they must now be silently turning over in their graves.

Item: I am extremely angry that after all these years—when we should have grown wiser together—that I now end up with Walcott's version of the *Odyssey* (1993) specifically *commissioned by the Royal Shakespeare Company*. Why? And, insult on insult, Walcott attempting to rework Homer into that poor, culturally deprived fisherman, Achille. Why?

Now, dear reader, you might well say to me: Have you not, dear man, accorded your writer the right to write? Why are you insisting on holding this one back? I don't want to reply by falling back on postmodernism, but perhaps on the words of my dear mother who always intoned, "If you don't have nothing good to say, is better you don't bother say nothing at all." Instead, I will argue that I find it very strange that the only hideous distortions I find in Walcott and Sir Vidia (V. S. Naipaul) are those specifically invented by the West, to keep Walcott, Naipaul, and me in check. And in a new century I've had enough, and that is why I speak so strongly. As my mother always warned me about my friends' speech, you can and must be more selective about your orality.

No, we cannot return, despite what Walcott says in "The Muse of History" (1974) to a pre-Adamic innocence. His poetry in *The Gulf* had recognized all too well that there was a connection (I would say an unfortunate one) that links us to this great barbaric mainland called North America. But we don't have to be forever prostrate; we can get up. We don't have to be always kneeling; we can walk—or as a character tells Macak, "What you kneeling for? . . . Pray for the day . . . when niggers everywhere could walk upright like men."[34] I am.

I don't pretend that it is not easier to "get on" if you are Sammy Davis or Louis Armstrong, but somebody needs to walk tall and firm, and sound out our alarms for us. Orality always did this—in the village first, as, for instance, when the family *griot* was displeased, there were certain things that the person being praised would have preferred not to hear. I remember once attending a farewell reception that the Emir of Zaria in Northern Nigeria was giving before embarking on his *hajj*. A sour note was struck because the Emir had totally ignored his Keeper of the Stables (who was only requesting to be paid). All his employees felt threatened. Suddenly, the Jester's good humor was not quite as funny as before—there was now an acerbic edge to it. The Emir paid the Keeper. Life went on.

Walcott says it is quite wrong to view classical Greek literature as "the language of the master."[35] Instead, he says, that the world—this Adamic New World of his—only makes sense if we claim victor, not victim status. But can we, given the terrible conditions that *post* hyphenated coloniality have continued to place on us? We can't just declare we won the war and go home. Where do we go? Do we forever have to be positing the polarities (empty and artificial) of choosing "Between this Africa and the English tongue I love?"[36] It sounds indecent to be always playing Africa against Europe, White against Black, civilization against barbarism ad infinitum. It is neither exciting nor interesting, and indeed sounds a little crass after the nth time. Especially, if when you mention it, you say it's not a game and you're not in it.

The monkey figure, the self-loathing, undesirable Africa and Haiti, and the White Goddess are all states of mind bred in the neurosis of being colonized and living in the diaspora. And since few of us have *read* much of this (although granted it comes to us with American movies like Tarzan, television, and advertising), most of the concepts about an anti-Africa are *heard* through *negative orality.* Indeed, it is passed on in the family itself.

ORALITY IN THE TEXT: SOME CONCLUSIONS

What develops then is that there are three types of oral inheritance, each with a "positive" and "negative" side to it. First, there is the genuine, unspoilt, direct, orality, that may or may not have survived in Africa and the New World. I see Soyinka as being a part of this, but I must insert a quick caveat. Reading *Aké: The Years of Childhood* (1981) would convince the most hardened romantic, even if one did not know Soyinka, that Soyinka had experienced a virtual English Victorian middle-class upbringing with a large family, much discipline, churchgoing, respect for authority, and happy, innocent, frolicking days at play.

Second, there is the invented orality in Africa and the New World, occasioned by need and function. I see Morrison as being part of this process, and I don't see her in this role merely because she is New World, detribalized, *deraciné.* I think that when you are placed in this kind of situation, you have to invent something to buttress the daily assaults from the "master" discourse. And so you may either loudly refuse to play, or go along with the beads and the palm oil, and Maulana Karenga's Kwanzaa, and Molefi Asante's Egyptian fetish. In a way this is what Edward Brathwaite settled for. He said as much in a particularly revealing (unpublished) interview he did with Vincent Cooper of the University of the Virgin Islands.

Third, there is the orality that is unrelated to function, has nothing to do with past, but is constructed to serve the interests of helping former colonial powers maintain hegemonic control. This orality is the most powerful, not restricted to any one small geographical area, but prevalent as "policy" wherever the West has sought to impose otherness on its objects, to render them useless and immobile. All the writers discussed have inherited part of this—they were all part of a colonizing/ghettoizing experience—with its notions of the dark Other as ugly, benighted, stupid, slow-witted, and obnoxious. This seems, unfortunately, to be the main aspect of orality that Walcott has so happily embraced.

ORALITY, THE TRIBE, AND THE WORLD

However, it seems to me that if people write novels and poems and put their names on them, they can't continue to pretend that they are scribes, serving the interests of the people. And just as the orality of village Africa asserted itself differently in towns and in the diaspora, less self-consciously, more provocatively, even with a degree of super-individuality, then the same will occur wherever novels, poems, and plays are composed. The "orality" that is imported into the written text is not the orality of the spoken word. The spoken was guarded, and it belonged to no one and everyone. Chinua Achebe had Okonkwo break almost every law in *Things Fall Apart* (1958), and Amos Tutuola's so-called traditionalist hero of *The Palm Wine Drinkard* (1952) did what he liked *on his personal adventure* to Dead's Town. I am suggesting that Tutuola's Drinkard broke the cardinal village rule when, *on his own* and without a by your leave, and only because *he* wanted to, *he* set out to find *his* dead tapster. This is a very Western thing. Tutuola once told me it wasn't, that indeed it was part of his own wish to travel all over Africa and collect stories, but I was never convinced that there was anything remotely Yoruba (even in the manner of his model Yoruba writers like D. O. Fagunwa) about the personal adventure for self-gratification. So, despite how the critics choose to present them, neither Achebe's Okonkwo nor Tutuola's Drinkard are oral/folklore heroes; they are relatively modern men going about their own personal pursuits.

Perhaps this is why the palm wine Drinkard has to fail. However, when he comes back, he returns in the manner of every folklore hero that Joseph Campbell would have recognized (although Campbell seems to have avoided Africa like the plague). Drinkard bears back the boon, in this case an egg, and resuscitates the village. This is the nature of quest. It is not an African thing or a New World thing—it's a people thing, and in this way we can't pretend that African orality is unto itself; it takes in and takes on the world. Similarly, when Manuel set out in Jacques Roumain's *Masters of the Dew* (1971) for Cuba, it is to glean knowledge that would be utilized at home later on; how to live with the land, pacify the people, and teach them farming techniques. On his return, Manuel transmits this. Note that in both cases of Drinkard and Manuel, the departure is *away from* the tribal group, and the return is *to* the tribe/group. Both Tutuola's and Roumain's characters are motivated by self-generating impulses; they see ways in which they wish to affect change, not necessarily in consultation with anyone else. And they do just that. So the departure from home, and the personal consolidation of change make Drinkard and Manuel into world figures, expressing a global orality.

Although Morrison locks up her characters in houses, they are *not* a tribe or a village, but very much part of a closely allied group. She once joked in an interview about her penchant for always having characters in houses. But if we look closely we see that the structure of the house is the nearest approximation to the idea of containment in tribe/village/clan. Here again, however, the characters act out of their own motivation. There might, eventually, be a larger purpose that could be read into their actions, but they are neither tribal people nor Western-type individuals.

I feel that, despite whatever our wishes are to the contrary, neither modern Africans who write their texts in a European metropolitan language, publish them abroad, and plug them on Western television, nor their New World counterparts who do the same, can lay much claim to the authentic use of much original orality. Orality has transferred itself into a new signifier, that has split the sound image, so that it is neither sound nor image, but a new sign in the text. Janheinz Jahn once told me that all "neo-Africans" use the "language of the drum"; I will not try to argue that one either way. Instead, I will contend that the ghettoizing/colonizing experience has not left us bereft, and those of us who write inevitably use orality, because it distinguishes us as people expressing an experience of *difference*. For we are all different from one another—there is no essentializing Blackness—and orality is how we convert our logocentrism into phonocentric terms.

NOTES

1. I am, of course, using Gayatri Chakravorty Spivak's term here, not Antonio Gramsci's. I want to convey the idea of a people totally cut off from the normal intercourse of everyday life. At this point I am more concerned with how and what they *say* rather than how they *eat*.

2. Here I am referring to the writers of the so-called Harlem Renaissance. The only way I have ever been able to understand this is that it was a cultural movement, first manufactured in France, then approved of in the United States by such stalwarts as Carl van Vechten, Vachel Lindsay and Eugene O'Neill. When the Blacks climbed on board, they went out on field expeditions, like Zora Neale Hurston (dispatched by Papa Boas, as she affectionately termed Franz Boas). Even Langston Hughes, Hurston, Claude McKay and Alain Locke shared the same generous "godmother," Charlotte Osgood Mason. She presided over her charges from the grandeur of her Park Avenue penthouse with two injunctions—that they never reveal her name and that they always be "primitive." The threat was that she would cut them off from the wealth inherited on the death of her physician husband. For some details, see Langston Hughes, *The Big Sea* (New York: Knopf, 1940); Zora Neale Hurston, *Dust Tracks on a Road: An Autobiography* (Philadelphia: Lippincott, 1942); David Levering Lewis, *When Harlem Was in Vogue* (New York: Knopf, 1981), 151–55; and Arnold Rampersad, *The Life of Langston Hughes*, 2vols. (New York: Oxford UP, 1986).1: 153–58, 163–65, 183–200; 2:208, 259.

On the other hand, rich heiress Nancy Cunard felt that she best knew about the direction in which Black writers should proceed, and she dismissed the whole lot of the Harlem Renaissance set. Instead, when she published *Negro* in

1934, she called on Ezra Pound (who wrote on Frobenius) (393–94) and contacted all and sundry across the British Empire. My next door neighbor, a solitary, sullen, very Europeanized Black man, A. A. Thorne, M.A. (he never forgot the M.A.!) wrote (and I almost fainted when I read it in this country years ago) a fierce and nationalistic piece about (of all things) the need for Black pride (308–12). According to Hughes, Salvador Dalí claimed he knew everything about the "Negro problem." He asserted quite simply, "I've met Nancy Cunard!" (Hughes, *Big Sea* 253). This was probably a snide comment on her Black lover, Henry Crowder, to whom *Negro* was dedicated.

3. The major problem with the english/English game is that it is a trifle foolish. Since "english" does not guarantee success, *especially* at the periphery, again it seems like nomadism to be a rather romanticized way of looking at the "folk." Additionally, it ignores the very thing we are talking about here, namely the vast amount of spoken and written literature in indigenous languages—Arabic, Swahili, as well as Afrikaans, French and Portuguese. I sometimes worry that this aspect of "postcoloniality," which the Australian academics play with gusto, often seems like a cheap substitute for the old "Commonwealth Literature."

4. Spivak has argued cogently both in *Outside in the Teaching Machine* (1993) and elsewhere about the need for the academic to be wary of the all-embracing power of the institution. However, she is at times quite capable of dismissing what we engage in as a "trivial discipline" (122).

5. Frantz Fanon, *The Wretched of the Earth* [1961] trans. Constance Farrington (New York: Grove, 1966), 180.

6. I realize that all this sounds terribly personal, and it is, but I need to say it because it is right and true. I think we heap too much praise on some of our writers, and fail to tell them that what they are sometimes doing is misguided and in poor judgment. Someone should have made a point of doing this to V. S. Naipaul (now Sir Vidia) as well.

7. Wole Soyinka, *Collected Plays*. 2 vols. (Oxford: Oxford UP, 1974), 2:8.

8. These textbooks were hugely successful. I remember that when I lived in Nigeria, the publishers would fly Grieve up and down as he went about the business of revising yet again his series for the Nigerian education market. The publishers paid for a large team of so-called experts to advise the great man on what should be retained and what discarded. To my shame I should add that I was part of the illustrious team.

9. Ngugi wa Thiong'o, *Decolonising the Mind: The Politics of Language in African Literature* (London: James Currey, 1988), 12–13.

10. In the final analysis, Ngugi is right. Although one does wonder whether there is not more than a hint of the poseur. The revelation only came after he could afford it, with the success of his first three novels. And even now, I am able to quote what he writes, because after his British publishers—Heinemann Educational Books—went off in new directions to Oxford, one of its former editors, James Currey, formed his own publishing house and seems to have walked away with much of the business, including Ngugi's English writing denouncing English writing.

11. Homi Bhabha, "Signs Taken for Wonders," (originally published in 1985) in *The Location of Culture* (London and New York: Routledge, 1994), 102–22.

12. I hesitate over the now popular usage given to this word. When first conceptualized by Deleuze and Guattari, if I read them aright, nomadism is a

metaphor for a new existence. They write, " . . . keep moving, even in place, never stop moving." Gilles Deleuze and Félix Guattari, *A Thousand Plateaus* (Minneapolis: U of Minnesota P, 1987), 159. This is scarcely intended as some type of advocacy for mass emigration, but rather a way of emancipating representational stasis. I deal with this more fully later on.

13. Edward Brathwaite, "Timeheri" in *Is Massa Day Dead?* Ed. Orde Coombs (Garden City, N.Y: Anchor/Doubleday, 1974), 30.

14. Brathwaite, *Roots* (Havana: Casa de las Américas, 1986), 240.

15. Brathwaite, *The Arrivants: A New World Trilogy* (Oxford: Oxford UP, 1978), 77.

16. Ibid., 40.

17. When I read Brathwaite, I always remember a joke that Sir Vidia (I like the sound of his knighthood and his Hindu first name) shared with his British audience in the early days of "Calling the West Indies." He claims (true or not) that he once asked a would-be Caribbean writer why she wrote poetry, and she responded, "It shorter."

18. Frantz Fanon, *Black Skin, White Masks: The Experience of a Black Man in a White World* [1952] (New York: Grove, 1967), note on p. 162.

19. I am not just arguing that New World writers are the only ones guilty of romanticizing the past and its oral traditions. Over and over again, we see it in Chinua Achebe and Wole Soyinka. In the 1950s and 1960s, only two African writers dared laugh, and those were Ferdinand Oyono and Mongo Beti. We didn't know much about Oyono, but everyone said they had both been Frenchified and lived in Paris anyway. We never said the same about Félix Tchicaya U'Tamsi, who was also Frenchified and worked for UNESCO in Paris, because he wrote in support of tradition.

20. Disappointingly, beyond Bhabha's words, there is a very conservative mind at work. Once we understand quite clearly the ideas behind the "interstice" and "hybridity," we are left with an almost indecent desire to be united with the master. And, as I suggested before, I am pretty sure that not much of what we do or say as former colonials impacts very seriously on the center: the center holds.

21. For a good, knowledgeable, warm-hearted, and level-headed broadside on Edward Blyden and Alexander Crummell, and their mistaken ideas and motivations in wanting to "civilize" Africans by teaching them the Bible, good table manners, and the English language, see Kwame Anthony Appiah, *In My Father's House: Africa in the Philosophy of Culture* (New York: Oxford UP, 1992). He also takes a few swipes at Du Bois, since Du Bois both wants and does not want his racism. We can be fairly certain of Appiah's objectivity, except when he deals with his father's contemporary Ghana. "Pops" was one of President Kwame Nkrumah's rivals whom Nkrumah had to lock up. He was a lawyer who in the 1960s had shocked Britain by marrying the daughter of Colonial Secretary Sir Stafford Cripps and sailed for home. Appiah is not too kind to *Osagyefo*—the Redeemer—as Nkrumah liked to be called.

22. The urbanization of tradition is really not as dramatically sudden as I suggest. There were clear signs in books written in English forty years ago, but this was seen even earlier on. For instance much of South African indigenous writing, because it was missionary sponsored, decried the advent of the Black person in the city. Thus, Alan Paton's English novel, *Cry, the Beloved Country* (1948), was well along these lines, and certainly no attack on apartheid as had

been assumed. Paton's mission school-type aversion to the raw native exposed to the rigors and corrupting ways of the city—a little (he thought) like the Prodigal Son. But this was all part of the thinking of Afrikaaner officialdom. After Paton, the new and exciting impact of the city was presented in Peter Abrahams's early work before he left for England and Jamaica, and Alex La Guma's *A Walk in the Night* (1962), and in Can Themba, Lewis Nkosi, and Bloke Modisane, the *shebeens*, and, of course, *Drum* and *Classic*. This is a period that is not too well known in the West, and deserves some serious study. Add to this the entire corpus of Onitsha market literature, and the writers' fascination with city life. The Onitsha authors seemed to be saying that the urban evils could corrupt, what with good drink and bad women, but a good time was had by all for the duration of the novelette.

23. Alessandro Triulzi, "African Cities. Historical Memory and Street Buzz," in *A Postcolonial Question*, ed. Iain Chambers and Linda Curti (London and New York: Routledge, 1996), 78.

24. See, for instance, Ulli Beier's article on sign-painting in Nigeria called "Naive Nigerian Art," in *Back Orpheus*, 19 (March 1966), 31–32; followed by eight unnumbered pages of illustrations, then page 39. They are mainly advertisements for hairdressing salons, tailor shops and restaurants. Beier adds that "the artist dreams up the romantic world he came to find in the big city"(32). Compare the would-be writer in V. S. Naipaul's *A House for Mr. Biswas* (London: Andre Deutsch, 1961), who uses sign-painting as his first expression of writing beyond orality. Also note how Sam and Willie *verbalize* their dream of the waltz as an escape from their humdrum, segregated lives in Athol Fugard's, *Master Harold and the Boys* (New York: Penguin, 1982), and the photographer's *spoken* dreams of a better life in *Sizwe Bansi is Dead* (produced 1972).

25. I want to suggest three possible areas where the idea of the flight away from/back to could have originated. First, at home in rural Ohio to this day people tell stories of the flight back. This could have been reinforced by what Morrison picked up from her then Jamaican husband in the early years of their marriage, for there is also a re-enforcing Caribbean account of taking flight back to the motherland. Before Sylvia Wynter became Black and radical at Stanford, she had a good laugh at this in her resuscitation of Prophet Bedward in her novel, *The Hills of Hebron* (1962). A third source is possibly the work Morrison did at Random House with many Caribbean and African writers. One such contact was a Senegalese academic at the University of Wisconsin, Edris Makward, with whom she did the major work in editing an early Black anthology. Furthermore, her job exposed her to meeting a number of writers from overseas—indeed that is how she and I first met in 1970.

26. Gerald Moore and Ulli Beier, eds., *The Penguin Book of Modern African Poetry* (London: Penguin, 1984). "Abiku" by J. P. Clark is on p. 199, and "Abiku" by Soyinka on p. 193.

27. The Caribbean spelling is "jumbie," and the Sierra Leone spelling is "jombie." See Eldred Jones and Clifford N. Fyle, *The Krio-English Dictionary* (Oxford: Oxford UP, 1980), 155. They provide an explanation of the Krio meaning of "jombie" and the "wan foot jombie," both (despite the editors' rather strange assertion that the word is from English "jump") probably taken back to Sierra Leone during resettlement by Jamaicans in the nineteenth century. I wish to thank Dr. Tom Spencer-Walters for helping me locate this source, especially as he was one of the consultants for the dictionary. Compare Richard Alsopp,

Dictionary of Caribbean English (Oxford: Oxford UP, 1996), 317, for possible African linkages.

28. Peter Stallybras, "Shakespeare, the Individual, and the Text," in *Cultural Studies*, ed. Lawrence Grossberg, Cary Nelson and Paula A. Treichler (New York: Routledge, 1992), 394.

29. Derek Walcott, *Dream on Monkey Mountain and Other Plays* (New York: Farrar, Straus and Giroux, 1970), 217.

30. Ibid., 236.

31. Walcott, "What the Twilight Says" in *Dream*, 39.

32. Ibid., 9. On the personal note, *The Chronicle of Higher Education* reported on February 2, 1996 that graduate student Ms. Nicole Nieme was suing Walcott for sexual harassment. This followed, the *Chronicle* stated, a previous incident reported at Harvard, and another at Boston, with different females. "This is the third time he has been accused of sexual harassment," the *Chronicle* triumphantly concluded (p. A17). The *Chronicle* did not detail if these were all "White Goddesses."

33. Walcott partly tries to explain the problem in *Drums and Colours* (1992 ed.): He was, he says, only nineteen; he was conscious of, and fearful of, the poverty round him. He adds, "Full of precocious rage, I was drawn like a child's mind to fire, to the Manichean conflicts of Haiti's history. . . . The fire's shadows magnified into myths. . . ." (Walcott, "Twilight" in *Dream* 11). This is twenty years, too little, too late.

34. Walcott, *Dream*, 254.

35. Walcott, "The Muse of History" in *Is Massa Day Dead?* Ed. Orde Coombs (Garden City, N.Y: Anchor/Doubleday, 1974), 3.

36. Walcott, "A Far Cry from Africa" in *In A Green Night; Poems 1948–1960* (London: Jonathan Cape, 1962), 18.

Chapter 2

New World/Old Word: Viewed, Visionary, Verbal, and Visual in the Construction of Text

> . . . Dürer's portraits of a black man, from ca. 1505–6, and of the enslaved woman Katherina, from 1521, [are] to be found on the same wall, a few feet from the Leonardo. Suddenly I am caught between the master and the enslaved. . . the black man dressed in what looks like a Venetian cape, the black woman who has had her hair "confined within a European headdress." In its spirit of parallelism, the catalogue suggests that Dürer goes beyond artistic and cultural stereotypes and shows himself "sensitive to the personality as well as the exotic potential of his sitter." Can the two be compatible when exoticism erases rather than enhances personality? . . . Can the "mean and measure of all things" frame this radical heterogeneity of the human condition when the catalogue entry states that circa 1492 there were between 140,000 and 170,000 African slaves in Europe? (Homi Bhabha, British Council, "Re-inventing Britain Conference," 21 March 1997, keynote address, <http://www.britcoun.org/studies/stdsprog.htm>. [Accessed Oct. 9, 1998]

In *S/Z: An Essay* (1974)   Roland Barthes rightly contended that the "writerly" (*"scriptible"*) text may simply not exist since it is "the novelistic without the novel, poetry without the poem, the essay without the dissertation, writing without style, production without product, structuration without structures." As such, it inhabits a pure netherworld beyond art and artifice, apart from any neat interpretations. And, since the author is "dead," s(he) cannot establish any sacrosanct position in determining the direction of the work. Language, with all of its powerful prejudices imposes its own format, albeit at times subtle, whereby subject and other become most manifest.[1]

Any examination of the literature of "encounter," between Europeans and Native Americans reveals how very often language itself serves as a device for invention. The European language does not merely relate, but creates its own non-European culture—a savage, a native, a non-Christian, a barbarian.[2] And, since much of what was written in the wake of Conquest falls within the purview of a propaganda heavily dependent on narrative codes, these types of "readerly" ("*lisible*") texts reveal a great deal about what Jonathan Culler has referred to as the manner through which the text and the reading process are all linked "within the modes of order which culture makes available"[3]—in this case a European culture.

CONSTRUCTING AMERICA

"America" is loaded with meanings, derived not from the place itself (although this could also be contested in a different context), but more specifically from what is said, referred to, and defined in the context of a European language. First, there is the "mythology," in particular Jacques Derrida's "white mythology," that must restore the *"sens propre."* However, a quandary occurs in that even when stripped of this through *"usure,"* we are still left with surplus metaphors that accrue to the original coin.[4]

Assuming then that at some stage there is a desire on the part of the narrative writers to relate "America," perhaps merely to write down the word, the European composer is beset with initial difficulties. At the most basic level, the debate over authenticity begins almost as soon as the current usage is initiated. Sebastian Cabot, as early as 1517, dismisses Amerigo Vespucci's voyage of 1497 as one "which Americus says he made." Bartolomé de Las Casas condemned Vespucci as a liar, and Peter Martyr simply omitted him. In 1836, Alexander von Humboldt concluded that the 1497 voyage was impossible, and as late as 1856, no less a personage than Ralph Waldo Emerson regretted that Vespucci, "a thief," had placed his name on the continent, during "an expedition that never sailed."[5]

If "writerly" texts could exist, demanding little reconstruction or evaluation on our part, but simply engaging the reader as a kind of accomplice, then within the supposed words of a fictitious Vespucci we should be able to find and locate the actual. But Barthes has warned us that (a) the author is dead, (b) the author is unreliable, and (c) the reader (even one several centuries removed) must take over and regulate the work, becoming a coinventor of the text. And, since the text is no longer anonymous, we must read beyond its margins, taking in the multifaceted ramifications of its intent.

Supposedly Vespucci made four voyages between 1499 and 1501. In the first, he traveled southwest from the Canary Islands to the Gulf of

Paria, north to Haiti, and back. In his second, he journeyed from Europe via Cape Verde, and made it as far south as the northeast corner of Brazil, as far as the Cape of San Augustin. He then traveled west along the northern coast of Brazil, the Guyanas, and Venezuela, north toward Hispanola, and then returned. On his third voyage, he came first south to the African coast, then moved down the coast of South America as far south as presentday Santa Cruz. Finally, on his fourth journey, he cut across the Atlantic from Sierra Leone, moving partly down the east coast of South America, before returning directly. If these accounts are reliable, they show that with time, Vespucci was able to utilize Christopher Columbus's experience, especially with regard to the utilization of ocean currents. The further south he sailed toward Africa, the greater his chances of exploring a larger swathe on the east coast of South America. Columbus's designs are therefore imprinted on Vespucci's plans, even without Columbus's words or their body of shared beliefs.[6]

This is important when we consider the extent to which the Columbus/Vespucci text bears startling similarities. Essentially, the journey was identical—to a "different" place; Columbus termed it "otro" and Vespucci deemed it "novus," but they meant the same—the area was not a version of Europe, but an un-European "other," located at the edge of "place" and, therefore, conjuring up representations of distinct opposites in landscape and people. It mattered little what they "found"; the text merely served as a device for justifying the "non-" existent, "non-" reality, "non-" sameness, "non-" entity. "America," in concept, as realization, challenged the very nature of known space and place.

Indeed, as a result of the projection of one type of fancy, Martin Waldsemüller's 1507 world map continued to rely on Ptolemy for Europe and Asia. For Africa, he utilized what was known through Portuguese travel; for China, he relied on Marco Polo. But for the New World, he relied on Vespucci. The twelve sheets that constitute the map therefore represent an "agreed" assembly of images of the world, not just Waldsemüller's. Rodney Shirley comments in *The Mapping of the World* that Waldsemüller's map therefore still suggests that this New World region is so remote, so "ultra," so removed from even the known "other" (Asia), that it deserves its own "legend."[7] Out of this cultural desperation, "America" comes into being and thus is, in actuality, "discovered."

According to Vespucci, the people he encountered are described in this way:

Let me say that after our journey had turned northward, the first land we found to be inhabited was an island ten degrees from the equator; and when we were near it we saw a host of people on the shore looking at us as though at something wondrous. We anchored about a mile from the land, equipped the boats and went ashore with twenty-two well armed men, and. . . the people saw us land and saw that we were different from them in nature.[8]

In this, the so-called *Mundus Novus* letter (an English translation from Latin of a lost Italian original), Vespucci indicates the direction we are attempting to pursue. This journey had presumably taken place between May 14, 1501 and July 22, 1502, and Vespucci had supposedly landed somewhere in the vicinity of Brazil and Venezuela among a people totally contrary to Europeans.

What this early part of the letter does reveal at the subtextual level is first and foremost that Vespucci, like Columbus, had entered into a no-man's-land of "uninhabited" places with people before he came to one that was "inhabited." Additionally, since this is no ordinary "letter," but indeed a public document that would utilize the new printing press, and would be read and reread all over Europe, it takes on the added significance of existing as an anthology about a belief system. As such, returning briefly to Culler, the reading process in order to be understood must make use of "modes of order" of the culture or, put differently, must be "recuperated" into an order comprehended by the reader of this very readerly text. Thus, from the onset, Vespucci evokes the metaphor much beloved by "discoverers"—strange natives gazing with awestruck reverence at the arrival of Europeans.[9]

Next worth noting is that the twenty-two "well armed men" constitute clear evidence of the not-so-hidden belligerent message in the text. Here, the reader is told quite clearly of at least one reason why the European is triumphant: Not only are "natives" constantly in terror, but they are also easily controlled by the use of superior European force. This heralds their imminent suitability for enslavement, kidnapping, torture, and death,[10] and prepares the way for their total domination by old words in the new world.

Vespucci's very readerly text continues to fit neatly into Barthes's formula in that, especially (in the context of self-affirmation of values), it "declares itself to be historical."[11] But this cannot be, for surely despite Edward Said's anguish over the need for origins (as seen in his *Beginnings: Intention and Method [1985]*), Vespucci's text is both within and outside history. Vespucci both represents an "origin" in that, for instance, his world is "novus," unexplored, undescribed, and only superficially, explicated. At the same time, his world is "antiquus," existing prior to any new experience and, in a way, "ante," predating even time itself.

European representations of "different" people are fashioned by this "ante" world, outside of time itself, where a specific European mind-set has failed to come to terms with the new social realities of a new world. In a few words, what Vespucci observes is not so much the dialectical opposition of novus/antiquus, but a failure to recognize the projection in terms of one on the other, the distant on the near, the familiar on the odd, and above all, the safe on the unknown. Out of this failure to acknowledge an imaginative extension, the text falls back on familiar echoes of ancient reference points, unable to expand into the new directions of a dramatically challenging experience.[12] I am therefore suggesting that both Vespucci and Columbus failed to relay New World reality for one major reason only—they saw the "old " in the "new," and were thus unable to translate one experience into the other, or to completely substitute the "One" for the "Other."

European readers had been fed on palatable tidbits that gave them assurances about the safe condition of their own Christian world. Vespucci had stated quite directly, as he compared his European crew to the people of Trinidad, that ". . . the people saw us land and saw that we were different from them in nature"[13] (emphasis added). "Nature" is an important code word in this sentence. By 1550, when the disputation between Bartolomé de Las Casas and Juan Ginés de Sepúlveda took place in Valladolid, Spain, the issue had reached a fevered pitch of excess. Indeed, "nature" established the basis for heated discussion, violent disagreement, and ultimate dismissal—did Indians have a "nature" that predisposed them toward barbarism? For Las Casas, Native Americans could not be barbarians, since even if they did not possess a "written" language, their speech observed certain methodologies that Europeans could appreciate. In rebuttal, Sepúlveda merely conceded that "they are as inferior to the Spaniards as. . . women to men. . . as monkeys to men."[14] I don't think the women/monkey analogy is too far removed from the consciousness of the time.

CARIB CANNIBALS AND THE "OTHER" SAVAGE

Both Columbus and Vespucci, almost as if by intentional collusion, fabricated texts that were identical. Thus indeed, the readers become "producers" in this new way: They have helped "engineer" the final product. They can, for instance, claim common kinship with ideas that belong not merely to Columbus or Vespucci, but which, through being shared by both, validate the readers' own. So, even as Columbus in Guadeloupe, in stressing the Ultimate Other, identifies the Caribs as man-eaters,[15] Vespucci in Trinidad "discovered that they [the inhabitants] were of a race called Cannibals."[16] They were utilizing the commonly agreed super text.

Logic in both instances dictated that the blessings of European christianization would be accompanied by enslavement. Columbus reasons that having been saved from their miserable lives, Native Americans "will be better than other slaves."[17] Vespucci, noting that slavery is indeed no strange custom among the people he sees, suggests that it supersedes the doubtful benefits of cannibal fare.[18]

Regardless of what may or may not have been actual social reality, it is not surprising that the explorers' depictions remain the same well into the period of eighteenth-century Pacific exploration. Indeed, the themes of exploration are so closely interwoven that the readers obtain the feeling that they are encountering, over and over again, samples of a kind of protoreaderly text. William Dampier, James Cook and others all embark into the "unknown"; all encounter nubile and willing "native" women and men; and all discover Paradise in the Pacific.[19] This seems a little surprising, especially since they were not Columbus "wannabes," blindly stumbling across the Ocean Sea bound for Cathay, but representatives of the European Enlightenment, whose very much professed reason for departure was often connected with scientific observation. Yet their texts had to be informed by, and conform to, the expectations of "Home."[20] The Plinian and Alexandrian monsters may have disappeared, but Vespucci's "femme sauvage" (especially in the Age of the Noble Savage) was given a renewed lease of life.[21]

One should not, and cannot therefore regard either Columbus's or Vespucci's narratives as personal creations. They are group compositions, manufactured from the accepted notions of the public. And to make sure that the "text" continues to be a shared view, components are added to help with our understanding or, in reality, our willingness to accept. Thus, the process of composition operates in this way,

Verbal (word/text/metaphor) + Visual(image/map/picture) + Visionary (Religion/Paradise/God/king) = Viewed

Thus the "text" performing in real life space (its words, meanings, connotations) has to be supplemented by maps and pictures, which in turn contribute to, and bolster up the "visionary." As a result, the accepted worldview is maintained, since the woodblock illustration (much like an untouched photograph) provides objective analysis.

For us to come to real terms with the literatures of the period, we have to understand that not only is the European verbal skewed, but the important and missing part of the equation is quite obviously the "visual." This is where Martin Waldsemüller's map constitutes such a tremendous aide to the racial memory. It confirms with the single implantation of "America" on the southern part of the "new" continent, that it was the property of a single European person who had "discovered" and "named" it for an entire community. The word, the mere act of its creation and reproduction, seems simple enough unless we clearly see, as with Barthes, that it constitutes one of the "cultural codes [which] are references to a science or a body of knowledge."[22] The problem is that here, although this does draw on a body of accepted, known European knowledge, it is nevertheless still structuring the culture.

CODICES AS HISTORICAL MEMORY

One very obvious example that I shall mention, but not discuss in any detail, is the instance of the so-called Aztec codices. One instance is Fr. Bernardino de Sahagún's attempts at transmitting information about the nature of "Conquest" via "native" informants in the *Florentine Codex*. Despite the accompanying pictographs, these illustrated chronicles say more about the "conqueror" than they do about the "conquered." The account, Sahagún tells us, is to make the Indies better known to the Spanish. In so doing he gives in several books a background of the customs and traditions of the Aztec people, and in Book XII, their confrontation with the Spaniards.

As scholars have looked closer at the work in question, what has emerged is not only that the indigenous painters and transcribers have been heavily influenced by a posterior Spanish interpretation of events, but in addition, since the pictures are often drawn after the verbal account, they obviously lack any first-hand authenticity. If we also consider the very pertinent fact that the composers of both the Nahautl and Spanish texts are at least a generation removed from the events they describe, this presents us with an additional quandary. This is hardly aided by Sahagún's own words in Spanish, which according to at least one scholar, mention Hernando Cortés much more often than does the Nahautl text.[23]

One would, not unnaturally, have hoped to have seen realized in the codices, particularly the Aztec (earlier versions of which the enthusiastic disciples of Cortés took such care to destroy), ideal elements whereby the "visual" and "verbal" come together in a new and revealing way for us to inspect, evaluate, and commend some four centuries later. But the truth of the matter is that, apart from works that can be authenticated without doubt as "pre-Cortésian" (and note how we date time itself, as if it had among the greatest timekeepers in the world never existed before European contact), there still exists an element of contamination. After all, even in these "authentic" accounts that postdate the Conquest (and Sahagún's is the most thorough that we possess), what is essentially being written down is a version of the occurrence for "home" consumption. There are giveaway lines in the text, such as the parts where the Spaniards are referred to, much as they call themselves, namely "Christians" or "people of Castille."[24] The account itself is hardly a history of the Aztecs, or even the Aztec view of Conquest; it remains a parochial version of events from a rather small part of a people of Mexico (afterwards renamed the Aztec by Alexander von Humboldt).

What the visual codices definitely tell us does not guarantee their verbal authenticity. After all, for all indigenous peoples of Spanish America, according to Enrique Florescano, Conquest had meant "the annihilation of their historical memory. . . their past memory destroyed and made anathema."[25] Utilizing our previous equation, it is evident that the "viewed" is skewed, since the word/text of the "verbal," the image/picture of the "visual," and indeed even the "visionary" have been filtered through the controls of an alien manipulator. But we have already noted this with Columbus and Vespucci, and it becomes even more evident in subsequent accounts, well into the nineteenth century, as Europeans begin a new exploration for a different Paradise in the South Pacific.

Being there, in the case of the composers of the codices, is compounded not merely by the transported myths that are played out in the heads of adventurers as disparate as Columbus and James Cook. Being there, indeed, for the sixteenth-century scribes, seems merely to confirm the appearance of authenticity from the "native" viewpoint, whose very status is considerably compromised by their being "pupils" of the very people for whom they are claiming to write an objective account. One may even argue that this exists today as one of the major problems for writers who seek to create a "postcolonial" text utilizing the tools and media of the colonial center.

Adam's task, we are reliably informed, was to name things. To gain "universal" (European) acceptability, the "visual" part of the equation would have to be present. Sebastian Münster (1489–1552) published his *Cosmographia Universalis* in 1544; the verbal helped along the visual and vice versa. In the 1550 edition, which became the standard geographical "legend" for a number of years, Münster excelled in verbal description even though, technically speaking, he was more interested in the visual. What interests us more is how Münster, via the English "translation" by Richard Eden (actually in a "version" of Vespucci letters), becomes a public spokesperson. Münster/Eden places Vespucci within the Columbus mythology, describing him as "being sent with Christopher Columbus, in the year of Christ, 1492, at the command of King Ferdinand of Castille, to seek unknown lands."[26] This is his supreme validation as "discoverer."

True, the visual is absent, but the basic message of encountering a strange, uncouth Other is very present. The depiction of this outsider from beyond the circumference of the world also occurs over and over again in Theodor De Bry (1528–1595) and his visual representations. His *Historia Americae* ran to fourteen volumes and began publication in 1590. With his utilization of engravings on copperplate, De Bry was able to illustrate a whole series of peoples and landscapes (which he had never seen), and which cut across European languages and hegemony, New World boundaries, or even the personal proprietorial egotism of the "discoverers." As a result, the illustrations continued to help unify the European view of the new as different, yet possessing a samelessness that could be understood. Richard Hakluyt, for one, was quick to utilize

De Bry, realizing that "he himself was technically incapable of producing illustrated books."[27]

De Bry's world confirms the verbal accounts in visual terms and, in this way, excludes four of Barthes's codes of actions. Certainly, the "proarietic," by which action can be organized into narrative patterns, is absent, as is the "hermeneutic," by which a problem may be formulated or solved. There is, after all, no "sequence" no "problem"—only a statement about the natures of the "other" world. "Semic" or connotative codes as well as "symbolic" codes abound, and indeed may now be clearly extricated from the verbal text, stressed, and placed within the narrative for new visual approval. Above all, though, the "(re)viewed" is now uppermost, for the picture now presents the cultural totality of what Ernest-Jean Sarrasine says everybody knows—at least what Honoré de Balzac says he says. Although Barthes contends that this may well be a "monster," he admits that "the locus of an epoch's codes forms a kind of scientific vulgate."[28]

A few examples must suffice of how European art was summoned to the aid of a European audience, how pictures began to serve the illiterate in understanding their own world, not another, and not a new one. Some of the issues already mentioned were first reinforced by De Bry—for example "worshipping the stone as an idol," monstrous creatures like hermaphrodites, naked women, cannibalism, and so on. De Bry's consciousness that these were indeed self and community encounters, perhaps even Freudian and Jungian in scope, may be realized in his own remarks that appeared at the end of his volume on Virginia. There are five plates of Ancient Britons, and beneath their representations, suggesting paganism, monstrosity, nakedness, cannibalism and so on, De Bry has written: "Some pictures of the Picts which in former times did inhabit a part of Great Britain." He continues that he had obtained the depictions from an "old English chronicle" and that it showed "that the inhabitants of Great Britain have been in times past as savage as those of Virginia."[29]

I can think of no single figure of the period who more than De Bry best represents our rather amorphous term, "European." Not only did his interests make him undertake a multiplicity of enterprises that crossed national and linguistic barriers but, in the process, his work truly became "continental," in that it represented no narrow parochial concern, but Europe itself as it would be defined four hundred years into the future. His work had become such a transnational undertaking that by 1594 a Milanese, Girolamo Benzoni, supplied the "words" to De Bry's *América*, Part IV, published in 1594, as part of the compendium begun in 1590. Earlier on, *América* Part I (1590) was written by English scientist Thomas Heriot, and *América* Part II (1591) was composed by a Frenchman who had visited Florida.[30] Wide dispersal was made possible in Europe through good translation methods: All parts were available in Latin and German. Part I was additionally published in English and French, and Part IV was so popular that it was also translated into Dutch and French, and published in several editions. [31]

The world of the "new" that De Bry introduced even to literate Europeans was one in which they saw proof of the monsters they had invented, and evidence of their own existence within a primitive background. The landscape was familiar; in one illustration entitled "The arrival of the Englishman in Virginia," David Beers Quinn has pointed out the "conventionalized" (Europeanized) "vegetation, figures and ships," adding that both "six or seven varieties of trees" and a conventional representation of an Indian village were present.[32] Side by side then with the "monster" is the "master," and this deliberate juxtaposing by De Bry stresses just why Columbus and Vespucci are utilizing a common backcloth to stress the contrast.

With printing and pictures, association between word and object had seemingly become discrete. Hence, both Columbus's and Vespucci's first letters were best-sellers, very much like De Bry's *Historia Americae.* They all gave assurances, especially regarding the immutability of religious belief, given an era that was certainly a period of anomie. All the old values had been seemingly questioned, but there needed to exist a degree of assurance beyond what Gerald Prince has termed the "disnarrated." These are devices whereby narrator and narrative evoke imaginary places in order to express discrepancies in life, when asleep or awake, and when beliefs or hopes no longer seem justified. If, pursuant to Reformation and Counter Reformation, "discovery" had the effect of "disnarrating" the steady flow of life itself, its age-old certainties, then the new travel accounts of Columbus, Vespucci, and De Bry could perhaps restore some elementary balance.[33]

The narrators/illustrators could best achieve this result of the new "viewed" as "reviewed" by ensuring that the texts possessed little continuity at a time of the seeming cessation of belief, and no closure, during a period that lacked finality or certainty. Instead, the text would derive its form from the urgency of the experience, and the new equation of the verbal with the visual that could more adequately describe, if not the "viewed," then at least the "reviewed" world. In the process, certainly there is distortion. Self and other are (re)constructed anew, and their New World creation, albeit through old words, has itself invented its own stereotype—Barthes' "mythologies,"[34] from which perhaps we can never free ourselves. Mythological interpretation becomes, at least for European readers, the complete components of the equation whereby the "New World" may be viewed. Yet not all exploration had the "visual," and in a way, this overemphasized the "verbal," since this could not totally portray the myth in the mind of explorer and audience.

OLD MYTHS/NEW WORLDS

Juan Ponce de León represents a fascinating case of Old World mythology at work in the New World as he sought out the Fountain of Youth. The revitalization of a European myth had made him explore Florida. Prester John, the legendary Ethiopian emperor, whose face, on contemporary maps, gazed stern-faced from northeastern Africa towards the East, was the repository of this belief. His 1165 fictitious letter had described a fountain stating that, "whoever drinks of its water three times on an empty stomach will have no sickness for thirty years. . . . A person who can bathe in this fountain, be he of a hundred or a thousand years, will regain the age of thirty-two."[35]

These were, of course, the mythologies of the East as invented by Europe, but they were replanted in the New World. Thirteenth century travelers, like Giovanni di Plano Carpini, William of Rubruck and Odoric of Pordenone had identified their presence in the East, while still not providing substantial proof. In order to ameliorate the ravages of plague within immediate memory, the quest for eternal youth continued: As late as his Second Voyage, Columbus recalls Prester John as did his earlier mentor Marco Polo and, of course, that armchair veteran, Sir John Mandeville.

Ponce de León initiates the process of the utopianization of North America—perhaps beginning with the idea of "America" itself as refuge to Europe, seen not only in Sir Thomas More's *Utopia*, but also embedded in the biblical meaning of an Eden before sin and a Paradise after death. Such an acceptance of place as symbol would witness the arrival of the *Mayflower*, William Penn's Quakers, Shakers, Hutterites, the Transcendental experiments at Brook Farm, Robert Owen's New Harmony, and even down through D. H. Lawrence's "Rananim" in Taos, New Mexico. Every one of these sought to establish a break from the old world of Europe and a foundation of a newer and freer order in America. In this process of self-centered search they continued to displace the Native Americans. Furthermore, all the experiments failed, because the perfection they sought, like Ponce de León's, was located in the heart not the heartland, and because America was only continuing to respond to European mythologizing, partly started by Vespucci himself.

Seeking "utopianism," of whatever variety, essentially strips away the physical reality of place. For Ponce de León, the quest was really for an America of the mind since he had already understood its elusive nature in his earlier sojourn with Columbus. He understood how the naming of the thing sought often conferred a "reality" which it did not have—so his name is associated with "Puerto Rico." For Ponce de León, it seems that the true wealth was within. He was 53 years old when he "discovered" Florida at Easter (*Pascua* in Spanish), a time of death and resurrection.[36]

And this is the underpinning of this middle-aged man's faith in the possibility of restoration.

Antonio de Herrera writes that "Ponce de León went ashore and took possession." At least in Ponce de León's case, this act did not merely indicate that the land was the property of his prince and his government. "Possession" now meant that Ponce de León could at least take hold and point with some assurance to his lifework, crystallized in spiritual fulfillment. And, once having found a spring that had been utilized by Native Americans, he felt that success had been achieved, even if somewhat arbitrarily.[37]

With Ponce de León, Vespucci's "America" therefore assumes a nonworldly, almost spiritual quality. Until Ponce de León's time, "America" had to be filled in, its contours flushed out with the imaginative pointers of the rest of the world. Up until then, "America" had not existed; the United States (which has practically monopolized the terminology) was, as Waldsemüller noted, "unknown." In making it "known," these earliest travellers initiated a process of idealizing the real.

First, Alvar Núñez Cabeza de Vaca, in the eight years (1528–1536) he spends in North America, rewrites the travel narrative. True, the equation persists in that the "viewed" is still partly visual, partly verbal, and partly visionary, but the "viewed" has to be perceived from a different "viewpoint." The standard travel narrative, as the new translation of *Castaways* shows, is turned upside down. Gone are the zealous Spanish Christians who seek to conquer and convert native pagans. As treasurer for an ill-fated expedition that was shipwrecked, Cabeza de Vaca and his party were forced to assume a totally different role. Now the "Indians" are Spaniards, as the ethnographic equivalence is totally capsized. As he wandered through latter-day Florida, Texas, and Louisiana, Cabeza de Vaca alone (of all the conquistadors) must have clearly known the meaning of being one of the "conquered." He learns to gesture and sign, to endure the delicacy of horse flesh, to experience the loss of power, and, above all, cut off from his ship, to experience the aloneness of a man adrift in a world of uncertainty.

What helps keep him and his party alive is that they are able to substitute Ponce de León's "Fountain of Youth" for a new mythology, a new faith, in the Seven Cities of Cíbola. This remains, however, a mere spiritual hope; all that is real exists in the tortured nature of their experiences as they, at times, embrace the Indians and receive their blessings and, at other times, endure captivity among the inhabitants of Galveston and the Queuenes. In the process of exploration (sincere enough although they remain quite firm in their adherence to God and Spain), the humbling experiences aid them in the process of role reversal and the feelings of the other.

Interestingly enough, one of their party is Estebanico, one of the earliest Afro New World explorers. They begin to see through his eyes—another humbling experience, since as a Moroccan he would have been one of the hated rulers of Spain, most of whom were expelled in 1492. They learn a little of what today we would term the multicultural nature of the New World. Cabeza de Vaca's world is no longer the neat assembly of One and Other, West and Indian, Christian and pagan, White and Brown. Instead, because of its many hued variety, Cabeza de Vaca's New World anticipates, indeed heralds, the creation of modern Latin America.

Within these novel experiences of this New World, Cabeza de Vaca can empathize, as the Indians become more humane, more forgiving, in spite of their own fear of Cabeza de Vaca's fellow Christians. At one stage, Cabeza de Vaca movingly writes:

They brought us blankets that they had hidden for fear of the Christians and gave them to us, and even told us how on many occasions the Christians had entered the land and destroyed and burned the villages and carried off half the men and all the women and children, and that those who had managed to escape from their lands were wandering and in flight. We saw that they were so frightened, not daring to stay in any place, and that they neither wanted nor were able to sow crops or cultivate the land but rather were determined to let themselves die, and they thought this was better than waiting to be treated with such cruelty as they had endured until now; and they showed great pleasure in us, though we feared that once we reached the Indians who had a frontier with the Christians, and were making war on them, these others would treat us ill and make us pay for what the Christians had done to them.[38]

Here he is certainly no apologist for Empire, grantedly a still dormant one, but nevertheless on the rise, with few questions asked about the roles of victors and victims.

I would not wish to suggest that Cabeza de Vaca is above the pretensions of his age. He is always conscious that he is "Christian," and that there is a difference between his party and the people they encounter. But the gulf is not as wide as that maintained by Columbus and Vespucci, and realized in the work of De Bry. Cabeza de Vaca's world is one in which an ordered universe, regulated by hierarchy and Spanish control, has broken down. Perhaps this, in more than one way, explains the ease with which Estebanico moves both with Spanish and Indians, with "conqueror" and "conquered." Perhaps, one reading is that as a so-called "slave," he is best equipped (especially given Moorish history) to understand the relationship of the Spanish toward Indians. So he himself, almost until the end of the narrative, seems fit enough to act as a leader and guide (in a strange place unknown to him), altercating both with Europeans and Indians.[39]

Columbus had found an "otro mundo," Vespucci a "nuevo mundo," but for Ponce de León and Cabeza de Vaca the spoils seemed less practical, less worldly, and yet more global. The symbol of the Fountain of Youth and the Seven Cities of Cíbola would remain as the El Dorado we all seek, to regain springtime and to live again in a young lifetime where the entrance to Paradise is not denied, as it had been to Columbus. For these quests into the places of the heart, men would be disgraced, suffer infamy, and die. The fever for fame, for their fifteen minutes of glory had driven Columbus, Vespucci, Cortés, and Francisco Pizarro to spend their lives in ceaseless hassles over alleged wrongs. Estebanico remained in the New World and was finally killed during another expedition seeking the elusive Seven Cities of Cíbola. Ponce de León kept up his ceaseless search until 1521, when he was also killed during a Native American attack in Florida. Yet people must pursue the things they dream and if in so doing they die, then their deaths at least have meaning, for they followed the beliefs of their hearts to the furthest shores, away from "Home" and the familiar, to a land beyond the real, where myths perhaps are realized.

As the dream became less concrete and more idealistic, later conquistadors would pursue its essence. Hernando de Soto, having become disgusted with Spanish in-fighting, and the later murder of Atahualpa by Francisco Pizarro, returned to Spain. Francisco Vázquez de Coronado would later be the subject of much official disapproval. But within them both they kept alive the possibility of the Seven Cities of Cíbola, at times called Quivira, not so much a search for gold (although it was that also), but rather a quest for spiritual fulfillment. So that when they encountered the Zuñi and the so-called "Pueblo Indians," they could not claim to have found the elusive dream.

Perhaps this is what Garcilaso de la Vega (contemporary and indigenous writer) meant. He stated that had the Spanish remained in Florida, they would have found not just gold and silver: "For not everywhere are there gold and silver, yet people do live in all places."[40] Of course Garcilaso is an apologist for the Spanish empire, but often beneath his overblown patriotism he hints at the possibility not merely of Spanish hegemony, but of a perfect world——"America"——where the ailments of Europe had been left behind. In such a province, all things become possible: the African, the European, and the Indian may now coexist in a place that is both "otro" and "nuevo." And where, because the ancient "mythologies" of caste and class no longer apply, new dreams are dreamt within the secure walls of the Seven Cities of Cíbola where humans live forever, always young, in Paradise.

ACTS OF CONQUEST

Once we begin to conceptualize, we can agree that Cortés, Pizarro and the multifarious copycats who follow in their wake are, in fact, "enacting" or "playing out" the earlier Columbus/Vespucci scenario. As such it is not difficult to note how self-consciousness helps reproduce theatricality. And if the encounters between Cortés, Pizarro, and the other conquistadors are a replay, then we should try to construct the basic elements of the five-act drama in which they are all engaged. We shall use Columbus as our model, as the protoscriptwriter who devises the "plot" that subsequent players follow, adapt, and imitate.

Act I could well be (if we deal mainly with the moment when two unwritten texts come together) a period of Silence. Within this we can argue that there are a variety of scenes. Quite early in Act I, Columbus/Vespucci/Cortés/Pizarro embark on the ancient archetypal heroic journey towards the Other. In such a script, devised by the West, the Other waits supine, silent, for the moment of "revelation." But, if we examined this in another way, we would easily see that the first act also demonstrates that neither of the major players assumes the mask of otherness.

At this stage, there are two Ones/Selfs; they are on a collision course that will define them historically forever with respect to each other—call this, if you like, the making of the Other. Therefore, at this early moment of pre-action, before the speech act has occurred, before Columbus writes Guacanagari, Cortés writes Motecuhzoma II, and Pizarro writes Atahualpa, all demonstrate the same neutral relationship (or nonrelationship) toward each other. Guacanagari's attitude towards Columbus is that "he was proud to call me, and treat me as, a brother," Columbus maintains. (I am aware that we are still relying on Columbus.) According to Bernal Díaz, Cortés admitted to Motecuhzoma that "we are all brothers." And Pizarro, so much the wiser after his own firsthand experience with Cortés, enunciates much the same "line." With Cabeza de Vaca, we need not defer or read against the grain; he tells us that (Christian and supposedly medicine-man that he was) he still only functioned in a subservient role.

This "line" is all part of the first act, which Stephen Greenblatt has rightly termed the "myth of brotherhood," arguing that "the oscillation between brother and other under the sign of wonder is one of the principal tactics in Cortés's strategy of conquest."[41] Quite rightly, one may assert that in Act I, there is therefore not the existence of equality— certainly Motecuhzoma sees Cortés as an intruder and wishes him to go away—but the "acting out" of the pretense of equality. On the whole, the motives exhibited are quite simple. Columbus/Vespucci/Cortés/Pizarro all have no doubt that, in order to sell their texts to their sovereigns, they have to create real life counterparts with whom the king, Ferdinand or Charles V, could presumably have some type of dialogue. In the course of this discourse (br)other becomes Other.

Their nefariousness is, however, not one sided, for I have every reason to feel that Guacanagari, Motecuhzoma, and Atahualpa harbored their own feelings of hegemonic superiority, except that there was not much that they could do given the imbalance of power. After all, at stake was their own position in the hierarchy, and they must have realized that the presence of Europeans off *their* shores, and within *their* domain, constituted a grave threat for them.

Obviously, they would also be concerned at how quickly they have become "conscripted" into the European "script"—how easily, it seems, they were being assimilated into a pretend "us." In looking at the original Spanish, Peter Hulme concludes as follows:

"Amistad" is a relationship of mutuality, in which trade and other forms of exchange can develop. It is entered into by equals, a point often emphasized in traditional societies by the ritual exchange of names. By the end of Columbus' sentence [in his letter about the First Voyage] the relationship has altered: In the original Spanish "tanto" governs not "our friends," but simply "ours"—"tantos nuestros" the possessive adjective signalling a relationship in which trade is not going to be necessary because everything and everyone rapidly become "ours"; ours to exploit as we will.[42]

Thus we note that Act I is a precursor to what will later take place—conversion to Christian and "civilized person" as a pretence for friendship, and brotherhood as a substitute for bargaining. Both are subterfuges to obtain power and wield control.

With Act II, the earlier silence is shattered and the two Ones/Selfs now meet. They touch, they sign, they speak (or attempt to speak) through a "translator." At this point (and we have to reverse the narration a little), they still have not acted out their own fear of Otherness: Columbus, imagining that he is in the province of the Great Khan, is circumspect; Cortés, conscious of his own rebellious role in going against constituted Spanish authority and invading the Aztecs, is diplomatic; Pizarro, despite his comparative lack of sophistication, remained always aware that Atahualpa was royalty, until that fateful day when he executed him and paid dearly for it afterwards. Seemingly, royalty was related to one another across seas and languages, a very intriguing point that has received little consideration.

Since none of the parties comprehends one another's speech (for what they do is monological, hardly qualifying as conversation), any action could be wrongly interpreted. This is why we must give very little weight to the lengthy sermonizing on the part of Motecuhzoma and Atahualpa, or the supposed verbatim statements of Guacanagari. As constant intermediary, for instance, between Cortés and Motecuhzoma, Doña Marina articulates everything as seen by her. She has enormous power, for no one else is qualified to present even the most basic renderings of this moment of archetypal European history—all seen through the eyes, heard with the ears, and articulated with the tongue of the Other. From the very outset, for instance, Bernal Díaz recounts this very presence:

Montezuma bade him welcome and our Cortés replied *through Doña Marina* wishing him very good health. . . . Then Cortés *through the mouth of Doña Marina* told him that now his heart rejoiced at having seen such a great Prince, and that he took it as a great honour that he had come in person to meet him and had frequently shown him such favour. Then Montezuma spoke other words of politeness to him.[43] (emphasis added)

But how sure can we be of what was said? Was this (like Cortés's letters) intended mainly for the Royal eyes? Is Díaz being very careful to recount how the Spaniards were able to observe the rituals of courtesy and establish a dialogue, so that none will doubt what Díaz says? Díaz is himself recalling the events from Spain as an old man, intent on refurbishing Cortés's image, than in serious decline, and since he spoke no Nahuatl, he had no way of verifying if Doña Marina was "translating" or "inventing." Furthermore, since a major Aztec text, the *Florentine Codex* (grantedly completed under Spanish supervision) assures us that signs and portents from Heaven itself had heralded Cortés arrival, Motecuhzoma's greetings to a "god" seem mildly temperate. Of course, I grant you that the god thing could have been played down, since I don't think that Charles would have welcomed any aspiring god in his kingdom.

At this stage of our discussion, in Act II, with the touching of hands and attempts at communication, it would be useful to say a few words about the idea of god that accompanies the scene. God, indeed, is an unseen actor, both promise and threat, as decreed by One (Aztec, Christian) on the Other (Aztec, Christian). But, additionally, there had been notions of supremacy that the West had always harbored, and that, indeed, had now become part of its "act" towards this incipient Other.

Earlier travel narratives, as I have shown elsewhere,[44] were replete with several fanciful devices. There was the search for gold (later El Dorado), Prester John (later Manoa del Dorado), the Fountain of Youth, and the obsession with cannibals, marvels, miracles, and monstrosities. Some in part had been initiated by Pliny's overfertile mind, and later confirmed by Alexander the Great and the embellished narratives that followed his death. What had not been located in the legendary East by John of Plano Carpini or Odoric of Pordenone, Marco Polo, or Sir John Mandeville, would later be recycled and actively pursued (indeed found and so named) in New World territory: Amazonia, Patagonia, the Caribs (a possible corruption that became "cannibals"), the concept of the Fountain of Youth, and numerous place-names termed El Dorado, all testify to an everlasting optimism.

Apart from these inventions lay something a little less concrete— namely the manner in which earlier travellers (mostly devout Christians) often bordered on the heretical when they constantly asserted that the Other viewed them as gods. Beginning with the cult of Alexander, which he personally encouraged just before his death, and lasting well into the "Enlightenment" with Captain James Cook's "Apotheosis" in Hawaii, we note a degree of constancy in these narratives that can be no mere fortuitous accidents. Europeans obviously considered themselves as gods to these savages, and so wrote about the manner in which all and sundry worshipped them with zeal and great aplomb.

Within the entire format of the New World context, the Columbus/Vespucci/Cortés/Pizarro paradigm is no different. This, indeed, is the important "action" that follows the "act" of speechlessness: All are elevated to godhead status; perhaps European males were simply intoxicated with their own fictions, the lies they told so convincingly in their correspondence to king and countrypeople, and the dissembling they had done so widely on the New World inhabitants.

Columbus, before he saw fit to adapt "Christo ferens" as part of his signature, claimed that Native Americans saw the Spaniards as men from Heaven. Later Cortés would enact (always passively, for they only "reported" what the "natives" thought) the exact scenario. In Cortés's case, the Aztecs housed the Spaniards in the same buildings as their gods, "because they called us Teules, and took us for such, so that we should be with the Idols or Teules which were kept there."[45] Later, when Cortés orders the destruction of the Aztec deities, and the substitution of his Christian gods, an argument can be advanced that the Spaniards did not wish the minds of the unfortunate natives to be crowded with unnecessary alliances to the sovereignties of the Other.

Act III marks the point of Contact. Still Ones, both sides are now attempting to "read" each other's "texts," to understand what "roles" have been assigned to them, the parameters of the discourse, and how it should be "played out" with an anticipation of the dénouement. Mutually recognizable speech and signs are still in their infancy—done but without guarantee of comprehensibility. Hence the role of the interpreter is challenged anew. Since common signifiers are not shared, there can be no writing, no talk, no mutual intelligibility. Each side is locked off in a dark world of his own invention. Only, ironically in Cortés's case, the Other rises above the fracas to structure the disorder. But in what fashion? Is it a world of her own making?

Indeed, the interpreters of all the scenarios have now become more than language informants. They are now intermediaries who act between two cultures (both "foreign" to them) and who attempt to make sense of their unities and polarities, their conjointedness and disjointedness, their nation and alienation. The role of interpreters/intermediaries as "inventors" is now more than ever evident, for they can never seem to be in the dark, unknowing, and ignorant, for clearly this would operate to their own detriment. Their knowledge, real or assumed, will attempt to define the "space" between Columbus and Guacanagari, Cortés and Motecuhzoma, and Pizarro and Atahualpa. We have no way of knowing whether the "heard" or "reported" text of the discourse of Encounter faithfully or almost faithfully reproduced what occurred—ironically this is the history that the Other rendered for us—but we can be reasonably certain that they did not. For the accounts are twice removed from the languages of utterance—at first spoken by Native Americans to someone who may or may not have understood, and then "translated" to a Spanish-speaking conquistador, and then later "written down" in Spanish, and still later "translated" into English, the language I (hopefully) read best.[46] The problems resulting from this linguistic chaos may easily be imagined.

NOTES

1. I shall be arguing, with Ferdinand de Saussure, that the association between "signifier" and "signified" is fixed by the primary language-user. This becomes of great significance when linguistic signs are used to denote oral sounds. But in the instance of "codices," we should also note how these operate as "signs" fulfilling, to a greater or lesser extent, their roles as icon, index, symbol, and signal. See Ferdinand de Saussure, *Course in General Linguistics*, ed. Charles Bally and Albert Sechehaye, trans. Roy Harris (La Salle, IL: Open Court, 1986).

2. These terms serve as convenient monolithic handles to identify the "Other," thus making recognition and generalization easy but, in the process, depriving the "identified" from any kind of "distinction," one from the other. The only "distinction" established is between the "Name-Giver" and the "name-receiver."

3. Jonathan Culler, "De Man's Rhetoric," in *Framing the Sign: Criticism and Its Institutions*, ed. Jonathan Culler (Oxford: Basil Blackwell, 1988), 107–35.

4. My metaphor lays claim, of course, to no originality. I have borrowed the idea of the coin, and its *"usure"* from Derrida. See Jacques Derrida, *Margins of Philosophy*, trans. Alan Bass (Chicago: U of Chicago P, 1982).

5. Samuel Eliot Morison, *The European Discovery of America: Southern Voyages, 1492–1616* (New York: Oxford UP, 1974), 305–07.

6. References to Vespucci's voyages are in Amerigo Vespucci, *Letters from a New World* ed. Luciano Formisano (New York: Marsilio, 1992), xiv, xv.

7. Rodney W. Shirley, *The Mapping of the World: Early Printed World Maps, 1472–1700* (London: Holland Press Cartographia, 1984), 28.

8. Vespucci, *Letters*, 9.

9. It is, therefore, no accident that long before the fictions of Daniel Defoe, the male European as god became standard fare in travel narratives. In the New World, Columbus can claim first place when he described the attitude of the Taínos towards the "men from heaven," but he, in fact, was merely following Marco Polo. One can assert that the idea of the godlike European male was always within the European racial subconscious since the image emerges time and time again, even as early as Pliny and Alexander the Great. See O. R. Dathorne, *Imagining the World: Mythical Belief versus Reality in Global Encounters* (Westport, CT, and London: Bergin & Garvey, 1994), 1–127.

10. Then contemporary logic shows how at the highest levels the issue of Native American humanity was brought into question. See, in particular, the

1550 debate between Juan Ginés de Sepúlveda and Bartolomé de las Casas in Lewis Hanke, *All Mankind is One* (De Kalb: Northern Illinois UP, 1974).

11. Roland Barthes, *S/Z: An Essay*, trans. Richard Miller [1970] (New York: Hill and Wang, 1974), 32.

12. One way in which there is an obvious response to what seems like cultural passivity occurs most vigorously in language—in "english" to be precise. As the study shows, out of the thrown away remnants of "empire," a new "post-colonial" language is invented, vastly different from the "English" of the colonial overlord. See Bill Ashcroft, Gareth Griffiths, and Helen Tiffin, eds., *The Empire Writes Back: Theory and Practice in Post-Colonial Literature* (London and New York: Routledge, 1989). But it should be stressed that the dichotomy between english/English, does not hold good for the self-same post-colonial situations arising from the French and Portuguese languages. Few would contend that Léopold Sédar Senghor's French, or Oscar Ribas's Portuguese exists outside a nonmetropolitan, non-European world. Indeed, it is precisely out of the recognition of the artists as "copycat" that they became known to metropolitan readers. Perhaps, at a certain level too, a similar case may be made for English (but less so for Spanish) writers. As the writers of *The Empire Writes Back* themselves admit:

"The relation between the people and the land is new, as is that between the imported language and the land. But the language itself already carries many associations with European experience and so can never be 'innocent' in practice. Concomitantly, there is a perception that this new experience, if couched in the terms of the old, is somehow 'falsified'—rendered inauthentic—a the same time as its value, judged within Old World terms, is considered inferior." (135)

13. Vespucci, *Letters*, 9.

14. Hanke, *All Mankind is One*, 84.

15. Christopher Columbus, *Select Documents Illustrating the Four Voyages of Columbus*. 2 vols. Trans. and ed. Cecil Jane (London: Hakluyt Society, 1929 and 1932), 1: 28.

16. Vespucci, *Letters*, 9.

17. Columbus, *Four Voyages*, 1: 92.

18. Vespucci, *Letters*, 9.

19. There is no one satisfactory work that explores the continued preoccupation with the concept of Paradise. But interested readers might do well to follow up on at least one aspect of freedom as noted in sexual license. Both Dampier's "Painted Prince Jeoly" and Cook's Omai, were young men "befriended" by their English "friends." Both were taken to England, where Prince Jeoly died. Omai, it is said by Cook's biographer, wept bitterly when Cook attempted to return him to his people. See one study, that relates Cook as god (like Columbus, Vespucci, Cortés, and so on) and the ultimate feminization of the Pacific male, Gananath Obeyesekere, *The Apotheosis of Captain Cook* (Princeton: Princeton UP, 1992), 129. Also see B. R. Burg, *Sodomy and the Pirate Tradition* (New York: New York UP, 1984), 123.

20. See Mary B. Campbell, *The Witness and the other World: Exotic European Travel Writing, 400–1600.* (Ithaca, NY: Cornell UP, 1988). Campbell establishes a serious understanding of the validity of "Home" in travel writing of the Middle Ages, showing that what European travellers feared and how they fared were often anticipated in conceptions of "Home."

21. See also John Block Friedman, *The Monstrous Races in Medieval Art and*

Thought (Cambridge, MA: Harvard UP, 1981). Friedman painstakingly shows how Plinian and Alexandrian writing influenced what European travellers saw and experienced. Unfortunately, he only deals with New World travel in an addendum.

22. Barthes, *S/Z*, 20.

23. James Lockhart, "Sightings: Initial Nahua Reactions to Spanish Culture," in *Implicit Understandings*, ed. Stuart B. Schwartz (Cambridge: Cambridge UP, 1994), 218–48.

24. Ibid., 238–39.

25. Enrique Florescano, *Memory, Myth and Time in Mexico: From the Aztecs to Independence* (Austin: U of Texas P, 1994), 68.

26. Sebastian Münster, *A Treatyse of The Newe India* [1533], trans. Richard Eden of part of the fifth book of Münster's *Cosmographiae Universalis* [1550] (N.p: Readex Microprint Corporation, 1966), not paginated.

27. Theodor De Bry, *Discovering the New World*, ed. Michael Alexander (New York: Harper & Row, 1976), 88.

28. Barthes, *S/Z* , 97.

29. De Bry, *Discovering*, 24, 27, 67, 97.

30. Ibid., 89.

31. Perhaps De Bry is hardly as "European" as he might appear. He was born in Liège, and often saw himself as a self-made man and an outsider by temperament and religion—he was Protestant. Above all, he knew he was not an Englishman (De Bry, *Discovering*, 8).

32. David Beers Quinn, *The Roanoke Voyages, 1584–1590*, 2 vols. (London: The Hakluyt Society, 1955), 1:413.

33. See Gerald Prince, "Introduction to the Study of the Narratee," in *Reader Response Criticism*, ed. Jane P. Tompkins (Baltimore: John Hopkins UP, 1980), 7–25.

34. Barthes contends that we should develop a mode of reading that goes beyond the language that the text imposes on us. If we can "unlearn" what is "natural" and "conventional," we can reach for the mythic. This may very often be at odds with former surface renderings, and would emerge despite the wishes of the "dead" author.

35. Ysevolod Slessarev, *Prester John: The Letter and the Legend* (Minneapolis: U of Minnesota P, 1959), 72.

36. Morison cites Antonio de Herrera as the primary source for Ponce de León's voyage, written some eighty years later in his *Historia General de los Hechos de los Castellanos* (Madrid, 1601). It appears, Morison argues, as if Herrera had access to "an original journal." See Samuel Morison, *The European Discovery of America: Southern Voyages* (New York: Oxford UP, 1974), 530.

37. Walter H. Fraser, *The First Landing Place of Juan Ponce de León* (St. Augustine, FL: Walter H. Fraser, 1956), 9.

38. Alvar Núñez Cabeza de Vaca, *Castaways* [1528–36], ed. Enrique Pupo-Walker, trans. Frances M. López-Morillas (Berkeley: U of California P, 1993), 107–8.

39. Ibid., 111.

40. Garcilaso de la Vega, *The Florida of the Inca* [1605], trans. and ed. John Grier Varner and Jeannette Johnson Varner (Austin: U of Texas P, 1962), 635.

41. Stephen Greenblatt, *Marvelous Possessions: The Wonder of the New World* (Chicago: U of Chicago P, 1991), 138.

42. Peter Hulme, "Tales Of Distinction: European Ethnography and the Caribbean," in *Implicit Understandings: Observing, Reporting, and Reflecting on the Encounters between Europeans and other Peoples in the Early Modern Era*, ed. Stuart B. Schwartz (Cambridge: Cambridge UP, 1994), 159.

43. Bernal Díaz del Castillo, *The Discovery and Conquest of Mexico, 1517–1521*, ed. Genaro García, trans. A. P. Maudslay (New York: Farrar, Straus and Cudahy, 1956), 193–94.

44. Dathorne, *Imagining the World. Mythical Belief versus Reality in Global Encounters* (Westport, CT., and London: Bergin & Garvey, 1994), 10–12.

45. Díaz, *Discovery*, 194.

46. Of course, in the best of all possible worlds, where the signifiers have some common agreement, say in an English-spoken, specific place and time, you still come up with the issue, as William Empson recognized in my undergraduate years at Sheffield, and more recently Stanley Fish has ably shown: that meaning still remains elusive, hard to track down and to agree on. So we are playing a dangerous game when we isolate a few incidents in the "historical record," especially given the many intermediaries through whom they have passed, and yet attempt to make meaning of them, valid for all time. See Stanley Fish, *Is There a Text in This Class? The Authority of Interpretive Communities* (Cambridge, MA: Harvard UP, 1980), 158–73.

Chapter 3

"To Wash an Ethiop White": Royalty, Gender, and Race in the Early Modern Period

And with my power did march to Zanzibar,
The eastern part of Afric, where I viewed
The Ethiopian sea, rivers and lakes, . . .
And by the coast of Byather at last
I came to Cubar where the Negroes dwell.
And conquering that, made haste to Nubia,
There having sacked Borno the kingly seat,
I took the king, and led him bound in chains
Unto Damascus. . . . Christopher Marlowe,
Tamburlaine the Great, Part II [I.VI.67–69, 73–78]

It is to understand, that the people which now inhabit the regions of the coast of Guinea and the middle parts of Africa, as Lybia the inner and Nubia, with divers other great and large regions about the same, were in old time called Ethiopes and Nigrite, which we now call Moors, Moorens, or Negroes, a people of beastly living, without a God, law, religion, or commonwealth, and so scorched and vexed with the heat of the sun that in many places they curse it when it riseth. (*The First Three English Books on America [?1511]–1555 A.D.* [1555]), 384.

Whether called Aethiops, Moors, Negars, Blackamoors, or a rose by any other name, Black people were known in the England of Queen Elizabeth I and her successor James I, whose reign united the kingdoms of England and Scotland. There seemed to have been a strange and conflicting attitude present regarding Blacks. On the one hand, they were welcome at court as interesting curiosities; on the other, they were given very stereotypical roles on the stage, made to look and sound monstrous, and, at one period, actually ordered out of England. This contradictory approach to the other is reflected in public policy and in popular theater, whether plays were performed on the stage or at court masques. Furthermore, we can additionally see through the character representations, how in the conventions of beauty and fairness, loaded messages that were passed on regarding concepts of aestheticism that were narrowly defined as "white" and "ladylike." This, in turn, introduced the elements of gender and class into the already loaded racial definition of what constituted whiteness, why it was undesirable, and thus why a contrary logic prevailed.

I am going to look at some of Ben Jonson's plays to show how classist notions enter into equating aristocracy with moral goodness, and that in a way this is understandable, since royalty were the great patrons and patronizers of dramatic art. I hope to demonstrate that there is a spillover from gender to class, as embodied in the figure of woman, and finally into race, with one notable exception: Gender issues were controlled by the fact that men played women, women were seen if not known, and for a long time, the head of state was a woman. No such restrictions applied to race; there was no apparent controlling device that urged caution in the depiction of the racial Other who, in any event, was definitely not known. Indeed, this was a time when there was widespread belief in the monstrous races, and who better to apply the label to than Blacks, whose mere presence stressed difference as necessary to the understanding of Englishness and whiteness in a burgeoning developing of race.

MADE IN HER IMAGE: ELIZABETH AS VERY WHITE MALE

When Ben Jonson was born, Queen Elizabeth I had been on the English throne for fourteen years. When she died in 1603, he had been subject to her reign for thirty-one of his sixty-five years.[1] This is perhaps the first claim he makes on the attention of anyone who would seek to enquire into his concerns with female characters. His monarch was female, he was Elizabethan, and like his peers who wrote plays and poetry, he was part of the virtues and vices of his time and their ambiguous attitude towards women.

In many respects, when one examines women in canonical Elizabethan literature, one is struck by the fact that they are usually observed through the eyes of men Since male writers create women, they seem incapable of projecting an internal essence. Instead, what men make of women, how they view and relate to them, and how realistic these viewpoints are, become an important concern.

In large measure, women in the West tend to be the objects of excessive artistic adoration. Predictably, this is possibly an inheritance from the era of Romance of King Arthur and his court. However, when juxtaposed with exaggerated virtues, the vices of women seem all the greater. Since women were expected to shine, if they glowed only dimly or not at all, they seemed unworthy of artistic assessment.

Thus, woman is often the source of the imagination of the Elizabethan writer—witness Jack Donne the player before he became the Rev. John Donne—and the direction of flights of fancy into his artistic excursions. Therefore, she has to perform a dual role: The woman must be a saint in order to give spiritual pleasure to the creative writer and his audience. Additionally, she has to be a sinner so that the tensions inherent in the situation can be exploited to the full. She must therefore be temptress, seductress, whore, and, at the same time, nurse, midwife, and mother. Perhaps this sums up all that Elizabeth as Gloriana represented a kind of ambivalent trope.

From the onset, it should be noted that there is a double irony involved in presenting women on stage. Not only are they manhandled by their male creators, but their parts are played by men as well. The Elizabethan audience will know that they were therefore conscripted into a grand kind of elaborate fakery: women created by men, played by men.

Obviously, this distracts from any realism one would wish to see evident in female roles. However, females have to be understood and accepted within these constraining constructs of the times. Still, the modern critic must therefore be wary in any examination, since the playwright and audience shared a contemporary pact of understanding that allowed for the easy manipulation of gender roles.

There is another aspect to this, mainly that, because in an admitted understanding of what will be termed artistic bisexuality, both are equally prepared to accept certain fluidities that seem almost postmodern—women are not much different from men, except in external characteristics seen in clothing. And when this is altered, so does gender, as Shakespeare knew so well. Females are part of a male-ordered universe and, at the same time, express their femininity in a manner that states the masculine condition of both genders. The relative absence of females on the stage, and subsequent cross-dressing contributed to the ambivalence that made up the fluidity of gender.

Such an attitude is often seen as perverse, and leads to harsh criticism. Gamaliel Bradford comments about Jonson's women:

Hardly anyone has studied Elizabethan Literature at all closely has failed to pay tribute of admiration to the robust and manly author of *Volpone*. Everyone recognizes his energy, his dignity, his close and earnest observation, his keen insight into human character; yet—perhaps it would have been better for him if he had lived in an undramatic age and come down to us simply as a profound and philosophic moralist, a sort of La Rochefoucault or La Bruyère. However this may be, Jonson was not the dramatist of women: Volpone, Mosca, Mammon, Bobadil could hardly be omitted in a general discussion of Elizabethan characterization; but where are the female figures to stand beside them? Of pure, modest, and charming women Jonson has few, though, for that matter, his men of an attractive order are not much more numerous.[2]

Yet there are female characters who stand out, not as male versions of women but as women in themselves. One such example is Grace in *Bartholomew Fair* (performed in 1614), who has been termed by William Gifford as "one of Jonson's few estimable females."[3] Equally, one may see a definite femininity in Celia in *Volpone* (1607) and Mrs. Fitzdottrel in *The Devil is an Ass* (performed in 1616). Furthermore, there are at least two women who serve as representatives of a type: Lady Would-Be in *Volpone*, and the repulsive Ursula in *Bartholomew Fair*.[4]

Jonson, given his interest in satire, might well have seemed to lack a degree of the gallantry of the time, because he portrayed women as possessing the same vices as men, while the Elizabethan Age itself projected certain kinds of myths. They were partly fostered by the Maiden Queen herself, whose reputation remained that of an unsullied virgin, despite her dalliances and liaisons with the dukes of Leicester and Essex. There was also the other image of a queen who had never married, apparently shut away from the world, and only gallantly wooed on staged occasions by such as Sir Walter Raleigh, cape on ground, which was bound to fire the imaginations of men whose courtly behavior partook of the theatricality of the time. Additionally, she was herself both lover and warrior, goddess and villain, whore and saint, woman and man. Thus, she proclaimed herself a type of cultural hermaphrodite when she stated that she had the courage of a man housed in the body of a woman. This may be part of the paradox of the period.

Contradictions certainly abound as soon as one begins to examine Jonson's plays. On the part of the dramatist there is an ambiguity of intent regarding gender. This does not only suggest his lack of certainty in the construction of female representations, but it also indicates that Jonson was equally aware of a perverse (yet human) admission of contrary motives. As an artist, Jonson would no doubt have grappled with this, for surely it provided the basis for artistic tension.

Sometimes, Jonson's women characters play out major roles. They exhibit all the vagaries of human behavior; they may be cunning, shrewish, witty or plain silly, but in large measure, they possess an underlying pragmatism. This is what helps them to come to terms with situations, and how they help their menfolk comprehend the varied nature of the world. In this respect, Jonson displays humanity at its best and worst, at times rendering his characters in clearly realistic terms. The other side of this is that this realism gives an element of completeness to the plays. Through the presentation of women who are as subject to human foibles as men, Jonson is able to show that sin and folly are the prerogatives of no one gender. Yet he does not go all the way and seems to shrink from utter condemnation that might mark him as more misogynistic than misanthropic. Perhaps Lady Would-Be is a good example of this. Lady Would-Be is obviously intended to be seen as an affected person. Volpone finds her pedantry tiresome, and she is indeed a bore. Note how she addresses Volpone:

> I have a little studied physic; but now
> I'm all for music, save, in the forenoons,
> An hour or two for painting. I would have
> A lady, indeed, to have all letters and arts
> Be able to discourse, to write, to paint,
> But principal, as Plato holds, your music,
> And so does wise Pythagoras, I take it
> Is your true rapture. . . . (*Vol.*, III.iii.188)

The affectation is certainly not redeemed when she adds:

> there is content
> In face, in voice, and clothes: and is, indeed,
> Our sex's chiefest ornament. (*Vol.*, III.iii.188)

Therefore, when Volpone asserts that "your highest female grace is silence," he seems just, and the antagonism of audience remains for the moment directed against Lady Would-Be, because of her superficial learning and her penchant for sounding out the names of great writers, a matter more of class than gender, and thus more palatable.

Lady Would-Be's character was not in keeping with the virtues of the queen herself, for she lacks the ability to balance extremities. Sir John Hayward comments in his *Annals* about Queen Elizabeth:

her haire was inclined to pale yellow, her foreheade large and faire, a seemeing sete for princely grace; her eyes lively and sweete, but short-sighted; her nose somewhat rising in the middest; the whole compasse of her countenance somewhat long, but yet of admirable beauty, not so much in that which is tearmed the flower of youth, as in a most delightfull compositione of majesty and modesty in equall mixture. But without good qualityes of mynde, the gifts of nature are like paynted floweres, without eyther vertue or sappe; yea, sometymes they grow horrid and loathsome. Now her vertues were such as might suffice to make an Aethiopian beautifull, which, the more a man knowes and understands, the more he shall admire and love. In life, shee was most innocent; in desires, moderate; in purpose just; of spirit, above credit and almost capacity of her sexe; of divine witt, as well for depth of judgement, as for quick conceite and speedy expeditione; of eloquence, as sweete in the utterance, soe ready and easie to come to the utterance: of wonderfull knowledge both in learning and affayres; skilfull not only in the Latine and Greeke, but alsoe in divers other forraine languages.[5]

The point is surely that, unlike Lady Would-Be, Queen Elizabeth's mind was seen to be alert, even as her very white body was physically pleasing.

Elizabeth is a mixture of perfection and imperfection: a "prince" with sallow skin, yet "faire" in complexion and beauty. And we should note that the word "faire" (as Kim F. Hall reminds us in *Things of Darkness* [1995]) is meant to contrast with the (male?) Ethiopian, the very nadir of beauty and fairness, whom Elizabeth will herself easily make "beautiful." Since the good book enjoins us that the leopard cannot lose its spots nor the Ethiopian his color, hence the literal logic of the conceit takes us to the point where Elizabeth must be raised to the status of godhead. Words like "spirit" and "wonderful" are intentionally clustered round "divine wit" to suggest more than a hint of some possible apotheosis that has transformed queen into king, woman into man, black into white, and human into God.

BEN JONSON'S WOMEN

Unlike Queen Elizabeth, many of Jonson's female characters are only superficially feminine. Perhaps this has as much to do with the opinion of the playwright and contemporary male bias, as with the realities of the actors, who were after all men playing women, that is men who were only women on the surface. Peregrine therefore finds that Lady Would-Be is much as her husband, Sir Politik, had affirmed:

> She is
> Were she not mine, a lady of that merit,
> For fashion and behavior; and for beauty
> I durst compare. . . . (*Vol.*, IV.ii.194)

And with this Peregrine concurs when he says, "Indeed your husband told me you were fair. / And so you are." The problem is that the mark of beauty is given almost as a redemptive quality, a gallant token that allows the constructor to be as disparaging as he likes to the point of downright mysogyny.

As I have already suggested, there is more than a degree of embarrassment in making fun of women of Elizabeth's gender. Jonson goes a little distance and then seems to make a hasty withdrawal: Lady Would-Be could be contrasted with Celia, also in *Volpone*, and Mrs. Fitzdottrel in *The Devil is an Ass*. In the latter instance, Mrs. Fitzdottrel is at the periphery of the play, which is concerned with making fun of the so-called witchfinders and monopolists of the day. Her husband Fitzdottrel is a fool and is cheated out of his fortune by a get-rich scheme. While Sir Politick is the male counterpart of his wife, Mrs. Fitzdottrel is sensible and realistic, and does not fall easy prey to her husband's wish to become a duke; thus, she is the more sensible of the two. And from the first she is suspicious of Pug, the devil's advocate. After Fitzdottrel has told her of his plans, he adds:

> Sweet-heart, if thou hast a fancy to one place
> More than another, to be dutchess of,
> Now name it. (*D.A.*., II.i.353)

Yet she does not fall victim to this. Her wry rejoinder is, "You have strange phantasies," showing that she is not easily won over by absurdities.

She is also a suitable contender for Wittipol's flattery and warns him:

> Sir, if you judge me by this simple action
> And by my outward habit, and complexion
> Of easiness if hath, to your design;
> You may with justice say, I am a woman;
> And a strange woman.... (*D.A.*, II.ii.354)

Thus, she seems to concede the myth of apparent feminine weakness and to assert a masculine strength. The double joke is in "habit," for as previously stated, the part would have been played by a man. There is a more sinister point made with "complexion" that carries both a contemporary meaning of "appearance" and a more modern, more loaded designation of race, derived from the dark complexion associated with vigorous males, as opposed to the fair, milk-white complexion of beautiful females.

In this case, Mrs. Fitzdottrel's "female" qualities are the uncanny ability to perceive a truth that seems to elude males. Perhaps because Elizabethan women are placed outside the total evils of the action of the world, they are able to be more neutral, like Marvel's Coy Mistress, beyond the reach of Empire and aging. In being able to rise to great poetic heights when he attempts to portray women at their best, Jonson is in keeping with the temper of Queen Elizabeth's projection of herself.

The queen herself was very much involved in what was going on. In fact, she had to be dissuaded from personally taking part in the attacks to repel the Spanish invaders. And it was as a male warrior queen that she delivered her notable address at Tilbury:

Let tyrants fear; I have always so behaved myself that under God I have placed my chiefest strength and safeguard in the loyal hearts and good-will of my subjects; and, therefore, I am come amongst you as you see at this time, not for my recreation and disport, but being resolved, in the midst and heat of the battle, to live or die amongst you all—to lay down for my God and for my Kingdoms and for my people my honour and my blood even in the dust. I know I have the body of a weak, feeble woman; but I have the heart and stomach of a King—and a King of England, too, and think foul scorn that Parma, or Spain, or any Prince of Europe should dare to invade the borders of my Realm; to which rather than any dishonour should grow by me, I myself will take up arms—I myself will be your general, judge, and rewarder of every one of your virtues in the field. I know already, for your forwardness, you have deserved rewards and crowns, and we do assure you, on the word of a Prince, they shall be duly paid you.[6]

Thus, is she both prince and princess, king and queen, man and woman and therefore possessor of the attributes and qualities of both genders. Hence, she ought to be feared even more, since she has assumed the garb of the Amazon, and by being above gender, she is now able to banish negative stereotypes as she reconstructs herself as a kind of super person. She can easily concede the myth of a feeble woman, and counterbalance this by stating that the "habit" of a woman (in fact she had dressed, controverting the model of theater, as a male warrior) was no detriment to her will and ability.

With this same pride, Mrs. Fitzdottrel states her case to Manly:

>   I am a woman
> That cannot speak more wretchedness of myself
> Than you can read; match'd to a mass of folly,
> That every day makes haste to his own ruin;
> The wealthy portion that I brought him, spent,
> And through my friends neglect, no jointure made me
> My fortune standing in this precipice,
> 'Tis counsel that I want, and honest aids;
> And in this name I need you for a friend;
> Never in any other.... (DA., IV.iii.367)

Her words, like Queen Elizabeth's, express pride and anger. Yet she is both desperate and hopeful. At this point, Mrs. Fitzdottrel achieves a new dramatic dimension; she is not just virtuous or pious: She becomes the very personification of the independent woman who reflects the image of the queen.

Jonson, therefore, is not merely content to see women as stereotypes. Though unable to direct the full force of his satire against them, he utilizes them as he does his male characters, to expose human folly and to praise human wisdom. Therefore, it is no accident that characters as disparate as Lady Would-Be and Mrs. Fitzdottrel still epitomize a collapse of contemporary understanding of gender roles, since they are not just beautiful or virtuous, but possessors of sound common sense.

Volpone was performed in 1606 and *The Devil is an Ass* ten years later. This would have been time enough for the dramatist to alter his portrayal of women. However, the writer's total intention is not to be found in chronological data, since both Lady Would-Be and Celia, the refined character, appear in *Volpone*. Equally, Grace, also a stable female character, appears with Ursula in *Bartholomew Fair* in 1614. Therefore, it seems that Jonson is out to demonstrate variety in gender and to show that these exist at both ends of the spectrum of class.[7]

Hence, a rounder and deeper version of Mrs. Fitzdottrel is noted in Celia. Again, she is not at the center of the action of the play, but her presence contrasts with the degradation of human duplicity. Corvino is prepared to sacrifice Celia, his wife, to Volpone, and thus she becomes the center of the vile conspiracy. Whereas Lady Would-Be is pretentious and even at times coarse, she is always aloof, removed, almost imperious. The evil around her affects her but leaves her uncontaminated. The audience easily sympathizes with Celia, if only because at first she seems so ready to please her greedy husband, Corvino. Here the feminine mystique emphasizes the physical grossness: Volpone must have a young woman "lusty and full of juice," according to Mosca. Corvino decides that Celia is most appropriate. She must wear her "best attire," "choicest jewels," and thus stress her "best looks." Again—but here for nefarious purposes—the outward is shown as substitute for, and to the detriment of, the deeper and more abiding human virtues.

As has been noted, this is part of what the queen herself was seen to project. But she herself reminded her audience that beneath the male armor she was a female warrior of merit, willing to offer the supreme sacrifice—her life. And since the total picture of woman made in Elizabeth's image was a combination of outward beauty and inner mind, when left alone with the foreign Other, Volpone, Celia's reflections became the conscience of the English Self, thus becoming the conscience of the play as she wonders, "Whither, whither / Is shame fled human breasts?" Naturally, she cannot be ravished by the evil Volpone, but Jason does seem to delight in dealing with the juxtaposing of opposing superlative polarities—here the pure, White English maiden and the wretched, evil, black-hearted foreign male villain.

The point must be stressed that the vagaries of the play and, in particular, the maintenance of the purity of an Elizabethan female typecast are the reasons why Celia cannot possibly come to an evil downfall and a fate worse than death. An aside forces me to add that it was this constant striving for the presentation of the purity of the English heroine in Elizabeth's mold that forced Henry Fielding, at first in *An Apology for the Life of Mrs. Shamela Andrews* (1741) and later in *Joseph Andrews* (1742) and *Tom Jones* (1749), to run counter to the precious values that Samuel Richardson had enshrined in *Pamela: or, Virtue Rewarded* (1741), stereotypical essentializations that remain part of Western literature until the late nineteenth century, like the good (albeit slightly dull) heroine who will not ever lie prostrate. This is why the "hero" has to seek his fodder in the grazing fields of the lower classes, and perhaps this is why the laboring classes were burdened with a supposed sexuality that the middle classes pretended to discard.

Incidentally, during the late eighteenth and early nineteenth centuries working-class women could easily be dubbed "black" since they supposedly shared this excessive sexual desire and low moral purpose with Blacks and sundry "others."

Celia is not saved through any inward grace or outward action. Though she calls on God, and appeals to Volpone, she seems incapable of taking a firm stand that would prevent her danger. Later she is given few lines that would deny Lady Would-Be's assertion that she is a "cameleon harlot," or her own husband's false accusations that

> this day she baited
> A stranger, a grave knight, with her loose eyes
> And more lascivious kisses. (Vol., V.iii.197)

At the closing trial, she eloquently pleads for mercy for her husband, but says a long nothing, despite her previous claims of love and affection, when the decision is made to send her back to her father. This is not because Jonson is incapable of having her speak up, but because the conventions of his day included (ironically) a female belief in the right of patriarchy. Furthermore, she was required to observe certain mores, since she was a merchant's wife and a person of some esteem.

Hubert Hall makes several relevant points in his discussion about one member of the merchant class in Elizabethan England:

Amongst the financial successes of an age unparalleled for its money-making activity, none was more complete or more instructive than that achieved by the founder of the Royal Exchange. Thomas Gresham, however, was no creature of civic fable, no self-made prodigy like Whittington. We can read the history of his life between the lines of account-roll and dispatch, pleadings and decree. Perhaps, even, for their sakes and our own, we know too much of his relatives, patrons, and allies; but then our knowledge will not have been acquired in vain. The greater master of exchange, the useful agent of the Crown, the financial adviser of ministers, the oracle of the city, the merchant prince, patron, and benefactor, becomes also, in his inevitable relations to the age in which he lived, as usurer, the son and nephew of usurers; a monopolist, the nominee of corrupt courtiers, and the associate of thievish contractors; and a landlord, the son, nephew, cousin, husband of a name as foul as any in the annals of oppression, eviction, and plunder. Yet if he were of these he was not like unto them; and higher praise than this can be awarded to no distinguished Englishman of the latter half of the sixteenth century.[8]

The connections then between merchant and royalty assume almost castelike proportions. At the same time there is a degree of noblesse oblige, and the familiar note that rising above moral turpitude and reconciling crass polemics is the equivalent of a national service of merit. At this point, morality and goodness merge into English/British nationality.

Without goodness, Corvino will sacrifice the virtue of his wife, Celia. Corvino was able to give Volpone pearls and diamonds, and had dowry enough to procure Celia who, in Mosca's words, was

> the wonder
> The blazing star of Italy! a wench
> Of the first year! a beauty ripe as harvest!
> Whose skin in whiter than a swan all over,
> Than silver, snow or lilies! a soft lip,
> Would tempt you to eternity of kissing!
> And flesh that melteth in the touch to blood!
> Bright as your gold and lovely as your gold! (*Vol.*, I.i.180)

Interestingly, Celia is the merchant class personified. The idea of "blazing" goes past the agricultural imagery of the harvest, to the passionate couplet that concludes this part. In these two lines there is a suggestion of God and glory, and religion and richness all easily yoked together. Seemingly, Jacobean merchant-class wealth has corrupted Elizabethan purity, as we move from the harvest with its nostalgic ring to the corrupting, destroying gold that would melt flesh to blood.

The national note is struck in the reference again to race. This is not subtle now, but quite blatant. The skin of beauty is "whiter than a swan" and it is associated not with Volpone's gold, but silver; not with the skin-darkening sun but with snow; and with the suggestion of lily-white and its connotations of virtue, racial purity, and the goodness of Christ. Celia is therefore not flesh and blood, but is the ideal, removed from immediate space. At the same time she is the very incarnation of sensuality. Jonson's language conveys to the lecherous Volpone the physical image of her presence that, coarse as he is, Volpone would best understand. The statement by Mosca is done in a language that relates to both Volpone (the fox) and Corvino (the raven) that of silver and gold.

Although Celia herself therefore says little, a great deal is spoken about her and she maintains a central position in the minds of the audience. Jonson is always conscious of the need for language to be moderate and never excessive, and he balances it as Queen Elizabeth did her own sexuality:

No precepts will profit a fool, no more than beauty will the blind, or music the deaf. As we should take care that our style in writing be neither dry nor empty, we should look again it be not winding, or wanton with far-fetched descriptions: either is vice, But that is worse which proceeds out of want than that which riots out of plenty. The remedy of fruitfulness is easy, but no labour will help the contrary.[9]

Thus, Mosca's description of Celia is dramatically appropriate. It is intended to lure Volpone into Mosca's trap. Celia thus becomes a vehicle for the exposure of evil and greed. She is not a mere character, but in contrast to Lady Would-Be is, at least, capable of an existence quite independent of the narrative structure. She provides the feminine quality to the play and adds a note of magic to the crassness of Lady Would-Be. In fact, it could be argued that she provides the audience with the necessary alternative to the pervasive villainy of the play.

CLASS: KING JAMES AND DIFFERENCE

If *Volpone* contrasted gender (with Queen Elizabeth as a kind of bisexual paragon), *Bartholomew Fair* deals with the issue of class. Grace in *Bartholomew Fair* does not share Celia's insubstantiality, but her class contrast appears in Ursula. Grace Wellborn, ward to Justice Overdo, has a surname that explains her outer social status, and a Christian name that hints at her innate goodness. By contrast, Ursula is a foul-mouthed, coarse pig-woman at Bartholomew Fair. Ursula's language is crude, whereas Grace's is cultivated; Ursula is rough, whereas Grace is genteel; Ursula is bawdy and freely employs vulgarities, whereas Grace is most ladylike in speech and action.

Their differences can only partly be explained by Jonson's attention to realistic detail. But indeed the text shows that it was performed before a royal audience; hence the aristocracy would be lauded, and the groundings disparaged. King James (and for that matter Elizabeth) would have expected no less. Neither ever claimed to be a democratic populist. The modern reader comes to *Bartholomew Fair* with the feeling that (as with *Volpone*), the female characters represent polarized extremities, with the scale of virtue tilted in favor of those who are rich, powerful, and British. This could not help but please a Scottish king, newly attempting an experiment that sought the unity of two kingdoms, and desirous of constant assurances of his own acceptability in England.

Jonson is more at ease with Ursula than with Mrs. Fitzdottrel or Lady Would-Be, because she belongs to the lowest orders. As such she is not expected to possess any ladylike characteristics. Her purpose is to provide loud comedy, and in this respect she is like no other character so far discussed. Since there is no hero or heroine in the play and the action takes place around different issues, Jonson has a freer hand in developing his class polarities.

Although one finds that Grace is the more agreeable of the two, she is as correct in her behavior as in her speech that her over-refinement is at times boring. Yet she is able to direct her own destiny in a way that Celia seemed unable to do. Finding herself confronted by two lovers, she argues quite rationally that she could not be expected to make up her mind after only two hours' acquaintance. But the method she utilizes to choose a husband seems silly. In the final act of *Bartholomew Fair*, Grace is more assertive. She is capable of wit when, for instance the following exchange takes place among Cokes, Winwife and Grace:

Cokes: Well then, we are quit for all. Come, sit down,
Numps: I'll interpret to thee: did you see mistress Grace? It's no matter,
         neither, now I think on't, tell me anon.
Winwife: A great deal of love and care he expresses!
         Grace: Alas, would you have him to express more than he has?
         That were tyranny.
Cokes: Peace, ho! now, now. (*B.F.*, V.iii.338)

Cokes is a simple foolish man, easily outwitted by Winwife, one of his rivals for Grace's hand. As an upperclass woman, Grace shows here her ability to grow, to learn from experience, to take charge in the macroscopic setting of the fair that is the world. For Jonson, the class ramifications, at least as presented here before a royal audience, indicate the ability to develop and grow.

Ursula is different, does not seem to develop, and is locked into postures of strutting and fretting, as Jonson himself had articulated when referring to the writer:

The true Artificer will not run away from nature, as hee were afraid of her; or depart from life, and the likenesse of Truth; but speake to the capacity of his hearers. And though his language differ from the vulgar somewhat; it shall not fly from all humanity with the *Tamerlanes*, and *Tamer-Chams*, of the late Age, which had nothing in them but the scenicall strutting, and furious vociferation, to warrant them then to be ignorant gapers. Hee knowes it is his onely Art, so to carry it, as none but Artificers perceive it. In the meane time perhaps hee is call'd barren, dull, leane, a poore Writer (or by what contumelious word can come in their cheeks) by these men, who without labour, judgement, knowledge, or almost sense, are received, or preferr'd before him.[10]

Is Ursula then like the poor writer, lauded for the wrong reasons? Even perhaps received into court through sheer duplicity? The final condemnation of those at the bottom of the social rung are those who deserve to be there, for they lack judgement, knowledge and good sense. It is of course a sweeping generalization, but this is a time totally committed to explaining the inborn inferiority of the lower orders, which seemed a natural and judicious response. It would spill over into racial issues, as noted in *The Masque of Blackness* (performed 1605) when Queen Anne and some of her ladies-in-waiting played the parts of Black women, completing our understanding of the theater as a place of legitimate alterity—a change of gender roles, class roles, and in this instance (to which I shall return) of race.

Perhaps the small role that women play is due to the aforementioned "capacity of the hearers." Jonson (like Shakespeare) was always conscious that production means the ability to attract an audience. At a time when—even despite the gender of the reigning monarchy—women had not gained an equal status in society, Jonson relegated them to the periphery of the stage. But their presence nevertheless helped him introduce elements relating to gender, class and race in the Britain of his day.

ELIZABETHAN PATRIARCHY

The Elizabethan Age was one of great expansion: in the arts, in navigation, in exploration, and in conquest. But the era was one dominated by *men* like Sir Francis Drake, Admiral Horatio Nelson and Sir Walter Raleigh. There are few women—apart from Queen Elizabeth herself—who occupied the limelight. Nevertheless England was powerful, as A. L. Rowse comments:

But there were certain factors that gave England greater strength than anyone realised at the time—certainly than her size and population warranted—and that made the struggle more even than anyone judging by appearances could have supposed. Some of these, the geographical for instance, have been continuing factors. The south coast control led the busiest thoroughfare of world traffic and the character of its harbours offered a decided advantage; deep water in close proximity to centres of trade, made admirable bases. Then there was length of coast line, the ease and cheapness of water transport. Land-powers have hardly any conception of the advantage here in speed of communications, flexibility and movement of resources to the required point. Anyone who knows Spain will appreciate the slowness and delays that hampered Philip's preparations, the difficulty of concentration: his resources could hardly ever be fully brought to bear, except in 1588, and then only after long delays and much loss, English mobilisation was so rapid and efficient that the Queen needed to keep only a small portion of her fleet in being.[11]

Much as Henry VIII had forged the alliance between Church and State, Elizabeth's task was the consolidation of state power. But this had little or no significance for women in general.

England was still fragmented by a deeply entrenched class structure. A woman was her husband's wife and few sought or attained independence. This is why it is impossible to seek for any modern counterpart in the characters that have been examined in Jonson's plays. They are not so much flesh and blood as dramatic performers of tasks, providing humor and humors (as with Ursula), expressing the feminine ideal (as with Grace and Mrs. Fitzdottrel), indicating female sensuality (as with Cecilia), or serving as comic relief to highlight the follies of the period (as with Lady Would-Be). However, they do indicate at specific points beyond the text, points where female characters, even as they are conflated into broad categories of the ladylike and the bawdylike, introduce actions that supposedly equate with their class element.

Ursula poses, however, another problem; she seems to indicate the inability or unwillingness of the dramatist to challenge the social caste system. Ursula is tiresome after a while, since she is simply the basic Elizabethan clown without any depth or any extra dimension that would have allowed her to address larger concerns. Of course the play, *Bartholomew Fair*, does not lend itself to any grave philosophical speculations, and perhaps it is requiring too much of any one character to perform a task that is not inherent in the dramatic form of loud farce. Within the framework of her occupation at the fair, Ursula is not conceived as having an inner life. In all fairness it should be added that this could equally be said for the other characters.

At a different level, Lady Would-Be is also two dimensional. She is intended to be a pompous show-off with pretensions to learning, and she performs this role throughout the play. One cannot fault Jonson for this, by claiming that he was unsympathetic to women. For not only was this not a major interest on his part in *The Devil is an Ass*, but also his comic intent supersedes any serious concern regarding the question of good and evil, as evinced by Christopher Marlowe in *Dr. Faustus*.

The more serious representations reveal varying degrees of depth. Grace, as her name suggests, has a certain spiritual essence. But she is not given a large enough role for the reader to determine the extent of her sincerity. Since *Bartholomew Fair* is the type of collage in which all the action takes place in one day around different people, the playwright cannot be faulted for failing to develop Grace as a character. Jonson, as already stated, is more intent on entertainment, and characters flit on and off the stage. As has been pointed out, they do show elements of growth, and, in this manner, Grace was seen to develop from a person with a zeal for game playing into a woman who seemed in command of herself. I remain convinced though that is limited to persons of her social and class stature. In a few words, pig-women do not grow.

Celia and Mrs. Fitzdottrel remain the most interesting of the female characters. They are both married to amoral and foolish men, yet they are both able to rise above the follies of their husbands. Therefore, in both cases, they exhibit an individuality that is most compelling. They are able to see through the guise of deceit and to attempt to achieve a higher level of moral reality. Both reflect pensive aspects in an environment that seemingly emphasizes the male, the materialistic, and the trivial.

Mrs. Fitzdottrel seems to be a stronger person than Celia. Celia merely acquiesces to her husband's whims and to the jurisdiction of the court, whereas Mrs. Fitzdottrel, while still admitting to her supposed limitations as a woman, establishes at the end of the play an independence that one would have liked to have witnessed in Celia. They are both victims of the actions of foolish men, but whereas Celia acquiesces to her condition, Mrs. Fitzdottrel is openly rebellious against the selfishness and crass unconcern that brought her to a condition of semidestitution. Mrs. Fitzdottrel does not possess Celia's physical charms, but did she, one suspects that she would have openly challenged the immoral jurisdiction of her spouse. After all, James was in constant feud with his Parliament, and his son would lose both his throne and his head in the antiroyalist revolution that would follow.

Other writers of the period attempted to deal with women, but the prevalent problem was that the female had to remain an object of wonder and admiration. True, she could be whore or witch, but aristocrats were always accorded certain kinds of privilege. Therefore, two inhibiting factors remained for Jonson and any writer of the period. They did not possess the ease with which they could write about women with the same carefree detachment they employed for men. In addition, in a play having a contemporary setting it would have been a mark of bad taste to have seemed to vilify women. No such constraints existed on playwrights when they came to crate the different Others of Elizabethan imaginings—the Moor, the Mongol, the Asian, and the Black. In such instances, stereotypes abounded and one set of notions coincided with another, creating a simplistic essentializing that merely made the racial other seem ridiculous.

"THOSE KINDE OF PEOPLE": RACE AND THE ELIZABETHANS

During Elizabeth's reign we first hear news of the presence of Blacks in England. Most likely they were part of the incipient slave trade that had brought Africans from West Africa to Europe, as curiosities, and later as domestic servants and status symbols. Writing in 1578, George Best wanted to convince Englishmen that exposure to the torrid zone would not unalterably change their complexions for the worse, and he gave this little bit of first hand knowledge:

I myselfe have seene an Ethiopian as blacke as a cole brought into England, who taking a faire English woman to wife, begat a sonne in all respects as blacke as the father was although England were his native countrey, and an English woman his mother: whereby it seemeth this blackness proceedeth rather of some natural infection of that man, which was so strong, that neither the nature of the Clime, neither the good complexion of the mother concurring, coulde any thing alter, and therefore, we cannot impute it to the nature of the Clime.[12]

Many of the British researchers into the relatively new discipline of Cultural Studies, including Stuart Hall's newfound allegiance to a Black cause, see the previous passage as marking an early Black presence in England—putting in a little stake for themselves, so to speak.[13] Not much is usually said about the "natural infection" of the man. I want to single this out, because I wish to stress how this becomes a new marker in the early Modern period of an alterity that went beyond gender. Indeed, Best argues quite cogently that the Blackness of the child remained, despite the "good complexion" of the English mother—there goes Homi Bhabha's much-vaunted "hybridity," whereby metropole and periphery blend easily together, mutually borrowing from one another. Certainly regarding gender/race marginalization, Best makes it quite clear that being Black and infected is really the worse of all possible worlds.

I wish to cite a further example of racial hostility from no less a person than Gloriana herself, who despite all of her own gender problems, and her need to assume a kind of politically useful transvestism, was quick to take hasty action to banish certain alien others from her kingdom. Queen Elizabeth's open letter dated July 11, 1596, as cited by Peter Fryer, was dispatched to several important officials in the country and went as follows:

On Her Majestie understanding that there are of late divers blackmoores brought into this realme, of which kinde of people there are allready here to manie. . . . Her Majesty's pleasure therefore ys that those kinde of people should be sent forth of the lande, and for that purpose there ys direction given to this bearer. . . . Wherein wee require you to be aydinge and assysting unto him as he shall have occacion, therof not to faile.[14]

Fryer adds that the matter did not simply end there, but was speeded up by the promise of monetary reward. He writes:

This was an astute piece of business, which must have saved the queen a lot of money. The black people concerned were being used as payment for the return of 89 English prisoners. The government simply confiscated them from their owners—there is no mention of compensation—and handed them over to a German slave-trader.[15]

The plan did not quite work, since as Fryer shows, we see her in 1601 issuing still more injunctions against "negars and Blackamoores."

Quite early, therefore, in African/European relationships the defining boundaries were established. Blackamoors, the queen stated, added to the number of mouths to feed, and since they were heathens they should expelled. Fryer states what he terms "the widespread belief, more firmly held than ever in the reign of a virgin queen of exceptional pallor, that whiteness stood for purity, virtue, beauty, and beneficence, whereas anything black was bound to be filthy, base, ugly, and evil."[16] I have already tried to show how Elizabeth's paleness was delicately hinted at by Sir John Hayward, who then proceeded to make a virtue of it. And we noted also that Celia's skin "whiter than a swan" became the subject of her allure, with the consequent corollary that blackness would have carried negative connotations.[17]

All of this would not impede the march toward trade. In 1601 a Khoi-khoi called Coree the Saldanian was abducted from South Africa and brought to England. Behind the kidnaping and abduction was the East India Company, and indeed some four months after Coree was seized he was brought to London and lodged with Sir Thomas Smith, merchant and governor of the East India Company. Despite his repeated wishes to be sent back home, the company held him in London against his will, even bribing him quite liberally.[18] Seemingly, they wanted his assistance in trading ventures, so at some point he ceased to be as nuisance and became a guest, however reluctant he might have felt.

JONSON'S *MASQUE OF BLACKNESS*: GENDER AND RACE

Jonson begins *The Masque of Blackness* with the assumption that Blacks themselves would wish to rid themselves of their troublesome color. Washing the Ethiop white thus becomes the aim of the masque, a conceit that will be enacted in all its manifestations. The heat of the sun, complained of so much by Shakespeare's lighter heroines, has turned beauty black and has sent the daughters of Niger seeking out a land named Britannia whose king will have the power to rid them of their burdensome skin coloration. It is particularly odd that James would have been chosen to represent a king that would rid them of their blackness. He himself was known for his love of the exotica, for the naked Black who danced in the snow when he married Anne of Denmark, and for forty-two black-faced revellers who accompanied the wedding procession. Kim F. Hall adds that "Blacks were a common feature in the Scottish court, kept there as dehumanized alien curiosities, on par with James's pet lion and his collection of exotic animals."[19]

Of course, this was no mere indulgence on Anne's part to play the part of one of the Blackamoors. Indeed, as recent critics are pointing out, with the expansion of the British Empire and the encounter with difference, plus the presence of Black people in Britain and the Scottish court, the *Masque of Blackness* and its follow-up, the *Masque of Beauty* (1608), are really ways in which the court can take an active role in foreign encounter and empire building. So, although the masque was at base a playful piece of fun, it carried with it the very serious message that Black/White encounter is one between ruler and ruled and, even more pertinent, one in which the ruled easily recognize their shortcomings and the need to rectify them. Race had not become fixed as yet, but I cannot agree with Kwame Anthony Appiah (himself part English and part Ghanaian) that racism is not endemic to English society until the eighteenth century.[20] We certainly note its beginnings here, and we would be hardput to call Queen Elizabeth's battle against her Blackamoors and "negars" by any other name.

By dazzling the American reading public with such an Anglicism as "racialism," and pretending that it only means racial awareness, and is not as loaded as "racism," Appiah does a disservice to his readers. Instead, let me refer to Stuart Hall's take on this which he clearly identifies as racist discourse. Quite rightly, Hall sees in Best a "binary system of representation [that] constantly marks and attempts to fix and naturalize the difference between belongingness and otherness."[21] Within the dichotomy of the fair, good-complexioned English woman and her dark, infectious Black spouse, is located the permanent and irredeemable nature of race difference and Black inferiority.

Best would reinforce his own point later on in his sixteenth-century text by stressing that Africa was a land fit only for Ham and his Black son, since the place had "cursed, dry, sandy, and unfruitfull ground, fit for such a generation to inhabite in."[22] Thus quite early in the literature of England, the demonization of the African—here firmly linked with biblical interpretation—becomes part and parcel of the ways in which the West conscripts and condemns the African continent. Elsewhere I have shown that there are earlier texts such as the Old English *Wonders of the East*, purportedly the adventures of Alexander the Great, which persist in locating Africanness on the outermost terrains of ultrahuman existence. The Others inhabit the Uttermost part of the globe.[23]

NOTES

1. I use the dates 1572–1637 for Ben Jonson, even though his birthdate is questionable. Elizabeth I (1533–1603) reigned from 1558 to her death and James I (1566–1625) reigned from 1603–1625.

2. Gamaliel Bradford, *Elizabethan Women* (Cambridge, MA: Riverside, 1936), 101.

3. Ben Jonson, *The Works of Ben Jonson*, ed. William Gifford (London: Edward Moxon, 1853), 180.

4. References to Jonson's plays are made from Gifford's edition and will appear in the text. *Vol.* will be used for *Volpone; B.F.* for *Bartholomew Fair*; and *D.A.* for *The Devil is an Ass*.

5. Kenneth Muir, ed., *Elizabethan and Jacobean Prose, 1550–1620* (London: Penguin, 1956), 2.

6. Gladys E. Locke, *Queen Elizabeth* (Boston: Sherman, French and Company, 1913), 225–26.

7. Dates are taken from Paul Harvey, ed., *The Oxford Companion to Literature* (Oxford: Clarendon, 1960), 419.

8. Hubert Hall, *Society in the Elizabethan Age* (London: Swan Sonnenschein, 1902), 58.

9. Ben Jonson, "Praecipiendi Modi" in *Timber: or Discoveries* [1641] in *English Critical Essays*, ed. Edmund D. Jones (London: Oxford UP, 1956), 96.

10. Jonson, "Propriety," in Muir, *Elizabethan*, 266.

11. A. L. Rowse, *The Expansion of Elizabethan England* (London: Macmillan, 1955), 246.

12. George Best, "A True Discourse of the Three Voyages of Discoverie, for the Finding of a Passage to Cathaya, by the Northwest. . . . " in *The Three Voyages of Martin Frobisher*, ed. Vilhjalmur Stefansson (London: Argonaut, 1938), 14–129. Originally published in Richard Hakluyt, ed., *The Principal Navigations, Voyages, Traffiques & Discoveries of the English Nation*, 12 vols. (Glasgow: James MacLehose and Sons, 1903–1905), 7:250–83. Extract cited is on p. 262.

13. Stuart Hall, "New Ethnicities," in *I. C. A Documents 7: Black Film, British Cinema*, ed. Kobena Mercer (London: Institute of Contemporary Arts, 1988), 27–30. There is "reprint" of this essay in *Stuart Hall: Critical Dialogues in Cultural Studies* ed. Davis Morley and Kuan-Hsing Chen (London and New York: Routledge, 1996), 41–49, where consideration of Best has been omitted. Hall's interest in Blackness and race is quite recent. The most casual glance at his work reveals that during the period of intense immigration of Indians, Pakistanis, and Caribbean people to Britain in the post–War II period, he along with certain liberal English intellectuals maintained a moral highground regarding race as a kind of unmentionable. Everything, it seems, could be explained away purely in Marxist terms—no one need be too embarrassed. Today Hall has been converted. A veritable welter of information is pouring out from him, including two recent video lectures in which he at least discusses race, even if he takes the now acceptable and more agreeable line that it is only a construct.

14. Cited in Peter Fryer, *Staying Power: The History of Black People in Britain* (London: Pluto, 1984), 11.

15. Ibid., 12–13.

16. Ibid., 11.

17. Kim F. Hall treats the issue of Blackness thoroughly, especially the manner in which it crept into the English language and became a negative signifier. I am aware, of course, that this is not limited to English alone, but is also found in several other European languages. See Kim F. Hall, *Things of Darkness: Economies of Race and Gender in Early Modern England* (Ithaca, NY: Cornell UP, 1995), 12–13, 97–98, 132–33.

18. Hans Werner Debrunner, *Presence and Prestige: Africans in Europe: A History of Africans in Europe before 1918* (Basel: Basler Afrika Bibliographien, 1979), 58.

19. Hall, *Things of Darkness*, 128.

20. Kwame Anthony Appiah, *In My Father's House: Africa in the Philosophy of Culture* (New York: Oxford UP, 1992). Appiah makes an excellent point when he deals with nineteenth-century Pan-Africanists like Edward Blyden and Alexander Crummell, contending that they were more motivated by Eurocentric motives and beliefs than "African" ones, which they could not possibly have known, and would have spurned in any event. But on this issue of the British and their racism, I fear that his heart has held preponderance over his head. His reasons may well be personal. His father, Joe Appiah, was a lawyer who had alarmed the British by marrying the daughter of the Colonial Secretary, and sailing off for Ghana. Appiah's father was treated quite badly by Kwame Nkrumah, and was tossed into jail for daring to oppose *Osagyefo* (the Redeemer), as Nkrumah had fondly christened himself. Understandably, Appiah most likely felt throughout many years of a lonely childhood that his British school chums were his true "tribal" pals, and England his home. He now lives in America, teaching at Harvard.

21. Stuart Hall, "New Ethnicities," in *I. C. A Documents 7*, 28. Hall has no such excuse as Appiah. He was born in Jamaica, and went to Britain as part of the

large migration in the fifties. Like V. S. Naipaul (and I for that matter), the English sent us to their universities to become British.

22. Best, "Discourse," 7: 264.

23. O. R. Dathorne, *Imagining the World: Mythical Belief versus Reality in Global Encounters* (Westport, CT, and London: Bergin & Garvey, 1994), 54–55, 12–14.

Chapter 4

Talking Indian: Written Hegemony and Oral Native American Narration

Indians turn out to be a population inhabiting the European mind, not the American landscape, a fictional assemblage fabricated over the past five centuries to serve specific cultural and emotional needs of its inventors. (James A. Clifton, ed., *The Invented Indian: Cultural Fictions and Government Policies* [1994], 313)

To be an "American" therefore was as much an image in the minds of the leading citizens of the United States as it was to be an "Indian," and for most, if not all of the two centuries of United States existence the two images were antithetic. (Robert F. Berkhover Jr., *The White Man's Indian* [1979], 136)

Throughout De Soto's rampage from modern South Carolina to the Mississippi River, slaves of African descent escaped and intermarried with the local Indians, making these escaped slaved the first Old World settlers throughout much of the Southeast and the Gulf Coast. (Jack Weatherford, *Native Roots: How the Indians Enriched America* [1991], 279)

In this chapter, I wish to consider some of the basic conflicts that involved contact between the European and the Native American in the United States to show that there was a discrepancy between "word" and "deed." I am not preaching morality, although a hefty dose of this would still be in order, rather, I am arguing that the discrepancy lay between the *sound* signifier and the *image* signifier in the ethno/languages of the Europeans who settled in North America. I think of English as a narrow language, exported from a small island, as contrasted with Spanish and Portuguese, which had experienced the impact of the so-called "Moor" (African, Arab, Muslim, and "pagan") for over seven centuries.

I would contend that for the members of the new English-speaking hegemonic order, the "word" was the language of the field, the outside, the practical; the "deed" was the script of the bureaucrat (in Washington, D.C.), the inside, the theory. The dual language mandate existed perhaps quite independent of whatever the speakers/writers may have desired. They simply found themselves caught up in the heteroglossia of a new discourse, conditioned by a different geography.

The numbers of Europeans who arrived in America were so overwhelming, that they were very much able to brand Native Americans as "different" from them. Second, Anglo Europeans had come to settle in a way that neither the Spaniards nor Portuguese had visualized, namely to assume total control of the indigenous people and their land and, above all, to declare indigenous institutions totally irrelevant to the body of the majority. The Anglo adage about no good Indian did not translate into Spanish or Portuguese.[1]

MOVING WEST: DOERS AND WATCHERS

Once the Civil War was over, the United States devoted its full efforts towards bringing about the extermination of the Native American population. By 1889, part of the Oklahoma District had been officially designated "Indian Territory," where it was expected the various bands, groups, "tribes," or nations could be conveniently herded and forced to settle. The land itself had been confiscated from Creek and so-called Seminoles, and by treaty deeded to them forever. But on April 22, 1889, still another sorry spectacle would be enacted, the Land Run, whereby 160 acres of "free" land would be guaranteed to each "boomer," all of whom had been loud in their advocacy of taking away even the little their own government had promised to the Native Americans.[2]

This illegal distribution of land is the dramatic symbol of the Western need to possess and own. The debate never took place regarding whose land it rightfully was, as affirmed by a treaty from Washington itself. As with the opening of the so called Oregon Trail and the Mormon Trail, those who journeyed west during the California gold rush, indeed as with the occupation of the eastern seaboard itself, continued to assume that this was a "wilderness," occupied by no one and meant for the taking by those strong and agile enough to seize it.

Native Americans watched as the strangers descended on what were now inscribed as "Indian Lands," to participate in the "Land Rush." All of the elements of earlier Native American Conquest came together: old photographs show covered wagons and the U.S. cavalry armed with guns whose sound would signal the beginning of the race, itself a microcosm of the slower move from the east to the west coast. The scene would be replicated over and over again, in an atmosphere of happy partygoing, simply because the "settlers" neither cared nor wanted to understand what was at stake. Between 1845 and 1861 in Texas, for instance, the writers of *The Native Americans* speak of how "ferocious attacks on Indians by Texas irregulars and land-hungry settlers virtually eradicated from the state its longtime native occupants."[3]

Since the Native Americans were watchers and not participants in these dramatic reenactments of the "Land Rush," they were presumably confirming their place in the history of the West as the losers. However, this is clearly a European/Euro American perception of existence, I suspect partly to be rooted in Darwinian theory. Truth is that Native Americans did survive, deprived of liberty and land, subjected to monolithic assumptions about them as "a people," and deprived of an ethnicity which truthfully identified them with their gods, ancestors, family and languages.[4]

At least even if they could not to this day, merely for the convenience of Euro Americans, see themselves as one, a basic issue is still apparent: Since they had never "owned" the land, they would neither "cede" nor "lose" it by treaty or conquest.[5] For instance, the area itself that would be wrested from them in Oklahoma had been home to Cherokee, Muscogee, Creek, Chickasaw, Chocktaw and so-called Seminoles. These "Five Civilized Tribes," so-derived because they were more readily and easily adaptable to European culture, would fare as badly as all the others. They had been "relocated" from the southeast to the west; the Cherokee were positioned to the northeast, the Muscogee in the center, the Seminole in the West, and the Chickasaw and Chocktaw in the southeast and southwest. Their division into "nations," each separate and distinct, showed that as early as the 1830s when they were moved, their distinctness had been officially recognized, even though they were grouped together en masse as "Indians" who had to live in "Indian Territory," and who were unfit to live among Euro Americans. Supposedly, they possessed ultimate rights to the land, once they had conveniently agreed to surrender Georgia, Alabama and Florida—but such legitimation was always denied by the controlling power. And this was done by a very logocentric method of treaties and promulgations—always confirming the instability of whatever was spoken about and agreed.

Additionally, their new nomenclature and place name made for what Christian F. Feest calls "an easy reduction of the tremendous diversity of native cultures. . . into a few comprehensible categories."[6] Along their "Trail of Tears" many perished, but they moved from the southeast in what seemed like a last, desperate bid to rid themselves from the marauders to the east. There they rebuilt their former lives, different though this was, secure in the hope that they would now be left alone. There in the west, they existed in "traditional" style, with land held in common, although others chose a newer version of private property. With the assumption of the Civil War, they were placed in an impossible position, since they were now wooed by both sides.[7] Their loyalty one side or the other mattered little. The reservation system, and the super-reservation that Oklahoma offered, seemed to be the answer even if, as Robert M. Utley remarked, it "tore down the traditional culture without substituting the new at which it aimed."[8]

Terminology like "Five Civilized Tribes" was certainly not, at that time at least, considered degrading. Indeed, to be civilized was very desirable, since marginalization hardly carried with it the nostalgic traces it now does. After all, if the White European was the apex of perfection, it could hardly be considered ridiculous to aspire to what he stood for. This included continuing to own slaves, their own indication of their mark of outsiderdom. In effect, this not unnaturally was one of the issues that appealed to the wealthier and more powerful members of their own Native American group.

Their economy was securely linked with the south, utilizing the Mississippi for goods, barter and Black slaves down to New Orleans.[9] Therefore, in a way, they saw little relationship between themselves and Washington, faraway and unconnected, indeed the very agency that had moved them west from their ancestral lands.[10] Southern overtures made even more sense, when the federal governments pulled out its troops in 1861. Logically, they signed still another treaty, this time with the south. John Ross, designated leader and himself part-Native American, was the main signatory. He had resisted southern importunings until it seemed as if, once again, his people would suffer at the hands of mounted and armed confederate troops, riding roughshod over the area, shooting and killing in their wake.[11]

Hence, the war between the states was exported to Native Americans. In effect, this meant that there was not just the original breakdown into "tribal" patterns, but pragmatic alliances with Union or Confederate forces, forced a new image upon the old groupings—a view that was totally alien to their original sense of self, and more in keeping with the practical realities of a war no one quite understood. For, if there was an original concept of patriarchy—the "White" man, good or bad—now a new chaotic intervention, marked by new symbols of uniforms and dialects, introduced a confusing and conflicting element. In brief, the master discourse articulates its orders in a narrow, confined language, whereas the minor(ity) listeners hear what they can in a myriad of languages. This is truly a moment of rupture, and there is no one to identify the suture and bring the divergent meanings together. English lacks the elasticity for world interaction.

Even when desperate efforts were made to claim neutrality, as with a band of Creek Indians on November 5, 1861, they were still forced to take sides. In effect, by attempting to flee to the Union side in Kansas, the Creeks were attacked by Confederate forces from Texas. At the Battle of Chustenaheahin on December 26, 1865, Colonel James "routed," as a plaque proclaimed, what were "Loyal Union Indian Forces." Ironically, their loss was due to others from the so-called "Five Civilized Tribes" fighting with the Confederates.[12] The new alliance not only signalled the virtual end of their old compact, since they were now engaged in internecine conflict, but also eroded what little was left of group loyalty.

New leaders arose: Among the Cherokee, Chief Ross found himself seriously challenged by the power of Stand Watie, now designated a "colonel" in the Confederate army.[13] Indeed, the very fact that there was disunion among the artificial grouping (the so-called "Five Civilized Tribes") gave the victorious federal government the opportunity it had long sought of negating former treaties. When, for instance, the few Cherokee who had made it to Kansas returned to "Indian Territory" at war's end, they were as badly off as before.

Euro Americans first invented the "Five Civilized Tribes" as a way of administering and controlling a multiplicity of people who had little in common. The Civil War, an external disorder for them, then forced a new pattern on them, whereby by aligning themselves with Union or Confederate, they brought about temporary relationships outside clan, and totally independent of the original concepts of "tribe" that predated their own corporation into the artificiality of the "Five Civilized Tribes." The end of the Civil War made them all "losers," since they could not and were not allowed to revert even to the invention of the old grouping of the "Five Civilized Tribes." Forced to surrender sovereignty, "Indian Territory," created as a fiction, was now totally discarded. By 1866, shorty after Chief Ross' death, the old lands were confiscated by a hegemonic administration bent on expansion.

"CIVILIZING" INDIANS

There is a reminder of Derrida's injunction that there is nothing outside the text, when more and more treaties were signed by a people who by now must have come to regard the ritual of paper, document, witnesses and words, as temporary formulae that assured nothing. For this had all happened before, and nothing had held in the real world beyond the signifier. The so-called Seminoles were moved east and wedged in with the other groups. One interesting sideline, pointed out by Robert M. Utley is that, with the new zeal for "freedom," abolition of slavery was also imposed on this Native American grouping. Indeed Utley argues that it was because "[m]any of these people [Native Americans] owned slaves [that Native Americans] felt a natural affinity for southerners."[14] For them abolition went further than it did in the rest of the United States: Their slaves, some of whom were Black, were made "citizens" of specific Native American nations, and this was made even more ironical since it was done when neither Native Americans nor African Americans were U.S. citizens.

Next came the railroads on which poured in all the n'er-do-wells from the rest of the country.[15] Among the new intruders were the better known Kit Carson, Jesse James, and the Dalton gang vigilantly pursued by the "Hanging Judge" Isaac Parker, who operated justice long distance from Fort Smith, Arkansas, as well as the best known promoter of the "Wild West," William F. Cody, better known as Buffalo Bill. Abundantly clear now, considering that indigenous sovereignty was a thing of the past, was that Native Americans had no control whatsoever over these new marauders. And the federal government was not really in a position to control its citizens in "Indian Territory."

The advent of new adventurers further increased the extent to which the west was blended as part fact and mostly fancy. As Frederick Jackson Tucker sought out a metaphor for American individualism, the West became a natural reference point. He asserted:

In the settlement of America we have to observe how European life entered the continent, and how America modified and developed that life and reacted on Europe. Our early history is the study of European germs developing in an American environment. Too exclusive attention has been paid to institutional students of Germanic origins, too little to the American factors. The frontier is the line of most rapid and effective Americanization. The wilderness masters the colonist. It finds him a European in dress, industries, tools modes of travel, and thought. It takes him from the railroad car and puts him in the birch canoe. It strips off the garments of civilization and arrays him in the hunting shirt and moccasin. It puts him in the log cabin of the Cherokee and Iroquois and runs an Indian palisade around him. Before long he has gone to planting Indian corn and plowing with a sharp stick; he shouts the war cry and takes the scalp in orthodox Indian fashion. . . . The fact is that here is a new product that is American. At first, the frontier was the Atlantic coast. It was the frontier of Europe in a very real sense. Moving westward, the frontier became more and more American.[16]

Thus the West became not a mere space, but an enormous testing ground for White manhood as it transferred itself from European to American genes. Somewhere, lost in all this, were the unfortunate Native Americans who were expunged in the process. The West is still the unfortunate word easily utilized (even in well-meaning documentaries) to represent, stand for, symbolize masculinity.

New arrivants saw the railroad as their way to wealth. They could purloin timber from the "Indian Territories" and ship at ease. Add to this that the new White "settlers" (often "invited" by the Native Americans who had little respect for them), conceived of their "lease" as "freehold" in a country where everything was up gratis and up for grabs. By 1880, "Indian Territory" was a mere name, since Euro Americans outnumbered Native Americans. In turn, they began to press for closer alliance with Washington for "Oklahoma" (a Choctaw term meaning "Red People") to become U.S. territory with U.S. schools and aid. So, if "Indian Territory" had ever existed, its fiction was now proven. It was, in reality, U.S. land waiting to be taken over by its rightful heirs.

Not unnaturally, the Native Americans protested. But the Red People in their Red Land had little voice now, and matters would move, not as they wished, but as the "Great Father" in Washington deemed. Recall too, that this was a time of expansive self-approbation, when the new country merely saw Native Americans as a stumbling block to progress. What finally emerged, again because of the monolithic assumptions that every group was the same, was the government's action at simply cramming all Native Americans together. Joined, therefore, with the old remnants of the "good" "Five Civilized Tribes," were shunted in the Nez Perce, Cheyenne, Modoc and so on, all shunted together into this one appointed space.[17]

From the east, even the "humanitarians" would now gaze out at a problem that seemed to have a simple solution. Since Native Americans could not be exterminated, perhaps they could be "educated." In other words, the old adage of the only good Injuns being dead ones, gave way to the enlightened promise that a good Injun was one who had been taught to speak and write English, whose "Americanization" would finally destroy him, in a way that even genocidal efforts had not.

From the viewpoint of official America, the Native American narrative is basically the same and equally as brief: they came, they were seen, they were conquered. Apache, Cheyenne, Dakota, the so-called "Five Civilized Tribes," the Nez Perce and everyone else had coexisted (not necessarily at peace) in contiguous places. After the Jefferson expedition of Lewis and Clark—actually a spying mission—and the 1849 discovery of gold, eager Easterners pushed their way West. At first, "treaties" were utilized, partly to stem Native American concerns, but they were just as easily broken. The U.S. Cavalry, under various generals, often Civil War veterans, were handpicked by Washington to mollify or crush unwilling opposition. Finally, despite heroic efforts by leaders like Geronimo, Sitting Bull and others, Native Americans were driven off from their ancestral lands, and forced to occupy "reservations."

THE INDIAN PRINCESS

The Indian maiden/queen is somewhat of a contradiction. The master narrative assumed that the male Native American was aggressive, militant and dangerous. On the other hand, from the earliest attempts of Hollywood, the assumption was made that the "squaw," was both harmless and part of the background scenery. Additionally she could be utilized, with her face appropriately tanned, to provide an off-scene love interest that would titillate but not offend White audiences. A good example of this is *The Lost Horizon* (1955) with Charlton Heston, where the writers insist on including a love interest. Disney would do as much in *Pocahontas: Journey to a New World* (1998), as the storyline stressed a "love affair" between an elderly Captain John Smith and a pre-nubile Pocahontas.

Sacagawea is only the most recent of Native Americans who see the incoming foreigners as objects of awe and devotion. The "good" Indian Guacanagarí was supposedly loyal to Columbus, even helping to salvage the contents of a ship which had sunk. But another cacique, Caonabó, was hardly as cooperative, and received the major blame for the destruction of Columbus's first New World settlement. And mentioned with these polar opposites was a *cacica*, Anacaona, who was hanged by the Spaniards in 1502.[18]

Additionally many fascinating people grace the fringes of the explorer narratives, and it requires a degree of Foucauldian archaeology to lay bare these important texts embedded in the master text. In another study I pointed out what seemed obvious that for Enrique of Molucca to have joined Ferdinand Magellan and Antonio Pigafetta on their "first" circumnavigation, meant, in effect, that he had already journeyed through Asia and Africa to Europe, and was now going back by way of the Americas and the South Seas.[19] Hence, in reality, he was the first circumnavigator, not Magellan.

At this stage, however, I should like to examine the narratives of Malinche (or Doña Marina) and Cortés in 1519; Pocahontas and Captain John Smith in 1607; and Sacagawea and Lewis and Clark in 1804–1806. The women have some of a number of elements in common: First, they are either royalty, or made into royalty. Second, they welcome the coming of the West, and in some accounts actually fall in love with their conquerors. Third, they all are able to move easily between at least two, and often more, languages, leaving the historical record with an enormous question mark, as regards the accuracy of what was said or not said. Fourth, they are guides; they know the land, and help open it up for the newcomers. And finally, because of their role, suggesting both indigenous patriotism and Western allegiance, they are claimed by both conqueror and conquered, colonizer and colonized, victor and victim.

The two names of La Malinche and Doña Marina tell us something about the dual and doubtful nature of what she stands for. "La Maliche" means plaything, whore, and is the none-too-flattering sobriquet bestowed on her by her kinsfolk.[20] The Spanish chroniclers instead preferred the more formal "Doña Marina"; it seemed more appropriate in the context in which she was represented in dispatches from Cortés to his emperor, or even later on when Díaz del Castillo compiled his semi-official history of Conquest, a sort of *apologia pro sua vita* for Cortés, at a time when Cortés was out of favor.[21]

However none of these women are mere shadowy, insubstantial beings, what Anne McClintock sees as boundary markers, "planted like fetishes at the ambiguous points of contact, at the borders and orifices of the contest zone."[22] Yet Malinche is a real person, however distorted by the majority narrative. As such she is an enabler, if not the the equal of Cortés, at least someone who inhabits the same space, moving toward the same goal.

Malinche is rendered in the pages of history through the letters of Cortés, the indigenous account supervised by Fray Bernardino de Sahagún, or the narrative of Díaz del Castillo.[23] Thus, we are able to glean some concept of what at least various Spaniards saw in her. Díaz describes her as "the mistress and cacica of towns and vassals" (Díaz, 66), and "a person of the greatest importance. . . [who] was obeyed without question by the Indians throughout New Spain" (Díaz, 67). This sounds like an exaggeration, unless an assumption was made that since she was the companion and lover of Cortés and had borne him a son, she had a measure of authority that was derived from him. Sahagún's informants are less expansive in what they say, "And when Moctezuma's address which he directed to the Marquis was ended, Marina then interpreted it, she translated it to him. And when the Marquis had heard Moctezuma's words, he spoke to Marina; he spoke to them in a barbarous tongue; he said in his barbarous tongue. . . ." Then follows Cortés's words. But the point I wish to stress is that in the quasi-indigenous text, in Nahautl and Spanish, Marina (termed Malintzin in Nahautl) is presented as the center piece of the dialogue. She is the mouthpiece for the West, and it must be stressed that no one (neither Motecuhzoma II nor Cortés) knows the actual meaning of the signifier.

Sandra Messinger Cypress feels that Días is emphasizing the ultimate in cultural synthesis, what she terms "the assimilation by Marina of Spanish culture." Hence, because of this she can forgive her relatives who had earlier sold her into slavery, and she can even be constructed as a good "*Spanish* mother" because she has forsaken the evil ways of her ancestors.[24] To Cortes himself, she is none of these. In his letters to Emperor Charles V, she is mentioned in an almost off-handed manner, when he talks about his interpreter as "a Native Indian girl who came with me from Puntunchan (a great river of which I informed your majesty in my first letter) . . . ."[25] The description is laughable, making her sound as if she had nothing personal to do with Cortés, but was merely part of the landscape.

Initially, the Indian princess must be wild and untutored in the manner of the Noble Savage. Her body awaits transformation into a Christian, even a European. And this can be best done even as she becomes the progenitor of future owners of the land—the Creoles who will assume the place of departed Europeans. Pocahontas was ten when she supposedly met Captain John Smith. Her youth plus her ethnicity contributes to what Donna J. Kessler sees as to how "she occupies an ambiguous position between savagery and civilization, both physically and mentally"[26]

There is a problem of credibility with Pocahontas, since Smith gave four versions of his 1607 captivity, and it is only in the last, published seven years after Pocahontas had died, that she is resurrected as an admirer who saved Smith's life.[27] The reasons are not difficult to suggest— there may have been an element of self-glorification (in a tale of adventure that had few witnesses—certainly none among his reading public). Additionally, as Peter Hulme suggests, there is a more serious element here; there is the very colonialist desire to conscript the other, to make it Self, so that it will obey the Self and follow its dictates.[28] Although Pocahontas did not marry Smith, she converted to Christianity and married another Englishman, John Rolfe. Neither, did Malinche marry Cortés, although she bore him children. The gatekeepers seem to be fit to bed down with the Conquerors, but not to become their legitimate spouses.

Smith had found the ten year old "the only Nonpariel of his [her father's] Country" and he adds "not only for feature, countenance, and proportion. . . but for wit and spirit."[29] This is their first meeting, according to Smith. By the time he writes his 1624 book, it is much more dramatic; Pocahontas put his head in her arms, and placed her own head on his to save him from the chopping block.

By the time we come to the Meriwether Lewis and William Clark expedition of 1804–1806, the myth of the devoted princess is still not laid to rest. It was still essential then, as perhaps Disney still found with Pocahontas, to have as an Indian American heroine, a savage woman capable of understanding the blessings of the gifts of the West, one who would serve (even on a coin) as an emblem of diversity, modern feminism and ancient myth. In real life, says Erica Funkhouser:

She was very young. She was probably fourteen. She'd been traded back and forth between different Minitari braves, apparently, before she was won by Charbonneau [a French fur trader] in a gamble, in a game, in a gamble really. . . he won her from another Minitari brave. . . [and] when he won her, he had already had another wife, so I think she was his second common-law wife. . . . Within a few months she was pregnant.[30]

For Lewis, she is, however, the natural guide, quite at home with the landscape. On July 22, 1805, he writes, "the Indian woman recognizes the country and assures us that this is the river on which her relations live." Later Lewis acknowledges, "I had mentioned to the chief several times that we had with us a woman of his nation who had been taken prisoner by the Minnetares, and that by means of her I hoped to explain myself more fully than I could do signs."[31] The subplot is that the princess had been made into a slave, and will be restored to her former status through the goodness of Lewis and Clark.

She is the saddest of the threesome we have been discussing. Pocahontas dies and is buried in England; Malinche simply disappears from the written historical record. With Sacagawea, there are sightings of her, one particularly pathetic, near St. Louis in 1811 when she is wearing the cast-off clothing of white women. Yet Sacagawea has served in the capacity of mythmaker for a long time. There are two texts that show how Sacagawea has remained in the forefront of popular entertainment: In 1943 Della Gould Emmons published *Sacajawea of the Shoshones*, and in 1979 Anna Lee Waldo published *Sacajawea*. As I mentioned before, *The Far Horizons* came out in 1955. All these texts have a common element: Sacagawea is the traditional Indian princess in love across the color line. But she is (because America is) concerned with miscegenation, and this is why in the film her love can come to naught. As with every film that contains an Asian/White American love interest, the Other woman's love cannot be requited.

PERSPECTIVE OF THE INDIAN "OTHER"

What, however, do we glean from the perspective of this Other? Were they, as official U.S. history suggests, merely content to bemoan their fate, in the wake of great oratory on the part of the "chiefs" as they succumbed to official U.S. might? Or was there another side to the struggle for control? It is, of course, tempting to simply read Native American history backwards, as seen from today's situation, and simply give a reasoning to account for a subjugated and divided people. But it is also possible to view Native Americans not as is our current wont, somewhat fashionably, as ancient custodians of a land they no longer possess. If seen differently, they become representatives of values that have also run contrary, even counter, to those of the dominant U.S. power structure. Therefore, their "demise" was due not so much to inferior weaponry, but to their own concept of "place" that, still remains intact today. Therefore, despite the popularly orchestrated outcry of injustice (which is certainly true in a most basic sense), Native American presence represents a viable alternative to latter-day American lifestyle, the still untold account of an environment and peoples misnamed by their conquerors.

In attempting to situate Native Americans, one must begin with the obvious. These are not a group of monolithic "Indians"; in a way, the very invention simply manufactured a way that made the Other easier to label, comprehend, and destroy. And, since we must note from the beginning disparancies in custom, religion, language, and behavior, we should begin therefore with an admission of multifarious peoples who inhabit an area on which Europe has forced itself.

One type of "mythology" imposed on the present-day United States is the irony of "place." In particular, the southwest represents an area where the Anasazi, for instance, erected lasting and permanent monuments testifying to their validity and ownership of "place." There would be no mistaking their presence in the past—the crumbling remains are eloquent testifiers to this. There could be little confusion over their "invisibility," their "underuse" of land, their nomadic lifestyle that created the impression of God's Own Country being one open wilderness.

Side by side with their ownership marks—their buildings, temples, artifacts, and representations of a vital lifestyle—they were still largely ignored. The "Spanish-American War," like the earlier "French-Indian War," signifies in large measure that total dismissal of any legitimate place for Native Americans, since what the powers fought over was ownership of the very landscape that excluded any minority presence apart from theirs. And when, with the conclusion of the Spanish-American War, victory was declared, again the very process of declaring "winners" and "losers" excluded the very real presence of any third party.

Since the southwest is properly the territory of these Pueblo, along with Navajo, Hopi, Zuñi, and Apache, American history of conquest and hegemony had to conveniently ignore their presence. Instead, even as the gold rush provided a pragmatic reason for new "settlers," the government in Washington, D.C. declared "Manifest Destiny" as a godlike, "national," even patriotic urge to unsettle those who had already settled. Thus, the Native Americans after being created first as Noble Savages never really cognizant of their sense of place, were now revived as diabolic agents opposed to God-given change. As a result, they could be "displaced," since they never had comprehended the meaning of "place," and new reserves could be specially created to settle them far away from the determined advance of footsteps western bound.

This is all the more reason why present-day readings of their texts, zealously passed down by Euro Americans, must be regarded with the greatest suspicion. It seems extremely odd that the epic is played out all over North America with the sameness already mentioned. Particularly strange are the various and clear markers of contact: These include, first the obvious manner in which Native Americans are easily duped by "treaties," or spurred on toward internecine conflict, or urged toward an acceptance of the infallibility and omnipotence of what they supposedly all refer to as the "Great White Father." Second, in all cases, having easily succumbed to the blandishments of marginal westernization (its small accouterments, emblems, and insignia), they presumably then just as easily accept Western subordination. Third, those who revolt against what would seem to be widely accepted notions invariably are seen as outsiders. In this context Little Crow, Crazy Horse, Geronimo, Cochise, and even Sitting Bull are shown as erratic, misled men in mainstream American history.

If we look at this a little differently, we could confidently assert that Native American leadership became an intentional way in which a few could sacrifice themselves for the many. After all, in many of these societies, "sacrifice" as a specific way of obtaining a goal, was a logical and acceptable practice. Thus, the leaders who stand out on the pages of American history did not make a conscious choice, but either did what was expected of them, or were in effect, chosen to develop alternative strategies.

INSIDE OTHERS AND OUTSIDE OTHERS

Although the period of contact, collision/collusion, containment, and conversion is relatively short, seen from the many angles of a variety of nations, it is the time that causes the greatest social upheaval. Obviously, before the advent of the Euro American, Nez Perce, Madoc, Utes, Lakota, Dakota, Cheyenne, Navajo and Apache were all "contained" within specific unmarked boundaries. They married within their group, but hunted, fished and worked together and, above all, sought mutual assurances in the specific language of each "tribal" cluster. Diane Bell has referred to the manner in which nearby unrelated groups could be taken into a primary group as "inside others." She uses this term because she argues that they can be "accommodated" very easily within the lifestyles and norms of the original groups.[32]

This presents a small degree of Otherness, in that once being accepted into the primary groups, Inside Others might well (true enough) become slaves, but they never constituted a threat to the unanimity of the original, holistic group. Native Americans did not, I think it is fair to say, ever encounter the direct opposite of these Inside Others, namely the Outside Others, until the Europeans arrived. With their advent, the rules had to be rewritten, for now a new and different force and power existed that sought to alter tradition, and, indeed, threatened the very stability of the original cultural group.

I think that the root of the quarrel must have been over language. At its simplest level, this was basically about the "right" names for things and people. Perhaps, more than a little aided by Christian proselytizing, this was the first and yet most fundamental shift. By utilizing different words and signs, the power of the Outside Others began to assert itself at the most basic level of speech. And, since this would be passed on from one generation to the next (especially given the absence of a "script"), the new speech would be inherited with all its neologisms, prejudices, distortions, and concoctions.

Within at least one generation what is preeminently at work shows not an unsuspecting folk succumbing to superior skill, but very wary peoples without control of their own idiom. And with the death of speech, we can also mark the end of the agreed-upon "holy," and the substitutions of the newly mandated "sacrosanct." When a people can no longer agree on what is ethically correct, what the ancestors had sanctioned, indeed even whether the ancestors are relevant, their togetherness becomes a mere artifice. They were held together, not by one old language and belief system, but by two distinctions, neither part of their own indigenity.

INVENTING "THE INDIAN" AS ENVIRONMENTAL COP

First, from the time of Euro American contact Native Americans had all been essentialized into a rather haphazard and simplistic fusion known as "Indians." Second, they began to mark distinctions between this new concoction of self and the European Other—an interesting role reversal, but one that was put into play by an enormous ethnographic error. As the undifferentiated Other, the "Indian" now invented commonalities where none had previously existed.

Once such invention was clearly the self-visualization of themselves of a concept imposed from without—they began to articulate a legend that was clearly absurd within the context of their own previous existence as nomads and hunter-gatherers. I refer here to the omniscient theme of the latter-day "Indian" as environmentalist and keeper of the lost pristine uncorruptability of land and sky. In a way, willy nilly, they are assuming a new burden as well—one that seems to suggest that "Indians," having been absent from the decisions of the Machine Age, could now offer reassurances that all could/should be involved in the cleansing of the Earth.

Better, it seems to me, to have truly represented the historical hand that was played them: They were neither benefactors nor beneficiaries of the promised plenitude. And now, at the time for the gnashing of teeth, when the United States (indeed the West) seeks new scapegoats its global despoliation, they must not become the bearers of national guilt. They were simply not there, for again the historical narrative is direct and simple; they had been banished to Florida or Oklahoma.

This is, therefore, the Other side to the new, revived, version of the Indian as environmental policeman. By simply agreeing to the articulation of environmental catastrophe, they take on the burdensome problems that go with doom without ever having had occasion for shame in even a little of the boon. Nor have we come very far in the media portrayal (I suspect partly approved by Indians themselves). It is, almost, as if the media seems to be suggesting that "Indians" possessed only one noteworthy attribute, hastily summoned up for our delectability, and this was their   almost irrelevant power to warn us of dire consequences. And they. do this in a dark brooding voice, in sentences much addicted to hyperbole and metaphor, slowly and distinctly articulated, a little like the voice of doom.

In the American West, we have invented versions of Indianness that have little to do with the reality of the Native American "tribal" experience. Instead, we have preferred to vary our images, in direct response to the concerns of our own time. They have been altered from the cannibal, to the un-Christian savage, from the Noble Savage, to the blood thirsty "Injun" with a penchant for killing and forcing unsuspecting White ladies to compose morbid "captivity narratives." But we must not, and cannot, hold our own contemporary presence guiltless, for at this time we have seen the emergence of a new Indian, again in response to our needs. And, even as we look closer for assurances about our own folders, let us always recall that we might well be glancing into the mirror and simply seeing ourselves. Is this "Indian" of my imagination, the reality of my own Self?[33]

For instance, regarding the so-called "captivity" narratives,[34] it seems most pertinent to enquire regarding who was the captured, and who the captive? For even as we look at the construction of the world of the narrative, what strikes us is the deliberate resort to sensationalism, and to the depiction of this thing called the Indian as sex-crazed and over desirous of possessing White women, often as trophy companions, a substitute for the all-conquering master, but also as a symbol of achievement in the White/Indian clashes. Most of the accounts do not actually relate living Native Americans, but are content to indulge in stereotypical presentations that proffer the Indian as beast, savage, and rapist.

In some respects, therefore, the issue here is not so much about the potential rape of the White female, but the omnipresent disorder—in sex, hygiene, criminality, and moral attitudes—that the Native American represents for the Euro American. This is contrasted with the cinematic images of the border towns that seek to restore wholeness and order by recapturing the woman, destroying her captors, rewarding the (White) hero, and proclaiming a *pax Americana* on the land. The subtextual view of the narratives therefore is one in which the Indian is the actual captive, ensnared by the smugness of eastern encroachers (so sure of their own values), and by their belief system one that well into the twentieth century established a legendary hierarchy for "civilization."

In the various versions of "captivity narratives," when the captives return to their own group, the account (simply by the fact that it can only be *written* after the event) by its very existence confirms that the European present is promising, triumphant, and full of expectation, whereas the Native American past was pointless, savage, and empty of all hope. It still remains, at the linguistic level, the polarization between orality and the written word, half-belief and truth, minor and master discourse. The narrative was explosive, particularly since few doubted that firmer captives wrote them even as they recalled the horrendous events of their past lives. Their firsthand accounts lent little veracity to the ennobling nature of the Euro American experience, validating once more that Native Americans and Whites led lives that were totally incompatible one with the other. As such, the extremities in viewpoints said little for the future possibility of any easy reconciliation on terms of equality. One side had to be conquered, and the other subdued. History only provides us with the missing blanks of the grand narrative; we are still unaware of the total script.

NOTES

1. I would contend that this is the situation, despite the bad rap given to the Spaniards by Bartolomé de Las Casas. He argued from the position he best knew, but I would still insist that the British came to rule, whereas French and Spaniards were more interested in settling. I am not trying to pick favorites and exclude any single European nation from the wholesale destruction of Native American peoples. For a good refresher, consult Peter Nabokov, ed., *Native American Testimony* (New York: Penguin, 1978), 50–53. In addition, the following documentaries were of great assistance in writing this chapter: *The Great Indian Wars, 1840–1890* (Simitar Entertainment, 1991); *The Native Americans* (Turner Broadcasting System, 1994); *500 Nations* (CBS, 1995) Pts. 1–4; *War Against the Indians* (The Discovery Channel, 1995); *The Way West* Pts. 1 & 2 and accompanying book, *The American Experience*, PBS, 1995. Also see the older series *How the West Was Won* (The Discovery Channel, 1993); *The Wild West* rebroadcast The Discovery Channel, 1995, Pts. 1–7.

2. See Dee Brown, *The American West* (New York: Scribner's, 1994) for a litany of atrocities committed against Native Americans including the intentional destruction of their food supply, the unilateral abrogation of tribes, the disregard of their hunting grounds, and massacres, and American Western myths and legends about them. See pp. 85–89, 104–09, 126–27, 190–94, and regarding treaties 100–02, 107, 136, 215.

3. This text was published to accompany *The Native Americans* on Turner Broadcasting Service, 1995. See David Hurst Thomas, Jay Miller et al., *The Native Americans: An Illustrated History* (Atlanta, GA: Turner, 1993), 304. The writers add that with expansionism "the West might be 'won' for the Anglo-American newcomers, but it would be decidedly 'lost' for these Indian societies whose lifestyles, based on hunting, fishing, foraging, gardening and trading, had been developing for more than ten thousand years" (304).

4. See the last six chapters of Nabokov, *Native American Testimony*, 282–440.

5. Consult Janet A. McDonnell, *The Dispossession of the American Indian*

(Bloomington: Indiana UP, 1991), regarding how bungling government policy, particularly promoted by the Indian Office, helped bring about the loss of land, especially pp. 121–25.

6. Christian F. Feest, "Europe's Indians," in *The Invented Indian: Cultural Fictions and Government Policies* ed. James Clifton (New Brunswick, NJ: Transaction, 1994), 314.

7. For information on the role of Native Americans during the Civil War, consult Shelby Foote, *The Civil War: A Narrative.*, 3 vols. (New York: Random, 1958 [vol. 1], 1963 [vol. 2], 1974 [vol. 3]), particularly 2:46–47, 702, 703, 776, and 3: 725–27.

8. Robert M. Utley, *The Indian Frontier of the American West, 1846–1890* (Albuquerque: U of New Mexico P, 1984), 251.

9. The use of captives as slaves was, for instance, part of Sioux custom. In this instance, an account for 1843 simply states, "The Sioux Indians take the Crow slaves." See Frederick Turner, ed., *The Portable Native America Reader* (New York: Penguin, 1973), 148. For specific information on African slaves, see Thomas et al., *Native Americans,* 289, 319. Note that in many cases as with the Seminoles, Blacks and Native Americans intermarried.

10. This, in turn, led to demonization of Whites by Native Americans. Witness this account, for instance, told by Leonard Crow Dog in New York in 1972 and recorded by Richard Erdoes and and Alfonso Ortiz, *American Indian Myths and Legends* (New York: Pantheon, 1984) Crow Dog relates the encounter with Whites:

And out of this blackness they saw a strange creature emerging. He had on a strange black hat, and boots, and clothes. His skin was pale, his hair was yellow, and his eyes were blue. He had hair growing under his nose and falling down over his lips; his chin was covered with hair; he was hairy all over. When he spoke, it did not sound like human speech. No one could understand him. He was sitting on a large, strange animal as big as a large moose, but it was not a moose. It was an animal no one knew. (496)

Note that the news of the coming of the Whites is spread from village to village by Iktome, the Spider Man and trickster among the Sioux. The account begs the question—was Conquest and Encounter a "trick" from which the nations could one day dance their way to a different reality?

11. John Ross was part Cherokee and part White. For some recent details of the Civil War conflict and the Native American predicament, see Thomas et al., *Native Americans,* 322–333. Ross was himself a slaveowner.

12. The term "Five Civilized Tribes" was a most unfortunate misnomer. It included the Cherokee, Chickasaw, Choctaw, Seminole and Creek, but even terms like "Seminole" and "Creek" were concoctions. At best, the terminology sought to differentiate one set of groupings from another; at worst, it implied that every other Native American group was "uncivilized." In any event, following 1865 every "tribe" received the same, unfair treatment—all were banished via the Trail of Tears under the federal Indian Removal Act of 1830, signed by President Andrew Jackson. For good discussion on the debate and act of Native American removal, consult Robert F. Berkhofer Jr., *The White Man's Indian* (New York: Vintage, 1979), 157–75.

13. Thomas et al., *Native Americans,* 327.

14. See Utley, *Indian Frontier,* 73. Also note particularly the argument by Henrietta Buckmaster, *The Seminole Wars* (New York: Collier, 1966), where she

contends that "Runaway Indian and Negro were thus locked together and became allies in a life and death struggle" (13), and how, as late as 1946, a plan had been advanced "for an Indian and Negro colony in Mexico" (149). Master/slave relationships had given way to one of allies.

15. For a more in-depth discussion of railroads and American Western migration, see Dee Brown, *The American West,* especially 24, 35–37, 40, 78, 81. For Native American views and attacks on the railroads, see 115, 134, 237, 247, 248, 263, 270.

16. Originally, Frederick Jackson Turner had read this as a paper at the July 12, 1893 meeting of the American Historical Association at the 1893 Columbian Exposition in Chicago. The present text is reprinted in Frederick Jackson Turner, "The Significance of the Frontier in American History," in *America: One Land, One People* ed. Robert C. Baron (Golden, CO: Fulcrum, 1987), 247.

17. Most people are now agreed that U.S. assimilationist policy was wrongheaded and misguided at best, and racist at worst. See, for instance, Samuel C. Armstrong, *The Indian Question* (Hampton, VA: Normal School Steam P, 1883); Robert F. Berkhofer Jr., *Salvation and the Savage: An Analysis of Protestant Missions and American Indian Response 1787–1862* (Lexington: U of Kentucky P, 1965); M. L. Hutgren and P. Molin, *To Lead and Serve: American Indian Education at Hampton Institute* (Virginia Beach, VA: Virginia Foundation for the Humanities and Public Policy, 1989); and Robert Trennert, *The Phoenix Indian School: Forced Assimilation in Arizona* (Norman: U of Oklahoma P, 1988). But more recently, a former Native American student at Shilocco school has written about how the educational system helped create a sense of identity. See K. Tsianina Lomawaima, *They Called It Prairie Light* (Lincoln: U of Nebraska P, 1994); see especially xi–xxiii, 1–26 (including Table 6), and 171–76. Also of interest is Senate Report #91–501, *Report of the U.S. Senate Committee on Labor and Public Welfare, Special Sub Committee on Indian Education.* Chaired by Edward M. Kennedy (Washington, D.C: U.S. Government Printing Office, 1969).

18. See "Pacification, Conquest and Genocide," in *Christopher Columbus and the Age of Exploration: An Encyclopedia* ed. Silvio A Bedini (New York: De Capo, 1998), 533.

19. See my discussion of Enrique of Molucca in O. R. Dathorne, *Asian Voyages: Two Thousand Years of Constructing the Other* (Westport, CT and London: Bergin and Garvey, 1996). Also see, Simon Winchester, "After Dire Straits, an Agonising Haul across the Pacific," *Smithsonian* 22:1, 84–93. I want to mention here a fascinating woman that appears in the pages of Hernando de Soto. She is referred to as the Lady of Cofachiqui and met De Soto around 1542. She is described in the most elegant terms as a queen in her own right. When she confers with De Soto, it seems to be about negitiations. See Hernando de Soto, *The De Soto Chronicles: The Expedition of Hernando de Soto to North America in 1539–1543.* 2 vols (Tuscaloosa, AL: U of Alabama P,1993), II:284–7. Also see the version published by Garcilaso de la Vega, *The Florida of the Inca.* 1605. Trans. and ed. John Grier Varner and Jeannette Johnson Varner. Austin: U of Texas P, 1962, 297–330.

20. Meredith E. Abarca comments: "Her name [Malinche] is synonymous with that of traitor." Meredith E. Abarca, "The Ambiguity of Three Mexican Archetypes: La Malinche, La Virgen de Guadalupe, and La Llorona," in *genre* 16/1995, 66. Compare this with C. Alejandra Elenes, "Malinche, Guadalupe, and La Llorona: Patriarchy and the Formation of Mexican National Consciousness,"

in *Latin America: An Interdisciplinary Approach* ed. Julio López-Arias and Gladys M. Varona-Lacey (New York: Peter Lang, 1999), 87–99.

21. Spivak makes an interesting point in this connection, arguing that with regard to Rochester and Jane in Charlotte Bronte's *Jane Eyre*, "this is the register not of mere marriage or sexual reproduction but of Europe and its not-yet-human other, of soul-making." Gayatri Chakravorty Spivak, *A Critique of Postcolonial Reason: Toward a History of the Vanishing Present* (Cambridge, MA: Harvard U P, 1999), 122. The register in the account of Jane and La Malinche is a strident, male one that defines the insignificant colonized other.

22. Anne McClintock, *Imperial Leather: Race, Gender and Sexuality in the Colonial Context* (New York: Routledge, 1995), 24.

23. For the letters of Cortés, consult any of the following: Fernando Cortés, *Fernando Cortés: Five Letters, 1519–1526*. Trans. J. Baynard Morris. New York: Norton, 1969, which is the text I shall use; Hernan Cortés, *Letters from Mexico*. Trans and ed. A. R. Pagden (New York: Grossman, 1971); and Fernando Cortés, *His Five Letters of Relation to the Emperor Charles V, 1519–1526*. Trans. and ed. Francis Augustus MacNutt. 2 vols. Glorieta, NM: Rio Grande Press, 1977.

For Bernal Díaz del Castillo, see any of the following translations: Bernal Díaz del Castillo, *The Conquest of New Spain* [1632]. Trans. and ed. J. M. Cohen (Harmondsworth, U.K: Penguin, 1965) which is an abbreviated version with editor's summaries for omitted parts; Bernal Díaz del Castillo, *The Discovery and Conquest of Mexico, 1517–1521* [1632]. Trans A. P. Maudslay and ed. Irving A. Leonard (New York: Farrar, Straus and Cudahy, 1956), from which I shall be citing references; and Bernal Díaz del Castillo, *The True History of the Conquest of New Spain*. Trans Alfred Maudslay and ed. Genaro García. 5 vols [1632] (London: Hakluyt Society, 1908–1916).

For La Malinche, also see Fray Bernardino de Sahagún, *Florentine Codex, General History of the Things of New Spain*. 12 vols, ed. Arthur J. O. Anderson and Charles Dibble. Salt Lake City: School of American Research and U of Utah, 1950–1982. Book XII is mainly concerned with the Conquest and has interesting pictorial representations of La Malinche, but it is not possible to assert that these were realistic depictions, even though they were drawn very close in time to the events by indigenous people who might well have had some personal experience of what had taken place.

24. Sandra Messinger Cypress, *La Malinche in Mexican Literature: From History to Myth* (Austin: U of Texas P, 1991), 31.

25. Cortés, *Five Letters*, 56–57

26. Donna J. Kessler, *The Making of Sacagawea: A Euro American Legend* (Tuscaloosa, AL: U of Alabama P, 1996), 23. Although Kesssler's book is about Sacagawea, she devotes her early pages to making some comparisons between Pocahontas and Sacagawea. Also pertinent is Rebecca Blevins Faery, *Cartographies of Desire: Captivity, Race, and Sex in the Shaping of an American Nation* (Norman, OK: U of Oklahoma P, 1999).

27. For Smith's various versions, see John Smith, *The Complete Works of Captain John Smith (1580–1631)* ed. Philip L. Barbour. 3 vols (Chapel Hill: U of North Carolina P, 1986). See the following where Pocahontas' and rescue of Smith *does not* appear: *A True Relation of Such Occurrences and Accidents of Noate as Hath Happemed in Virginia* [1608]; *A Map of Virginia, With a Description of the Countrey, the Commodities, People, Government and Religion* [1612]; and *The Proceedings of the English Colonie in Virginia* [1612]. For the reference to Pocahontas and her alleged

devotion for Smith see *The Generall Historie of Virginia, New England, and the Summer Isles* [1624]. Pocahontas had died in England in 1617. For detailed discussion of the discrepancy, see Frederic W. Gleach, *Powhatan's World and Colonial Virginia: A Conflict of Cultures* (Lincoln, NE: U of Nebraska P, 1997), 109–18.

28. Peter Hulme, *Colonial Encounters: Europe and the Native Caribbean, 1492–1797* (London: Routledge, 1992), 136–73.

29. John Smith, *Works* I:93.

30. Erica Funkhouser, "Who was Sacagawea and How Did She Aid the Expedition?" <http://www.pbs.org/lewis and clark>[accessed October 26, 1999].

31. *The Journals of Lewis and Clark* ed. Frank Bergon [1904–1905] (New York: Penguin, 1989), 199–200; 238.

32. Diane Bell, "An accidental Australian tourist: Or a feminist anthropologist at sea and on land," in *Implicit Understandings: Observing, Reporting, and Reflecting on the Encounters Between Europeans and Other Peoples in the Early Modern Era* ed. Stuart B. Schwartz (Cambridge: Cambridge U P, 1994), 509.

33. Recent studies of Native Americans in film delve more deeply into what I am attempting to discuss here. See Gretchen M. Bataille and Charles L.P. Silet, *The Pretend Indians: Images of Native Americans in the Movies* (Ames, IA: Iowa State UP, 1980; Elizabeth S. Bird ed., *Dressing in Feathers: The Construction of the Indian in American Popular Culture* (Boulder, CO: Westview, 1996); Michael Hilger, *From Savage to Nobleman: Images of Native Americans in Film* (Lanham, MD: Scarecrow, 1995); Jacquelyn Kilpatrick, *Celluloid Indians: Native Americans and Film* (Lincoln, NE: U of Nebraska P, 1999); and Peter C. Rollins and John E. O'Connor eds., *Hollywood's Indian: The Portrayal of the Native American in Film* (Lexington, KY: The University Press of Kentucky, 1998).

34. Several of the so-called "captivity" narratives are loud in their proclamations of "Platonic relationships"—nothing happened. The reason might not be merely kind and forgiving Indians, but because of the time and place there was the definite impossibility of hoping to describe sexual encounters in clear terms, and expect to return to live among the unforgiving Puritans. I suppose this is why there is none of the troublesome sexuality of Malinche with John Smith and Pocahontas. I think in a way he establishes the format for captivity narratives that will follow. Incidentally, when Black men continue this in American literature as "slave narratives," they also omit any sexual references; with the women narrators it is different.

Chapter 5

(Re)Placing the Wor(l)d:
The Search for the "Half Sign"

each culture fixes its thresholds differently. This amounts in effect to allowing that the act of naming belongs to a continuum in which there is an imperceptible passage from the act of signifying to that of pointing. . . . The natural sciences put theirs on the level of species, varieties or subvarieties as the case may be . . . . The same method of operation is involved with the native sage—and sometimes scientist. . . . (Claude Lévi-Strauss, *The Savage Mind* [1966], 215)

Once knowledge can be analysed in terms of region, domain, implantation, displacement, transposition, one is able to capture the process by which knowledge functions as a form of power and disseminated the effects of power. (Michel Foucault, *Power/Knowledge* [1980], 69)

Regarding the intellectual colonization of the world, we should initially look to two leading intellectuals of the eighteenth-century period—specifically, Carl von Linné or Linnaeus (1701–1778), a Swede and an aristocrat on the make, and George-Louis Leclerc, compte de Buffon (1707–1788), an aristocratic and wealthy Frenchman—particularly because the European "scientific" endeavor has always been presented as truthful, nonsubjective, and "universal." Together, from the eighteenth century onwards, they began a system that would influence the world well into the late modern period, indeed as late as the present. Both creatures of the Enlightenment, they named and classified according to a so-called objective criteria that remained unchallenged until well into the postmodern period.

LINNAEUS: SEXUALIZING THINGS

Linnaeus, who used his penchant for classification and naming to earn himself a place among the aristocracy, believed that the world should and could be classified in Latin and according to certain basic principles and ideas, of which members of the Enlightenment were so sure, and over which Europe held sway. Accordingly, he and his "apostles" (as they called themselves with a quaint touch of religious fervor)[1] travelled throughout the world giving every plant two names, somewhat like a European person—a family and a personal name, one for the genus and another for the species.

Interestingly, even the so-called "objectivity" of Science was compromised from the very start. The earth would be labelled in Latin, surely the ancient language of everyone on the globe, and European values would be imposed on the plant, mineral, and animal world. I am, of course, not only interested in the "naming" process, but particularly in the unabashed "worlding" of gender, sexuality, and race.[2] For what European cataloguing of natural phenomena did was to accord everything and everyone a certain hallmark, if not of approval, then certainly a condescending and totalizing uniformity. Of course, needless to say, the old names persisted, but at the level of the folk, the uninformed, the ignorant, so no one would seriously think of writing a scientific paper without knowing the "right" moniker for golden apple or breadfruit or stir apple or stinking-toe or five-finger. Even now, as I write the words, I smell and taste the fruits, but I have to resist the temptation to use scare quotes around each one—for are not they after all, half signs, said but never written, the inferior signification of those of us who live on the margins?

Along with the new words, came new concepts, and most important in this regard was a different way of regarding race, class and sexuality. I am going to give one startling instance where they all combine in the name of a plant. I refer here to the marsh plant that acquired, indeed was identified with, the name Andromeda. Now, not just coincidentally, Andromeda belongs to European Greek myth, but the name is a particularly suitable candidate, since it denotes the Other, for Andromeda was Ethiopian. Second, she was chained to a rock. "Chain" suggests both the Chain of Being, namely her physical fixedness, as well as the chains of enslavement and her social immobility. We have, therefore, both imprisoned woman and enslaved Blackness in the name that is foisted on the unfortunate plant, with one being gender-controlled and the other race-dominated, hardly botanical qualities endemic to plants. Add to the conceptualization of all this within the Great Chain of Being, the way that a Europeanized God had seen fit to arrange the universe, with man (European male, of course) just beneath the angels and the godhead, and some humans lower than others. Thus we understand Andromeda's total "odderness" as Black Ethiopian and woman.

As Winthrop Jordan put it in *White over Black:*

The idea of the Great Chain of Being possessed all the power and all the weakness of any gigantic synthesis. The Chain of Being, as usually conceived, commenced with inanimate things and ranged upwards through the lowliest forms of life, through the more intelligent animals until it reached man himself; but it did not stop with man, for it continued upward through the myriad ranks of heavenly creatures until it reached its pinnacle in God.[3]

Thus, the naming said much; Andromeda was woman and Ethiopian, low on the gender and racial scale. Therefore, classification is not just an idle way in which Linnaeus and his followers simply set up convenient markers for agreed-upon world usage, but in reality the manner in which Europe imposed its obsessions and ethnocentrism on the rest of the world, and how we all readily accepted them as a step toward our own enlightenment.

The Greek myth is most appropriate in still another context; Andromeda is rescued by a very European icon, Perseus, and even, some might contend, "saved" by his marriage to her. No better illustration of European beneficence and goodwill is as readily apparent; it speaks much to the colonized everywhere about the virtues, strengths, and goodness available from the civilized offerings of Europe, because it was being willingly given, seemingly with no strings attached. In exchange for passivity, even some might contend for the feminization of the native, a rescue would be affected from the jaws of a chaotic and deadly monstrousness, and a resituating of the colonized, now united with the savior, to a secure place of order, peace, and law.

Andromeda's name was imprinted, first as a botanical specimen low on the Chain of Being, and later emblazoned as an astronomer's curiosity high up in the sky as "the chained lady" in a faraway constellation between what was named Pisces and Cassiopeia. There is much more that could be said about this additional instance, but lest I be accused of making too much of it, I will simply add that the depths of the swamp and the heights of the sky are physical but not cultural spaces. Whether colonized Other observers looked down or up, they would always be reminded of the wretchedness of their condition, apparently justified by the very nature of the God-centered universe itself.

Let me cite some additional remarks by Alan Bewell in "On the Banks of the South Sea" that help buttress what I have been contending:

Linnaeus reads the marsh andromeda as if, indeed, it were integrally expressive of the classical myth. Gazing upon the plant transports Linnaeus into a mythological Golden Age as yet unaffected by the darker elements of sexuality (though they are obviously present in the [what Linnaeus termed] "evil toads and frogs" that drench Andromeda "with water when they mate"). In this nostalgic pastoralist vision, Linnaeus does not distinguish between women and plants, but instead treats the sexuality of the marsh andromeda as if it were the same thing as the specific conception of female sexuality conveyed by the Andromeda myth—that of ideal innocence threatened by bestiality. It is not simply that Linnaeus continually passes from talking about plants to talking about women; he really feels that he has discovered their fundamental kinship. . . . To see the plant properly, therefore, requires a special kind of double vision, which allows us to see both plant and female as one, passing easily from one to the other.[4]

For Linnaeus, the marsh plant is almost one with woman and, as I have tried to stress, one with a negative concept of a racialized blackness. Linnaeus himself ecstatically scribbled in his notebooks:

I noticed that she was blood-red before flowering, but that as soon as she blooms her petals become flesh-coloured. . . . As I looked at her I was reminded of Andromeda as described by the poets, and the more I thought about her the more affinity she seemed to have with the plant; indeed, had Ovid set out to describe the plant mystically . . . he could not have caught a better likeness. . . . Her beauty is preserved only so long as she remains a virgin (as often happens with women also)—i.e. until she is fertilized, which will not now be long as she is a bride.[5]

This seems a trifle absurd, and rather far removed from a marsh plant, commonly called "rosemary." Gender and race demarcate class in this classificatory scheme, and although Linnaeus does not establish a hierarchical order for race, the next century would be rife with all and sundry who could draw on some of these notions to do just that.

Bewell went on to argue that for Linnaeus

plant and girl [were] juxtaposed. The fact that the same name "Andromeda," applies to both tells us that, for Linnaeus, the proper understanding of the botanical description requires that we constantly recognize the analogies established between vegetable reproduction and human sexuality.[6]

What we note in the apparently harmless triad of genus, pistils and stamens, and species, is the neat substitution of class, gender, and race. This leads us ultimately to plants, women, and blackness, as one and the same.

Linnaeus's typically Enlightened European obsession demarcates mere plants like the andromeda as innocent and virgin, or as possessing the human hermaphroditic constituents of a bodily hybridity, so beloved of earlier travellers to the East. This constant sexualizing of the plant world continued to leave its marked and distorted imprint on his system. Actually, it was a rather clumsy attempt to humanize the plant world.

The discoverer names what he sees; so any dictionary will reveal that a word like "monoecious" is a Linnaean neologism, between 1755 and

1765 from the Latin "Monoecia," for plants that have both stamens and pistils. However, since this would seem to be a common element among a host of plants, why would the difference be so important, except that it could be contrasted with "normal" humans? Does it have some eye-opening and macabre appeal because of its alternative method of reproduction? Are we looking at the majority of flowering plants as so-called "objective" scientific observers or curious voyeurs? Does this supposed "difference" further confirm these types of plants and their names as even more distant, more utterly Other?

As I have said, Linnaeus did not specifically establish a hierarchy of humans per se, but he did stress in *Systema Naturae* (1735) that there was an "objective" Scientific European way of regarding race. We were all of the genus homo, of the species sapiens, varying from the Wild Man, to the American (Native American), to the European who had "gentle" eyes and "was governed by laws," to the "sooty" and "black." The latter had "frizzled" hair, was "crafty, indolent [and] negligent" and "governed by caprice."[7] So readers, in accepting the obvious contrasts, could draw their own hierarchical conclusions.

On the other hand, Mary Louise Pratt quite rightly asserts that "[o]ne could scarcely ask for a more explicit attempt to 'naturalize' the myth of European superiority."[8] And clearly, by citing how Captain James Cook's expeditions sailed under secret orders, Pratt shows that Linnaeus's forays also marked still another official attempt by Europeans to inscribe the earth. As she puts it, "the naming, the representing, and the claiming are all one; the naming brings the reality of order into being."[9] These efforts would provide a reasoned justification for colonization. Peter Fryer mentions a pupil of Linnaeus's who was provoked to speculate that "one would have reason to think that the Moors had a rather strange origin."[10] The latter was suggested when the news spread that a rabbit had interbred with hens giving birth to some rather fluffy-covered chickens. Other students of Linnaeus helped to give scientific validity to the idea that the Khoi (or so-called "Hottentots") and the San (or so-called "Bushmen"), a group they referred to as the Khoisan, had little concept of God and had never speculated about life after death. Hence they were plainly inferior. As David Chidester concludes in his recent study, " 'Bushmen' shared with 'Hottentots', according to all reports at the end of the eighteenth century, this common feature: They lacked any trace of religion."[11] This made it much easier to visualize them as the natural objects of a slowly growing apartheid consciousness premised on an All-unknowing Self and a totally ignorant other. The un-Enlightened truthfully began to fear extermination, and the nineteenth century would witness their neurosis grow, as some of the most hateful racial claptrap that was ever published appeared under the aegis of "Science."

BUFFON: TALKING RACE

What is truly ironical about the eighteenth century is that Europeans were so certain about the rightness with which they conceptualized the world both known and unknown to them. But since they were preoccupied with themselves, issues of race continued to plague their enlightened minds. George-Louis Leclerc, comte de Buffon, and Linnaeus were bitter rivals and probed at the same issues with the same preoccupations. Buffon had the time and money to devote to a thirty-six-volume *Histoire naturelle,* the first of which appeared in 1749. It rivalled Denis Diderot's thirty-five-volume *Encyclopédie* (1751–1772), whose bold idea was to encapsulate all knowledge in a book, or rather several books. But whereas Diderot's venture was a joint enterprise, this was an individual man's work, very much on keeping with the bold claims of Enlightenment.

Linnaeus had been moving in the direction of the proclamation that there was in some way the inevitable connection between the African and the ape, the Black man and the monkey. Lisbet Koerner writes that Linnaeus had hesitated over the use of the term homo sapiens, since *homo diurnus* had the advantage of being contrasted with *homo nocturnus* "whom Linnaeus termed Homo troglodytes, and associated with albino Africans, in those days often exhibited as freaks . . . [claiming that] exotic apes shaded into humans."[12] Had he gone this route, it does not leave much to the imagination as to which race would have been day and which night, which wise, and which the troglodytes. We might still have been mired in that swamp of yet another invention by a precious Enlightened mind. But it seems as if Linnaeus had had his doubts, or rather his more ambitious flights of fancy were severely reined in by theologians. There were no such constraints for Buffon.

With the assurance born of his time and class, Buffon easily explained blackness:

as the east wind, which generally blows between the Tropics, arrives not at Nubia till it has traversed Arabia, it is not surprising to find the natives very black; it is less surprising to see the inhabitants of Senegal perfectly black; for the east wind before it reaches them, must blow over the whole of Africa in its great breadth, which renders the heat of the air almost insupportable.[13]

And he also ranges the world, like Linnaeus's disciples, from the Caribbean where "these savages, though they never think, have a pensive melancholy aspect," or cites Sir Walter Raleigh to explain that there was a group of Indians in Guyana "of which the natives are blacker than any other Indians."[14]

The European preoccupation with blackness goes back to the earliest contacts between Blacks and Whites. I will note the total and complete fascination of George Best over two hundred years before in 1578, when he describes an "Ethiopian" (quite black we are told) who marries an Englishwoman, but who never changes color, although he lives in England, and whose son retains the darkness of his father. Best speaks in length about the strange nature of skin coloration; as already shown, he talks about how black is not merely alien but an "infection."[15] Perhaps a different explanation is needed   for infection, and this would be advanced over and over again. Buffon took the position that albinos fitted into this category and that "white therefore seem to be nature's primary color."[16] Actually, by arguing that the two colors could be equated, Best was not really attacking anyone; instead, he was merely trying to show that all the various parts of the world were habitable, and that since the Ethiopian could live in England and never change color, then English people could travel elsewhere without hazardous results to their complexion.

This did not mean that the point made by Buffon was not part and parcel of European consciousness. After all, if all you see is "white," it does tend to assume an aura of its own. And it works the other way as well; as a mere tourist of no significance on the most mundane of visits to China, I was a minor celebrity as I went through Chinese villages, accompanied by a small squad of locals, who were intent on rubbing next to me, attempting to yank at my hair, or importuning me regarding the whereabouts of a certain "Mr. Michael"—Jackson or Jordan, it really did not matter. I have witnessed the same "curiosity" exhibited in African villages towards Whites. African villagers stared, touched, and wanted a closer examination of skin and hair.

However, there is a difference in that eighteenth-century Europeans were saying that they were doing all this in the interest of an "objective" prurience called "scientific evaluation." Hence, there is the recent argument that is made quite repeatedly—one I do not totally buy—between European "racialism" (or racial awareness) and "racism."[17] I cannot wholly accept the distinction, because when you possess the power, it becomes not an idle fetish, but rather an ability to transform people into your own construct. The Chinese did not physically affect me in this way, nor did the curious Africans examining the Europeans. But the Europeans named the world, named and misnamed me, and then went about the business of ordering/giving orders to what they had apparently brought into existence.

Despite the tendency of Jacques Roger's recent study to justify Buffon and account for his illusions, Roger must still conclude that:

It would be impossible here to examine the mix of errors, hasty generalizations, half-truths and exact observations that Buffon echoed. Despite his critical intelligence, he was at the mercy of his informants, who often added to their European prejudices those of their station.[18]

But all this merely places Buffon within the general, misinformed perspective of his time. Both he and Linnaeus were driven, not by horrible notions of the Other, but by a safe and contended feeling about their own center. They both saw nothing awry with armchair speculation as they listened to, or read from reports in the field. They then invented the theory, and wrote about it, learnedly and profoundly. The people about whom they wrote had nothing to say; they remained at the margins of the text.[19]

OTHER ODDER ODDITIES

Some of the native, human, suitably renamed oddities turn up in the texts of explorers like William Dampier (who bore back the "painted" Prince Jeoly) and Captain James Cook (who returned with Omai). The South Pacific was now the cultural arena of the Other, so the Enlightened traveled there, fully preened, exhorting in the wonder of their selves. Greg Dening places it in perspective:

It was a period in which the nations of Europe and the Americas saw themselves acting out their scientific, humanistic selves. Government-sponsored expeditions from England, France, and Spain followed one another, self-righteously conscious of their obligations to observe, describe and publish, to be humane and to contribute to the civilizing process of natives out of their superior arts and greater material wealth. It was a time of intensive theater of the civilized to the native. . . . [20]

Much like Linnaeus's plants, natives also had to be classified and studied.

In the sixteenth century, Native Americans had been kidnapped and dragged across the Atlantic by "discoverers" from Columbus on. Lewis Hanke mentions that Bartolomé de Las Casas, as a young lad of eighteen, had been in Seville when Columbus returned from his First Voyage with "seven Indians, brightly plumed parrots, Indian masks cleverly contrived from fishbones," and (in the words of Las Casas) "a large quantity of gold, including samples of finely wrought work."[21] Las Casas would afterwards become a fierce spokesman against the injustices of European enslavement of Indians, and indirectly, a proponent of African slavery in the Americas.[22] His observation of these early captives, and his later association with an unidentified Indian (supposedly "given" to him by his father)[23] seem to have bred in him a degree of sentimental exoticism, which made him all the more ready for the campaign he mounted to end Indian slavery in the Americas. But it was not apparent in anything I have read that he ever changed his mind that Indians were "barbarians," although deserving of Christian salvation.[24]

I do not want to go into any great detail concerning the arguments that were advanced by Las Casas and Juan Ginés de Sepúlveda. Suffice it to say that neither comes off today as particularly enlightened, since the argument advanced was not so much whether there ought to be slavery or not, but under what conditions. Aristotle, therefore, became most important in defining not just the slave, but those who had the right reason to make war in order to enslave. Las Casas could not seemingly have opted out of his time and century, and put forward a notion so radical (as he later did) that nobody should be enslaved. The Bible, St. Augustine, Cicero, and all the "right sources" that Las Casas cited, had asserted that it was wrong to enslave Indians because they were civilized.[25]

That was why it was important to argue, as Thomas Jefferson would in the eighteenth century, that Indians possessed artistic finesse, unlike Blacks.[26] In a curious way, then, these circus parades of the Other in European capitals could be reduced to a mere commodity spectacle, but the European viewers also registered pity, empathy, and a feeling of responsibility. Hence was born the Noble Savage, against whom war could not be justified. Thus the pity that abolished New World Indian slavery, but retained serfdom; thus the hypocrisy that introduced African slavery, but kept the Africans marginalized as totally outer, so no such misgivings as regards their humanity would hasten abolition.

Another sixteenth-century sympathizer with the Indian was Albrecht Dürer. In 1520, Hernando Cortés had dispatched six Aztecs to Spain, complete with a number of artifacts. They became a kind of travelling circus, as they toured Seville, Valladolid, and Brussels to mark Charles V's coronation.[27] In Brussels Dürer had witnessed the exhibition of these strange but nameless creatures and had written in his diary as follows:

I saw the things which have been brought to the King from the new land of gold, a sun all of gold, a whole fathom broad, and a moon all of silver of the same size, also two rooms full of the armour of the people there, and all manner of wondrous weapons of theirs, harnesses and darts, very strange clothing, beds and all kinds of wonderful objects of human use, much better worth seeing than prodigies. These things are all so precious that they are valued at a hundred thousand florins. All the days of my life I have seen nothing that rejoiced my heart as much as these things, for I saw amongst them wonderful works of art, and I marvelled at the subtle Ingenia of people in foreign lands. Indeed I cannot express all that I thought there.[28]

Dürer would later take an active interest in depicting some of the unusual faces he saw in the Europe of his day. One writer harks back to Dürer's visit to Brussels as a turning point in his art, citing his famous portrait of a Black servant, Katharina, twenty years old in 1521, and commenting that Dürer accorded her "the same attention as he shows in the delineation of wealthy merchants or fellow artists."[29]

Where both Las Casas and Dürer were mistaken, however

well-intentioned, is in interpreting Aztec orbs and discs in pure contemporary European obsessions, that is, as the Sun and Moon. They did not read them as calendars, as the signatures and signs of another culture, giving a significance beyond anything that Europe in the sixteenth century was able to imagine.

By the seventeenth century, Africans became fashionable as pets to decorate milady's chamber, to accompany her on walks, and to be painted with her next to her horses.[30] This did not seem to prevent the continuation of the African body as a floating and often contrary signifier. So that, for instance, the servant or groom turns up in other depictions as one of the magi (which is a carryover from the sixteenth century). Now two more contrary signifiers appear—Black St. Maurice[31] and the Black Virgin.[32] Therefore, even as Black figures were represented mainly as servants, somewhere in the European mind these representations carried along with them an accompanying but nonconnecting corepresentation as saints and virgins—all solemnly yoked together in the Christian church.

In England, by the eighteenth century, Blacks were so numerous that, even as they met and congregated around St. Giles Circus in London, the locals dubbed them "St. Giles blackbirds."[33] By then, however, the articulate "subaltern" was no longer silent, but still Eurocentric, as witness the work of Ottobah Cugoano, Olaudah Equiano, Ignatius Sancho (in England), Jacobus Eliza Capitein (in Holland), Anton Wilhelm Amo (in Germany), and Phillis Wheatley (in the United States). The problem was that very often we see their texts filtered through the European editors and readers. They too are very much imprisoned by the circumstances of their own time.[34]

By the eighteenth century, Indians and Blacks gave way to South Pacific islanders as objects of European curiosity. They were carted back to Europe, and subjected to the same humiliations as the Indians and Africans, but now in the name of Science. Additionally, the United States had begun to embark on its own genocidal hegemonization of its indigenous peoples, which would reach its apogee in the next century.

In the nineteenth century, there occurred a new twist, as race, gender, and sexuality combined in the indecent exposure of the "Hottentot Venus" in London and Paris, as crowds gazed at the bare bottom and vagina of Saartjie Baartman, observing its supposed excessive size with prurient interest. When she died in Paris, another Black woman was pressed into service under the same name.[35]

Let me add at this point that it was no accident that Saartjie Baartman was supposedly a "Hottentot," a vivid European construct that sought to place a kind of super-barbarism, an ultra-"negro" savagery on this perversion of the unfortunate Khoisan of South Africa. Winthrop Jordan contends that Europeans felt that "the Hottentots" were "the most appallingly barbarous of men," arguing that, for Buffon, polar peoples "shared honors with the Hottentots," whereas for Linnaeus there was a serious question about their human status.[36]

The perception of Hottentot inferiority went hand in hand with the generally current view that all "natives" were sub-European. Egyptians could not have built the Sphinx, nor could ancestors of present-day Native Americans be responsible for the Mississippi Mounds, much less could indigenous people have constructed the civilizations of the Aztec, Inca, and Maya, or the magnificent buildings at Great Zimbabwe.

Thus, Omai—Cook's "boy"—read back to Cook what was already in Cook's mind, namely that Pacific islanders could never have planned to make such extensive voyages. Their journeys had to be derived from whim, not good planning. In this connection, Ben Finney asserts that:

On his third voyage into the Pacific, before heading north for his fatal encounter with the Hawaiians, Cook had touched on the small island of Atiu in the archipelago later to be named the Cook Islands after the English navigator. There Ma'i (who the English called "Omai"), a Tahitian Cook was taking back to England, met four of his countrymen who told a tale of their drift voyage to the island. Some ten years earlier they were part of a group of twenty men and women who had set sail from Tahiti to Ra'iatea, a day and a half's sail away. For some reason, however, they missed the island and drifted for many days to the southwest until the canoe, which had by then been overturned, came within the sight of Atiu, at which point the Atiuans spotted the wreckage and rescued the five survivors.[37]

Cook used this one incident to demonstrate that this was the manner in which the islands were settled. Local people, it seemed, could not erect pyramids in Egypt, or found civilizations in Central America or Africa. After all, they were the colonial Other, and incapable of any positive civilizing endeavor.

Not only were these specimens "outcastes," or rather "un-classed" in a very class-conscious European society, but additionally they occupied the space at which sexuality, race, and gender intersected. Visitors paid to see the Hottentot Venus because she confirmed their worst feelings that she was the utter(most) Other, and Dampier was able to loan out Prince Jeoly because, again, Jeoly was conceived as being odder. Otherness became odder(most) became utter(most) when it inhabited a different body like the "Elephant Man," or especially when (as in these cases) the skin pigmentation of those observed was not the same as the observers. Later, these oddities would be exhibited at state-sponsored expositions and fairs, before becoming part of the private commodification of spectacle at exhibitions and travelling circuses.[38]

NOTES

1. Their mission was divine; hence the names "apostles" or "disciples" were fitting. Heinz Goerke points out in *Linnaeus* that Linnaeus himself "chose the term to indicate that their task was a missionary one. Their assignment was to travel all over the world, scrutinizing nature at his direction and according to his ideas, and at the same time spreading his fame." See Heinz Goerke, *Linnaeus* (New York: Scribner's, 1973), 149. Goerke also cites a source that had admiringly described Linnaeus as "God's Registrar" (89). Daniel Boorstin adds that Linnaeus had invented the syntax he used, but as he tried to make his ideas conform to reality, his descriptions got longer and longer. Boorstin relates how the various "disciples" went off to the East Indies, North America, Asia, the Middle East, South Africa, the South Pacific, and various parts of Europe. "Deus creavit, Linnaeus disposuit," (God created, Linnaeus classified), Boorstin sardonically concluded. In Daniel Boorstin, *The Discoverers: A History of Man's Search to Know His World and Himself* (New York: Vintage, 1983), 436–46. Let me add that I deal here mainly with primary sources. However, I recommend the additional work of such scholars as Lorraine Daston and Katherine Park, *Wonders and the Order of Nature, 1150–1750* (New York: Zone Books, 1998). Bruno Latour has several relevant publications; I particularly recommend his study with Steve Woolgar, *Laboratory Life: The Social Construction of Scientific Facts* (Beverly Hills, CA: Sage,1979), and his *We Have Never Been Modern* (New York: Harvester Wheatsheaf, 1993). For a good gender perspective, see Londa L. Schiebinger, *Nature's Body: Gender in the Making of Modern Science* (Boston: Beacon Press, 1993).

2. See Gayatri Chakravorty Spivak for her coinage of "worlding." She uses the word to describe how the unnamed but barbaric Other may be transformed as "human," and thus become suitably pliable for use by Western imperialism. See Spivak, "Three Women's Texts and a Critique of Imperialism" in *"Race," Writing and Difference*, ed. Henry Louis Gates Jr. (Chicago: U of Chicago P, 1986), 267.

3. Withrop Jordan, *Black over Black: American Attitudes Toward the Negro, 1550–1812* (Chapel Hill: U of North Carolina P, 1968), 219. Specifically, a number of scholars have written on cultural and racial constructions of Science during the Enlightenment.

4. Alan Bewell, "On the Banks of the South Sea," in *Visions of Empire: Voyages, Botany, and Representations of Nature* ed. David Philip Miller and Peter Hannis Reill (Cambridge and New York: Cambridge UP, 1996), 178.

5. Cited in Wilfrid Blunt, *The Compleat Naturalist: A Life of Linnaeus* (London: Collins, 1971), 56.

6. Bewell, "Banks," 178–79.

7. Emmanuel Chukwudi Eze, ed., *Race and The Enlightenment: A Reader* (Cambridge, MA: Blackwell, 1997), 13–14. Eze's book is very useful, since it has compiling in one place most of the audacious statements on race by Enlightenment thinkers.

8. Mary Louise Pratt, *Imperial Eyes: Travel Writing and Transculturation* (London and New York: Routledge, 1992), 32.

9. Ibid., 33.

10. Peter Fryer, *Staying Power: The History of Black People in Britain* (London: Pluto, 1984), 166. The allusion here is to Nicolaus E. Dahlberg in 1755 (see 530, n. 6).

11. David Chidester, "Bushman Religion: Open, Closed, and New Frontiers,"

in *Miscast: Negotiating the Presence of the Bushmen,* ed. Pippa Skotnes (Cape Town: U of Cape Town P, 1996), 54.

12. Lisbet Koerner, "Purposes of Linnaean Travel: A Preliminary Research Report," in *Visions of Empire: Voyages, Botany, and Representations of Nature,* ed. David Philip Miller and Peter Hannis Reill (Cambridge and New York: Cambridge UP, 19960, 123.

13. Eze, *Race and the Enlightenment,* 21.

14. Ibid., 19.

15. See George Best, "A true discourse of the three voyages of discoverie, for the finding of a passage to Cathaya, by the Northwest, under the conduct of Martin Frobisher; . . . " in *The Principal Navigations, Voyages, Traffiques and Discoveries of the English Nation* [1598], 12 vols., ed. Richard Hakluyt (Glasgow: James MacLehose and Sons, 1903–1905), 7:262–63. This passage, quite rightly, is used by writers in Cultural Studies to pinpoint (a) an early Black presence in Britain, (b) an early example of intermarriage there, and (c) establish proof that there had been a continuous Black presence in Britain.

16. Jacques Roger, *Buffon: A Life in Natural History* (Ithaca, NY: Cornell UP, 1997), 175.

17. See, for instance, Kwame Anthony Appiah, *In My Father's House: Africa in the Philosophy of Culture* (New York: Oxford UP, 1992), 13–17. Note the outright opposition in Kim F. Hall, *Things of Darkness: Economies of Race and Gender in Early Modern England* (Ithaca, NY: Cornell UP, 1995), 3–4, n. 7. Hall disagrees with Appiah's assertion that racism is an eighteenth-century phenomenon. In a way, this is really a great deal of fuss about nothing. "Racialism" is really the British English usage for the American English "racism."

18. Roger, *Buffon,* 176.

19. See illustrations in Hall, *Things of Darkness.* Also see an ongoing work in progress, *The Image of the Black in Western Art,* under the general editorship of Ladislas Bugner (Cambridge, MA: Harvard UP, 1976–1989), 5 vols. to date. A problem with the series is that it tends to stress how well Blacks integrated into European life and culture, ignoring any issues and problems.

20. Greg Dening, "The Theatricality of Observing and Being Observed: Eighteenth-Century Europe 'Discovers' the ? Century 'Pacific,' " in *Implicit Understandings* ed. Stuart B. Schwartz (Cambridge: Cambridge UP, 1994), 452.

21. Lewis Hanke, *Bartolomé de Las Casas, Historian: An Essay in Spanish Historiography* (Gainesville, FL: U of Florida P, 1952), 78.

22. For Las Casas's opinions on African slavery and his later change of heart, consult Juan Friede and Benjamin Keen, eds., *Bartolomé de Las Casas in History: Toward an Understanding of the Man and His Work* (De Kalb, IL: Northern Illinois UP, 1971), 22–23, 165–66, 291, 415–18, 505–6, 584–84.

23. Las Casas had been "given" an Indian by his father Pedro de Las Casas. Columbus, in turn, had made this "gift" to Pedro himself. The account states that Bartolomé had returned the Indian to the authorities for repatriation to the Indies. Few can vouch for the veracity of this—indeed it sounds a little like George Washington and the cherry tree. See Bartolomé de Las Casas, *The Devastation of the Indies: A Brief Account* [1552], trans. Herma Briffault (Baltimore, MD: Johns Hopkins UP, 1992), 3.

24. Las Casas had conceded as much in his famous debate with Juan Ginés de Sepúlveda at Valladolid in 1550–1551. See Lewis Hanke, *All Mankind is One: A Study of the Disputation Between Bartolomé de Las Casas and Juan Ginés de Sepúlveda*

in 1550 on the Intellectual and Religious Capacity of the American Indians (De Kalb,
IL: Northern Illinois UP, 1974).

25. See Bartolomé de Las Casas, *In Defense of the Indians: The Defense of the Most
Reverend Lord, Don Fray Bartolomé de Las Casas of the Order of Preachers, Last Bishop
of Chiapa, Against the Persecutors and Slanderers of the People of the New World
Discovered Across the Seas* (De Kalb, IL: Northern Illinois UP, 1974). This work,
unpublished until 1974, constitutes the formal Las Casas argument against
Sepúlveda in 1550–1551. Modern scholarship has tended to fault Las Casas for
arguing too strongly in "Manichean antitheses (innocent Indians, cruel
Spaniards), enhanced by the biblical image, repeated over twenty times in the
text, of docile sheep versus cruel wolves and tigers." See *Cambridge History of
Latin American Literature*. 3 vols., ed. Roberto González Echevarría and Enrique
Pupo-Walker (Cambridge: Cambridge UP, 1996), 1:96.

26. Thomas Jefferson had praised the industry of the Indians, arguing that a
Black person had never "uttered a thought above the level of plain narration."
See Thomas Jefferson, "Notes on the State of Virginia" [1785], *Writings* (New
York: The Library of America, 1984), 266. Jefferson's views on race are typically
those of the "Enlightened" European we have been discussing.

27. Later, the escutcheon of Charles V would be emblazoned with an Indian as
a "Wild Man" in the appropriate posture of submission. No doubt these early
visitations of humble Indians would have helped supply the necessary belief in
such a representation. See John Block Friedman, *The Monstrous Races in Medieval
Art and Thought* (Cambridge, MA: Harvard UP, 1981), 201.

28. From Dürer's diary, quoted by Jean Michel Massing, "Early European
Images of America: The Ethnographic Approach," in *Circa 1492: Art in the Age of
Exploration*, ed Jay A Levinson (Washington, D.C: National Gallery of Art, 1991),
515. Also see Hanke, *All Mankind is One,* 75.

29. Gude Suckale-Redlefsen, *Mauritius: Der helige Mohr/The Black Saint Maurice*
(Houston, TX: Menil Foundation, 1987), 103.

30. See Hall, *Things of Darkness.* Note the illustrations of numerous aristocratic
ladies and their prestigious "Blackamoors."

31. Concerning Black St. Maurice (d. 286), see Gude Suckale-Redlefsen,
Mauritius. St. Maurice was supposedly a synthesis of beliefs from East and West.
In the West, he is a combination of a forgotten Moor, and Maurice, commander
of the Theban Legion from Egypt. In the East, he was associated mainly with
martyrdom.

32. See Ean Begg, *The Cult of the Black Virgin* (London: Penguin, 1996). This is a
fairly comprehensive book, discussing Black Virgins, Black Christs, as well as
saints like St. Maurice.

33. See an early treatment of this in Wylie Sypher, *Guinea's Captive Kings:
British Anti-Slavery Literature of the Eighteenth Century* (Chapel Hill: U of North
Carolina P, 1942), 2–3.

34. Recent studies are appearing on some of these writers particularly from
England. Also see O. R. Dathorne, *The Black Mind: A History of African Literature*
(Minneapolis: U of Minnesota P, 1974), 76–88.

35. For more on Saartjie Baartman, see Fryer, *Staying Power,* 229–30, and
Sander Gilman, "Black Bodies, White Bodies," in *"Race," Culture and Difference*,
ed. James Donald and Ali Rattansi (London: Sage Publications, 1992), 174–76. She
was brought to Britain in 1810 by an Afrikaner farmer and put on exhibition in
Piccadilly. The show was so popular that her "stage" name, "The Hottentot

Venus," was revived in Paris by another woman in 1829 some years after the original Saartjie Baartman had died there in 1815. Also see George Cuvier's post-mortem of Baartman in T. Denean Sharpley-Whiting, *Black Venus: Sexualized Savages, Primal Fears, and Primitive Narratives in French* (Durham, NC: Duke U P, 1999), 16–31.

36. Jordan, *White over Black*, 226–27.

37. Ben Finney, *Voyage of Rediscovery: A Cultural Odyssey through Polynesia* (Berkeley: U of California P, 1994), 24. The account does not relate how the rescuers arrived there. Finney asserts that Cook would probably have changed his viewpoint had he not died.

38. The presence of "oddities" caused the Victorian mind to run rampant. Creations in fiction such as the creature made by Frankenstein, and Dracula are testament enough to the presence of a definite belief in the hideous Other, which, in reality, were all around, and constantly on display.

Chapter 6

Imagining Africa:
Space as Myth and Reality

> One of Western modernity's principles or basic ideas is individual-
> ism; another is antisupernaturalism, which, in the Western concep-
> tion, is closely linked with humanism. These principles would
> hardly find embrace in the bosom of the cultures that resiliently
> value community life and consider the religious life intrinsic to—
> inseparable from—their total way of life. (Kwame Gyeke, *Tradition
> and Modernity: Philosophical Reflections on the African Experience*
> [1997], 270)

> It has always been true that the West's vision of Africa has been the
> product of its own imagination rather than that of a serious interest
> in what actually happens on the continent. (Richard Werbner and
> Terence Ranger, eds., *Postcolonial Identities in Africa* [1996], 36)

Africa as "myth" or "legend" is most apparent even from the most
casual glance at a map. First, over centuries the Mercator projection of
the world has distorted its shape on maps, so that along with everything
south of Europe, Africa assumes a smaller proportion in relationship say,
to "Great" Britain. After all, as any standard map still made evident,
Greenwich is at the very center of the world. From there, space and time
are calculated. From this point, all other areas in the world are either
"west" or "east," "north" or "south." More importantly, from Greenwich
the entire problem of the earth, hurtling through space, is fixed and
"comprehended."[1]

The continent of Africa begins therefore as an appendage, almost an
afterthought, to the grand design of the mapmaker, indeed to the order
imposes by extrahuman considerations. The manner in which this is
fixed and secured is not seemingly subject to debate, since any
"educated" understanding or comprehension of the earth rests on the

basic assumption ordained by Mercator and the Greenwich prime meridian.

Add to this the "legend" of the borders that define Africa as a continent. Ali Mazrui had already raised the question regarding who decides where Africa stops, particularly when the Red Sea is singled out as an eastern landmark that defines its outermost limit, locking off the interacting cultures from Arabia and, in some strange and pernicious manner, totally cutting away the so-called "Middle" East.[2]

Here the problem only begins. For a closer look reveals that, since the greater part of Africa was "unknown" to Europeans until the fifteenth century, to this day academics and others delimit North Africa with an invisible line drawn in the sand. To the northeast, even though Egypt quite pointedly stares us in the face, it becomes a part of the "Middle East," linked more closely with the Mediterranean world than with the continent of Africa.[3]

AFRICA AS LEGEND

Within the continent proper, place names continue to assert the "legendary" nature of what we seek to conceptualize as a whole. First, the term "Moor" (meaning anything from Muslim to pagan) survives in "Morocco" and "Mauritania." And the root word is there because these areas impacted on Europe between the eighth and fifteenth centuries.[4]

Second, following further European encounters, place names assume the posture of identification from an external gaze. The Ivory Coast is one case in point that has survived, conjuring up terms such as "Slave Coast," "Guinea Coast," or "Gold Coast." This all had little to do with group ("tribal") identification of indigenous inhabitants, and spoke more to the needs of the Portuguese, Spaniards, British, and French.

Third, even when names are altered in the spirit of "independence," there is still a dependency on reacting to a colonial past. When, for instance, the "Gold Coast" becomes "Ghana," it merely substitutes one kind of myth making for another. "Ghana," of course, harks back to the ancient kingdom of the same name, but the present-day borders of contemporary Ghana bear little or no resemblance to the ancient empire. It becomes even doubly confounding that anti-imperialists who reject the notions of European colonization, should embrace its equally pernicious African counterpart.

Fourth, some names that survive into the present pinpoint issues beyond the external gaze. "Niger" and "Nigeria" seem to be hasty concoctions of what the One termed the Other: As the West reached back to a partly fictional Latin past, it came to the simplistic conclusion that these were lands of the Blacks, and so it triumphantly called them. Add to this, however, the manner in which the terms became acceptable, partly due to mutual "tribal" rivalries, and hence survive today.

Fifth, the West also invented areas that seemed to proffer solutions to its own dilemma. Britain and America, facing the problem of postemancipation and large numbers of Blacks in their territories, hastily invented two "utopias." One, a place of freedom, Freetown, and the other, an area of liberty, Liberia, were both hastily carved out of "Darkest" Africa for returned slaves. An irony worth pointing out is that those who did "return" were so far removed from African realities that they hastily dubbed the indigenous Africans "natives" and sought to lord it over them, successfully it seems until the recent civil wars in Sierra Leone and Liberia. I would contend that beneath the surface is the omnipresent need of indigenous "natives" to rid themselves of the "Creoles" who had bullied, ruled, and governed for nearly two centuries.[5]

Hence, when the name "Africa" is evoked it is quite definitely fictional, in that at "home," on the continent, the most basic identity is first by ethnic nationality. Never, ever, apart from those who seek to make a political point, do indigenous people ever refer to themselves as "Africans." The nearest that I have seen some attempt at this is in South Africa, where Xhosa and Zulu sought to establish common identity faced with the Afrikaaner/British. Hence, one was termed "Black," the other "White," but this easy alliance, particularly for so-called Blacks, was never deep. Note Chief Buthelezi's constant efforts to subvert Nelson Mandela's "Blackness" by asserting his own "Zuluness."

How else, though, could a place of origin be invoked in the New World of Canada, the United States, Central America, South America, and the Caribbean? Indigenous people from Africa who populated these areas were not only a mixture of "tribe," but in many instances, they were composite mixtures of Black, White, and Native American. Hence, the part of them that sought to recall one part of their own origin had to give it a name. I suggest that "Africa" as concept, and as reality, was a product of the New World, never of Africa itself.

AFRICA AS REALITY

New issues faced people who had been brought from Africa. One major significant difference was that they lacked the new code of language—English, Spanish, Portuguese, or French—sacrosanct in each specific area of hegemonic control. They could modify the language, and this they certainly did into pidgins and creoles, but the European languages were often removed from the reality of place, inadequate to describe inherited ritual and custom, and deficient in vocabulary to relay a totally new and distinct situation.[6]

Add to language the new structure of hierarchy in the New World, where a lighter skin pigmentation established preference and ascendancy. Thus, there must have come about a sense of profound anonymity, projecting itself in any number of ways, but especially in the manner in which the individual is first manufactured from the (Black) group person, and then cut adrift in what seemed like a world without purpose or reason.

Out of the disorientation came not an identity with the loss, for who could tell what it was? Instead, there grew an urgent need to become part of the very "One" that rejected the "Other," a desire to destroy Otherness and reconstruct a more agreeable whole that could merge with the One. Phrases abound to describe how the process, at the physical level, would best be attained: "limpiar la raza" (washing out the race) is the Latin American equivalent of what seemed mandatory.

De-emphasizing the African went hand in hand with (at first) the self-repression of language, religion, dress, and other modes associated with the mores of a despised continent. Few thought differently, since survival necessitated speaking like the master, praying to his God, and imitating his clothes and food. Washing out the race, then, is not merely the physical act of sexual coupling, but it is a suicidal encounter, in many respects, to kill the very inner self that had been sustained thus far.

Self-destruction many be witnessed in various ways, as we look at the history of African habitation of the New World. After the death of language, religion, and other mores, comes the stage of the mimic, the colonial who is most adept at aping and who, as a result (and this is the truest irony) is often socially elevated for his adroitness. The colonial language itself invented a host of names for this "phenomenon": "assimilação" (Portuguese), "évolué" (French), or "subject" (British), all address the possibility of inclusion, once certain conditions were satisfied. But note how the words all address the same intent namely that of making the object alter, change, and grow into the perfected embodiment of the subject. So Portuguese colonials could assimilate, whereas French ones could evolve; both grew into the apex of humanity, namely the Portuguese and the French themselves. For British colonials, Britain held out the promise of "Britishness" (only God could be an Englishman!), subjected to the Royal Crown and the Privy Council.

Nor did matters alter very much with the thrust for independence. Those who began to assume the mantle of power in the various territories in Africa and the New World were themselves products of the very system against which they fought. I do not mean to underplay the crudeness of European attempts at crushing these incipient, although somewhat modest oppositions. But I do wish to stress that the leaders were (and remain to this day) embodiments of the same system they attacked. Often, education, along European lines, in European capitals by Europeans (once the dust subsided), seemed to ensure that the recipients related more easily to the metropolitan centers than to the original indigenous periphery. In Frantz Fanon's words, "The colonized is elevated above his jungle status in proportion to his adoption of the mother country's cultural standards. He becomes whiter as he renounces his blackness, his jungle."[7]

This was how "Africa" often served as a rallying cry for the masses. It had the effect of excluding the metropolitan areas from the discourse, and of providing a weapon for the new leaders. At this stage, "Africa" added even more to its former legendary status. Now it became associated, at least in the early part of the century, with a "free" Ethiopia and Liberia. And radical African leaders, for reasons of expediency, bought into the mythology because it was a supreme weapon, which helped them associate with their equally radical New World colleagues.[8]

In may ways, it may be quite confidently asserted, "Africa" assumed a pattern vis-à-vis Europe, which was replicated in the reality of the New World. After European exploration and colonization, there was a break down in the "tribal" structure, and in a way, this meant that there occurred limited substitution of European norms for African ones. Although this did not penetrate very deeply into the fabric of African society, it nevertheless operated in two important ways that had ramifications for the extension of Africa into the New World.

CONTROLLING NEW ETHNICITIES

Europeans, for instance, tried to introduce, as noted, a different level of ethnic identity: French Africa, British Africa, and Portuguese Africa assumed distinctions that differed from each other, and helped to further distance ethnic groups, even those who seemingly could claim an affinity with one another. Next, as a direct result, of the introduction of elite educational systems, there was developed, in Africa itself, before the slave trade, a new type of hierarchy, solely based solely on colonial principles.

One of these was the ability to speak the language of the metropolis, to utilize it well, and to be able to employ it as a medium for control or mastering the masses. In turn, the general public would be expected to, and often did, admire the ability of their new leaders to masquerade in the image of the colonial overlords. This is trifle more than what V. S. Naipaul means by mimicry, and is best expressed by Gayatri Chakravorty Spivak:

Against this globality—or post-nationalistic talk—is representation—both as *Darstellung* or theatre and as *Vertretung* or delegation as functionary—of the financialization of the globe, or globalization. What I had earlier seen as the upwardly class-mobile metropolitan ruse of recoding mimicry as resistance, comes into its own in this dispensation.[9]

The colonized Native Informant looked like the colonizer, could articulate the language of the master, dress like him, and even some 'mes bear his name. But Spivak would argue that, far from being mere mimicry, this operates much like Gilles Deleuze and Félix Guattari's nomad reterritorializing space as "a nomad, and an immigrant and a gypsy in relation to one's own language."[10]

Language became the supreme device by which African indigenous culture was manipulated. As part of language, there were the concomitant issues of the new mores of Europe: its religion, food, dress, music, architecture, and literature. But I do wish to suggest that it is the establishment of the primacy of European language that permits, even necessitates, the acceptability of all the other "norms." They become normal, not alien, because they are backed up by the enormous, potential power of the colonial power.

I say "potential," because the power was largely one that only seemed to be there. Although thousands of civil servants occupied the various territories, there were never more than a handful of European soldiers. And these were mainly officers in control of compliant "native" troops whose sole task was to oversee their own majority and confirm, at the same time, the ability of the European minority to control.

What then, one must ask, permitted "colonialism" and a subsequent "grant" of independence? Political scientists often hark back to the concept of force, but as noted, this was merely potential, hardly ever exercised, and never real. It seems that what was actual existed in the manner in which, through language, alien rituals were transformed, transposed, altered, identified, domesticated, and therefore accepted.

At the most obvious level, the "school" became a new controlling mechanism, a class-making machine.[11] Through "education," the conscripted African could advance rapidly up the rungs of power within the colonial establishment. Such an "education" often meant taking the term literally—leading people away from ways that were "barbarous," that is, hostile to the colonial administration. Securely tied with "education" was the church apparatus since many schools were church schools, and it was often not possible to gain admission to such an institution, with the great promise of advancement, without adapting still more of the alien rituals.

Most basic was baptism, involving name change and religious adaptation. The new name conferred on the African had to be capricious, since parents (themselves well-wishing non-Christians) randomly chose names from days of the week, months of the year or books of the Bible. Once name-givers (usually parents or close elders) had abrogated the sacrosanct nature of a meaningful African name, children were often left with appalling appellations such as "Sunday" or "Genesis."

Name change did not actually even mean a personal change, for

Africans functioned still within a given community, and even those who were forced to speak English for long periods at the mission schools returned to their own home base during vacations, where they helped out with farming and assumed the normal duties and obligations of young people.

Equally, religious change did not ever mean a complete turnabout in religion, and a refusal to acknowledge the presence of what was actually the authentic spiritual experience. Who could deny the presence and viability of ancestors? Who would dare turn away from feeding them, paying them homage, or honoring them? At the important occasions of human development, at birth, initiation, marriage, and death, rituals continued much as before. But I would be overtly optimistic if I did not assert that the imposition of the new culture with its rewards did not carry with it great erosion of the African norms.

European mastery/magic over the landscape, place and time, and clothes and lifestyle seemed to possess an inherent superiority, irrespective of the people, but inherent in the thing itself. At base, then this uncertainty, this division of cultural loyalty actually brought about the collusion between the dominated and the dominant. The way to acquire the paraphernalia of the Europeans seemed simple: baptism, schooling, and going abroad to pursue a profession were guarantees in the process of social evolution. As I have stressed, above all this was the emphasis placed on signifiers, utilizing the imposed language so that often it could not be comprehended even by the language owner himself—when it became a dialect or a creole, or was written as "english."[12]

TALKING THE TALK

We note an especially good example of this new language in popular literature in Nigeria during the forties and fifties.[13] Here, "talk" on paper in the so-called Onitsha literature, was meant to convey, sometimes even teach, the use of the language. Many accounts, for instance, deal with instructions on writing love letters, or winning the heart of a would-be lover; still others, in heavy, ponderous language show how virtue triumphs. Onitsha literature, like its counterparts in Ghana and East Africa, as well as indigenous language compositions in southern Africa, took literature back to its functional origins. It could be and was often didactic, and it espoused Christian/European values. I would like to suggest that by the middle part of the twentieth century, the colonial emphasis had been definitely stressed, but it had also backfired. Africans, untutored in the metropolitan language, and unselected for advancement by the European power structure, could approximate very closely the sound of the signifiers, convincingly enough for anyone outside the metropolis.

Additionally, we note that African popular music had the same effect, although its historical input is a little different. William Megenney has shown the fascinating and interesting relationship between New World and African music, in that one feeds off the other, and then in turn exports its own new synthesis back, which comes back yet again.[14] This much is evident with soca and zouk, African-based, but yet, even as they borrow the African rhythm and melody, export them back and help (along with the residual Latin American influence from the thirties) to create soukouss, the rich vibrant heavy sound perfected by singer-composers like the Grand Old Man of Congolese music, Tabu-Ley Rochereau. He has been around since the early days with the late Franco, Nico, and Le Grand Kallé. Tabu carries on the tradition and personifies the changes that the music has taken.

We also note similar changes in the music of Tabu's former wife, M'Bilia Bel, and the younger Nyboma, especially in such stirring and energetic numbers as his "Papy Sidolo." For instance, Zaire musicians imported the sounds of Cuban rhumba, itself a synthesis of the sounds of Africa and Europe. In turn, the Zaire musicians utilized their own (albeit Belgian-imposed) African language, Lingala, European electric guitars, African choral singing, and European "romantic" themes to push the limits of the new sound. This was what subsequently became known as "soukous," and in the seventies and eighties was again reexported back to the Caribbean (particularly Martinique and Guadeloupe) where it was now termed "zouk." At this level we note how Africa and the Afro New World interact; "Mother" Africa takes turns at being both elder and child, and the New World offspring refashions its own mythology, and reexports it to Africa.

Thus, a specific pattern begins to be formulated in Africa before the dispersal of New World African, and then entails our recognition of an Africa that has become "detribalized," fragmented, even Eurocentered. I suspect that this is the concept that many slaves took to the New World, and one that was reinforced by the most influential latecomers, the Yoruba. By the time of the arrival of the Yoruba, their "tribal" identity had certainly broken down. Fierce contests had pitted the holy city of Ife against the lay power of Benin. Superimposed over all this was the new British concept of a thing called "Nigeria," understood by few and adopted by fewer still.

The New World Yoruba in Cuba and Brazil (latest to abolish slavery, and thus the places where the Yoruba influence was strongest) seemed to conform to this understood invention of "Africa" and the "African." Since few knew Africa firsthand by this time, Yoruba mores came to stand for an Africa conjured up in the imagination. Not unnaturally, the continent of Africa, recollected in fancy, became the symbol of a Utopia, a place of near perfection, that both counterbalanced the bad rap given by Europeans and Eurocentric Africans, and at the same time, an area equivalent to the kind of perfection Europeans had presumably found in the New World.

Quite simultaneously, therefore, with the acceptance of Africa as a real Utopian Paradise, there existed the rejection of the New World as such. In a way, this was a countermeasure, designed by the slave-thinkers, that would neutralize the effect of their own rejection from the promise that the New World supposedly held out to Whites. It was revolutionary and it became articulated as this more and more as it defied European idealism, substituting an African alternative that was equally as unreal.

EUROPEAN IDEALS AND AFRICANS

There are, of course, some obvious differences between what Europeans aspire to and what Africans may just settle for. The European hope of perfection lay in the acquisition of New World Territory—"wilderness" of the New World. The African wish for the ideal was located not in New World land, but in an unspecified place named Africa where there were no narrow boundaries. Africa became a leap of faith, a promise of freedom, a village to which the fettered could literally fly to, as free people. At the end of Toni Morrison's *Song of Solomon*, Milkman finally shared Shalimar's knowledge, "If you surrendered to the air, you could *ride* it."[15]

A second difference that is apparent in European and African conceptualizing of the New World was one relating to tense, in that for Europeans the promise of the New World lay in the future. For Africans it seemed fleetingly present, as an indicator of possibilities beyond what the Rastafarians conscripted as "Babylon" or whatever other metaphor served to describe it. The "Promised Land" for Africans was not here, in the present, but in an Africa of the past that of course could be associated with a physical escape to Canada or elsewhere, or a spiritual return to Africa or heaven, both synonymous with each other. The present visualization on the part of Europeans and the past validation on the part of Africans, probably, more than any other single factor, accounted for the way in which they saw themselves as part of New World reality.

Finally, Europeans, in the majority and the ascendancy in the New World, themselves imported a conceptualization of Africa that would, in part, be borrowed by Blacks. This was an Africa of their own conjecture, born out of earlier misunderstood contacts with natives, pagans, and savages. This "Dark" Africa, where "Blacks" lived, this place of horror and evil, was one from which forcible excavation could be justified. Slavery, then, could not be inhuman, if the wretched were being rescued from a place of horror. Indeed, it was an African no less, one who had been returned to West Africa after being "mistakingly" sold for a slave, who spread positive tidings about the goodness of the English. According to Francis Moore in his *Travels into the Inland Parts of Africa* (1738), fourteen months was about as long as Ayuba Suleiman could endure London. He managed to convince the English to send him back—he was himself an African slave trader—and we are told on his return, "he spoke always very handsome of the English."[16]

What is surprising is not so much that the propaganda of the time was concocted and even widely believed by its *European inventors,* but that it came to be firmly accepted by the *invented Africans.* Even as they were remade, remanufactured. and refurbished by the imaginings of Europe, Africans (like Phyllis Wheatley) could and did give thanks to a Christian God for rescuing them from a "pagan land." As noted, the new situation was not peculiar only to New World Africans, but had been insidiously introduced into the continent itself by missionaries. Were they able to speak to one another, both continental and New World Africans from the fifteenth to the nineteenth centuries might well have agreed that Europeanization, with its concomitant associations, was a most desirable alternative. There are, of course, exceptions, but in large measure, Europe as superpower, at home and in the Americas, reflected an aura of superiority few could dispute. And since few knew their history and believed that they were merely empty slates, waiting to be filled in by European civilization, it was not a difficult myth to accept.

Along with the idea of an inherent inferiority came the proof. From the fifteenth century until the twentieth, the Bible was utilized to situate Africans, at home and elsewhere, as those (like Ham) who had been cast out. After Charles Darwin, evolution had then been utilized over and over again to depict Africans on both sides of the Atlantic as Piltdown humans, one step removed from ape, and living proof of the theory. More recently, "intelligence" and testing devices have been used by Arthur Jensen, Charles Murray, and others to suggest "genetic" inferiority. The Bible, Darwin, and genetics all pointed toward the same inescapable conclusion: Blacks were doomed to occupy the lower rungs of society since they were by nature defective.

Again my purpose is hardly to point out the merely obvious but rather to stress how those "condemned" take on the beliefs of their judges. As early as the eighteenth century, an important thesis was composed by a first generation African, Jacobus Eliza Johannes Capitein (1717–1747), who zealously provided evidence that "slavery was not contrary to the laws of God."[17]

Acceptance of condemnation by the Bible was also assiduously debated. Indeed many "experiments" carried out by European intellectual and political leaders attempted to prove that "nurture" had as much say as "nature." For instance, Pope Leo X had been "given" a Moor, who he subsequently named Leo Africanus (c. 1485–1554).

Africanus converted to Christianity, travelled widely, and in his travel literature stressed the way of the Christian church, as much as the pope.[18] Later on, the Duke of Montagu had sponsored Francis Williams (c. 1700–1770) to Cambridge. Additionally, he constantly provided books to Ignatius Sancho (1729–1780), a West Indian grocer and letter writer in the manner of Lawrence Sterne. The German Duke Anton Ulrich von Braunschweig-Wolfenbüttel and himself sponsored Anton Wilhelm Amo (1703–?) to the University of Halle. Dr. Samuel Johnson employed Frances Barber (c. 1700–1770) at his home, often tutoring him in Latin and Greek, and later leaving him a generous allowance.[19] The experiment, with which the subjects readily acquiesced, was to determine, in the sentiments of the Duke of Montagu, whether a Black man with the proper training could be the intellectual equal of a White person.[20] Lest we dismiss their concerns too quickly, let us recall that in our own time the discussion seems almost moot to some researchers: the answer regarding whether Black equals White, propounded in *The Bell Curve* (1994) with much gloss and embellishment, is a resounding no!

What the Harlem Renaissance poet, Countee Cullen, termed the "diabolic dye" was therefore common to indigenous Africans and Westernized Blacks. Therefore, what some sought (and here many would disagree) was at least to show the extent to which they could not be castigated as children of Cain. The easiest way, within the belief system of the early twentieth century, was to opt for "class" rather than "caste." For W.E.B. Du Bois, the Black intelligentsia were the aristocracy among Blacks, and obviously missionaries to Africa such as Alexander Crummell and Edward Blyden shared these views.[21]

In arguing for special status (within U.S. cultural and social structure, many Black intellectuals had to concede a major point—what, again, no less a figure than Du Bois had referred to as the "low average culture" of Blacks, and how Marcus Garvey, the leading Pan-Africanist of the 1920s, had always utilized the trappings of European authority from his native Jamaica to symbolize the African way of life.

Both the adopting of Europe and its discarding as well as the substitution of "class" were channelled into interestingly new directions, that attempted to incorporate Africa as belief and idea. For Du Bois, this was effectively seen in his founding of the Pan-African Congresses; for Garvey, the "Back to Africa" movement served as an intending launching pad. But Du Bois's various Pan-African Congresses were all held in Europe, and Garvey's projected voyages were confined to New York, where with the help of Du Bois, his assets were seized by the U.S. government, and he himself finally expelled from the country.[22]

Garvey's reach was wider than Du Bois's in that Garvey's movement, under the general umbrella of the Universal Negro Improvement Association, had offices in several countries worldwide. Du Bois, on the other hand, remained very much a Black American intellectual with no mass support even in the United States. Although both men wisely utilized the print media, Garvey's *Liberator* was a newspaper with wide, general appeal, whereas Du Bois's *Crisis* and *Opportunity* were journals with limited intellectual interest.

Nevertheless both Garvey and Du Bois established a major yet unintended common front: both their movements were intended for non-Africans, outside Africa, with obviously limited or no appeal to those on the continent. In a way, therefore, one could plausibly argue that Garvey and Du Bois established the final severance between Black Africa and the Black diaspora, in that both movements indicated concerns that were distinct to nonindigenous Africans. Thus, in a rather ironical fashion, even as New World Blacks united, they were distancing themselves more and more from the reality of old world Africa.

Out of this distinction an even new and hitherto unformulated concept of "Africa" emerges. We have noted how the former European invention, buttressed by misinterpretations of the Bible, Darwin, and genetic theory, tended to lump Blacks together. We have also observed that New World Blacks, in seeking to establish some kind of cozy relationship with Whites, opted for "class" or what the Du Boisian intellectuals saw as natural leaders. By the time that we come to what is not really a Garvey/Du Bois conflict (although they saw it in this way) but rather an alliance of similar beliefs, the imaging of Africa assumes a different dimension in the New World.

From then on until the present, Africa can no longer be a place, but only a political concept, no longer an idea, but now a remedial reality. "Africa" could be summoned up to terrify the White majority, because this place of darkness and awe was part of their own creation. "Africa" would also be invoked by Blacks in the name of the most nebulous concepts, at any level, for any reason, at any time. Since it was no longer fixed, definite, whole, it became a shadow of the New World, assiduously following in the paths of Blacks and Whites, and waiting for some frightful moment when shadow becomes substance. These protean dimensions finally separated the concoctions of the New World from the reality of the Old.

AFRICA AS CONSTRUCTED LANDSCAPE

The Berlin Conference had carved up the African continent with little regard for its own indigenous ethnicity. Instead, the new norm that was imposed was more to do with Europe and its view of the world as made up of nation-states; indeed European "tribalism" itself was the new measure of what constituted an African. The "native" was therefore subdivided into British "subject," French *"évolué,"* and Portuguese *"assimilação."* These terms all seemingly offered some help for eventual and ultimate redemption; through European Westernization, "natives" could be made in their master's image, indeed could even aspire to becoming the master.

Not surprisingly, early advocates of this method whereby "subjects" could become their own masters, drew heavily on the European experience in order to put forward what was for the native not a bit ironical—how to become a European agent. Garvey, for instance, who founded the United Negro Improvement Association, proclaimed the need to return to Africa. But it was all done within the trope of a European mythology. His authority figure decked up in the manner of a colonial governor, complete with plumed helmet and horse, and his followers' regalia of dukes and duchesses were all lifted directly from the plenitude of British colonial pomp with which Garvey was most familiar.

All of Garvey's paraphernalia, even as it was passed on to the Rastafarians, was of course, mythological invention at its best. I do not mean by this to suggest any degree of invalidity; after all, social myths may originate in any manner, even as they promise a degree of political utopianism. And here it would be pertinent to stress that there is thus a great deal of difference that separates Black and White aspirations for the Promised Land. For most Whites, their arrival in the New World was in itself the fulfillment of the promise, the realization of the hope, the entry into Paradise. Place names throughout the America, and the transfer of European myths relating to abundance, wealth, and prosperity, confirm this.

For Blacks, the Promised Land lay not forward in a space to be conquered, but backward in a time to be reexperienced. Furthermore, even though there may have been an attachment to some faded and ancient notion of place on the part of Whites, there was no yearning for a permanent return. Europe was, after all, a place from which they had voluntarily fled. Contrast this with Africa as a village, not a nation nor a continent, what each succeeding New World Black generation had to remake and reclaim. This kind of attachment, albeit Romantic, would not have been possible in Africa itself, even though Africa also inherited not the glorified myths, but rather the ignoble versions of its own degradation that were part and parcel of New World faith.

The agents who reduced Africa to this concept of ignobility and ultimate denial were primarily European. On the one hand, colonialism had reinforced the pattern of belief on both sides of the Atlantic. On the other, and weighted more heavily, was the Western reinvention of "black," as defined and denoted in any European language, with its images of barbarism, cannibalism, and crude, naked people. The West, particularly the United States, had the means and the media to depict large-scale versions of this stereotype. Black arrival in the New World called for an arrangement of the stereotypes of the former land into positive and negative elements. In a way, these are only handles that allow us to describe the new references, for in reality they do not really possess endemic qualities. Since the Africa that is recalled is to a large extent invented, one can further assert that both the positive and negative elements are "true," since they permit a degree of interaction with the former continent from afar. On the "positive" side, whatever runs counter to majority opinion (whether colonial or ghetto imposed), or presents the continent in its imaginative totality, is asserted. On the "negative" side, since the very word "black" was utilized by European languages to mean and indicate all that was derogatory, this was echoed in the resulting dialects and creoles.[23]

Those who invented mythology perceived Africa in a holistic manner. Those who advocated the Utopian Paradise had to rewrite remembered history, and often to deny memory, that is assume that the villains were never, and could never have been Africans themselves. As part of the antithesis to the virtuous "Black" man, the troublesome figure of the "White" was erected as thief, robber, rapist, and, above all, in keeping with the rhetoric of the time, non-Christian. Thus came about a dual construct of "Africa."

Hence the need, as already discussed, to fly back to Africa, an inbred notion found in oral spoken literature, early spirituals, and later written material. The return to Africa represented more than "flying away" in a physical manner, but now assumed synthesized Christian religious significance, whereby the bosom of Christ was often associated with Africa, and the escape from slavery often meant more than "following the North Star," as has been pointed out. In both cases, flight and the North star, assumed cosmic proportions that went beyond the literal or even spiritual interpretations of New World theology. By transforming the idea of flight and star, the slaves sung themselves a new belief system. This surpassed the practical teachings of their Yoruba and Ashanti forebears, and asserted instead new notions that sought to stress mortal escape from the confines of the body to a new merging with the universe.

Above all, out of the misery of serfdom, and the relative absence of royalty, was born a new egalitarian system. Needless to say, none of this was present in the old, historical Africa. Instead, in Ghana, Mali, and Songhai, to name but three instances, the hierarchical nature of the society is most evident in that they are very often described as "empires," with kings and emperors as rulers. In time, perhaps, as we move more away from the Eurocentric leanings of European and African historians, it might be possible to construct a different model, one in which the various areas achieved unity not so much through coercion, but rather through a communalistic effort on the part of all the citizenry.

Not without some irony, the presence of a domestic slave trade in most African kingdoms reinforced this pattern of inequality. Add to this the latest hotbed of fierce debate, the presence of Jews,[24] and the accepted and known part played by Arabs and Europeans, it becomes most evident that a large mass of people existed who had little to say about the consequences and effects of their daily lives. Furthermore, note that even though both Judaism and Islam had entered into Africa quite late, after the turn of the Christian era, any recollection of an Africa, free from external influences, was hardly a reality.

However, what evidence does remain for us, particularly in the form of praise songs, is certainly not directed at the peasantry, but from the common folk to an elevated leader. In most of these panegyrics, the object of adoration is exalted, attributed with almost godlike qualities, and always solicited for some kind of gift. Of course, the idea of who the New World Blacks really represented derives from their new nomenclature. For they were no longer part of the old ethnic formation, rather they clung tenaciously on to the fringes of the New World nation-states, at least as hyphenated citizens.

Garvey's redemption, his promise of a new faith, would be taken up later on and popularized by the Rastafarians and, in particular, by Bob Marley in reggae music. Here the promise of Africa is focused on Ethiopia, now the promised land, and on Haille Selassie, the emperor, who is really Ras Tafari, or king of kings. The actual historical truth of Ethiopia and its emperor's predicament mattered little. More relevant was the fact that all through the immediate present up until Mussolini's invasion, Ethiopia was the only supposedly free African country. Liberia, the other, had received full attention by Alexander Crummell, Edward Blyden, and other nineteenth-century African Americans.

In a way we note an almost hierarchical New World dividing up of Ethiopia and Liberia. It was almost as if Liberia had been coopted by nineteenth-century "establishment" figures, with the blessing of the U. S. government. From as early as the eighteenth century, Paul Cuffee, a "Free Colored," had taken Blacks to Monrovia from America.[25] But there was nothing truly revolutionary about his act. It had been encouraged, and continued to be approved of, by the American Colonization Society. A larger irony was that the very people who sought to colonize Liberia were themselves Black spokespersons for the West and, second, they regarded the "natives" (as they termed the Africans) rather contemptuously.

Liberia, therefore, had created in Africa a new kind of colony, whereby the returnees had escaped from their New World status as untouchables, redeeming themselves in their anxious desire to Christianize the "savages" and make Liberia part of the Western world. Indeed those who wanted to lead their fellow Blacks there would be sure to receive the approval of the government, as Abraham Lincoln voiced over and over again in no uncertain terms. In the same breath as Lincoln could admit to equality between the races, he could as easily assert: " My first impulse would be to free all the slaves, and send them to Liberia, to their own native land."[26]

Ethiopia was further away in the Romantic mind, touched by the Western mythologies of Prester John,[27] but not perceived in this way by New World speculations. Ethiopia became for twentieth-century visionaries what Liberia had represented for nineteenth-century emigrants. There was, of course, one major difference: Ethiopia remained distant, a dream of a possibility, whereas Liberia was brought closer, the distinct possibility of the dream. The phantom had been corrupted by the advent of the American Liberians who quickly turned their own dream of Paradise into one of internal destruction and external collusion.

So-called Black Islam is a twentieth-century phenomenon in that it too was invented, independent of the Five Pillars of Islam, and bore more relationship to the resuscitation of Black pride in the United States than to a religious affirmation of Allah. One of the most widely held beliefs of the time was that Whites were created by a mad scientist, a fantasy that had nothing whatsoever to do with the tenets of multicultural Islam. This was a firm belief that Malcolm X held, even though this is scarcely mentioned today. The Nation of Islam had had the effect of creating a new, indeed a different set of "others." In a way, this was a bold, although clearly mistaken view. For one does not simply create the "other," merely by naming him. One has to possess the power to render the "other" as marginalized, even irrelevant. And so, despite the undoubted achievements of the Nation of Islam, one reason that it survives as a splintered faction today is that the power of the one deemed the other was never truly overcome.

The simplistic, frequently asserted view—that once Malcolm X completed the *hadj*, he was convinced of the unity of the human race—cannot be true. I encountered Malcolm X on his way back from his second trip to Saudi Arabia. I recall distinctly, that, as he addressed students at Ibadan University, he began his statement with "Brothers, sisters and others," still attempting to differentiate between Africans and Europeans. indeed, he delivered a race-baiting harangue, which seemed so out of place in Nigeria.

Malcolm X's speech on that May day in 1964 continued to extol most fervently an Africa of the imagination. He stated that he felt "free" as he walked through Africa, but the truth was that Malcolm X could hardly have accomplished his journey to Africa without actively utilizing the trappings and accoutrements of the West. And here I refer not only to his mode of transportation, and indeed his attire, both clearly Western, but particularly to his delivery in English. The language he had to employ in order to address his audience on that day, as well as in Harlem, and in the pages of his *Autobiography*, was English, and it was in that language that his audience understood him.[28] Although I will grant that for reasons that were beyond Malcolm X himself, indeed perhaps even inimical to his most cherished beliefs, his reputation did spread all over Africa. The reasons were, like tee shirts, Coca Cola and jeans, more to do with the willful act of imitating the victor, rather than the acceptance of the message he brought. For the argument that stressed color could hardly have made any sense to a people with no difference in skin coloration, but certainly much difference in tribe.

This was where the real irony lay, that Malcolm X—though he espoused an African line, what today we might even term an Afrocentric viewpoint—was very much a creature of the West. Unable to address the mixed audience in Ibadan in any of their languages (Igbo, Yoruba, or Hausa), he was forced back on the very thing he rejected: English. This had to be so, since even had he acquired one or two of the Nigerian languages, he would have been unable to communicate with perhaps one-half of his audience.

It is not without significance that English remains the national language of Nigeria to this day, as it does for a majority of other African countries. In passing, it should be stated that for Africans English is nonthreatening, and thus more easily acceptable to masses of differing ethnic groups, who would suspect an attempt at ethnic domination were some other indigenous language to be utilized. Like French and Portuguese, the early European language imposition carried with it a degree of prestige, an assumption of Westernization and learning, that helped establish a new order of social patterning.

The language "elites" in the various areas bought into two mythologies: one was the sanctity of the European-imposed nation-states, and the second was a belief in the new order. This is very relevant for our concerns, since the custodians of the old hierarchical patterns were often reduced to the status of clowns. Therefore, we should observe that both in the old world of Africa, and the New World of the Americas, a breakdown of traditional patterns occurred. At this point we can note how the loss of past affected the literature on both sides of the Atlantic, and the extent to which there is a degree of thematic commonality.

If one reflects for a moment, it is easily noticed that the articulation of Black people in the United States is little different from those in the rest of the New World. "Ghettoization" is a similar process to colonization, whereby people external to a culture impose their own norms and beliefs on the other. What is even more fascinating in the case of the United States is that spokespersons like Du Bois, an avid Pan-Africanist (at least in theory), promoting conferences in Paris and New York, articulated the concept of the "talented tenth," whereby subject peoples could be promised a process by which they could aspire to becoming part of the ruling class.

In a way, this was a continuation of the nineteenth-century wish that

Liberia had come to represent. Blacks had their own territory, where they could practice their own version of overlordship, mastered so well as underlings in the ghettoes of the New World. Pan-Africanism, however, had not one country, but the entire sub-Saharan Africa as its romantic realization. What this most certainly demonstrated was an inability (like their White counterparts) for Black Americans to be able to identify with a specific area. All that they both could hope to do was to lump every ethnic and area experience into one, small enough to be comprehended, large enough to possess the possibility of suzerainty.

As such, Black and White Americans, both Creoles in the New World, and unable to fit themselves with any specific certainty into any one given place, simply opted for an entire space. Much as they had called themselves Black and White, African and European, they began to identify with a larger terrain and to coopt imaginative landscapes for themselves. The process was the same; the major difference was that African Americans never had the power to impose a given view on Africa, but White Americans could and did on Europe, especially after 1945. And the West, in general, continued to fashion Africa after its own nightmare image—a model of persistent gloom and darkness inherited by Americans, Black and White, as the lair of the Other.

NOTES

1. Even as progressive a thinker as Young seems to have few qualms with the idea of Greenwich as center. See Robert J. C. Young, *Colonial Desire: Hybridity in Theory, Culture and Race* (London and New York: Routledge, 1995), 1–2.

2. Contrast Ali Mazrui, *The Africans: A Triple Heritage* (Boston: Little, Brown, 1986), 23–38; which was also made into a documentary.

3. See the recent academic debate in Martin Bernal, *Black Athena: The Afroasiatic Roots of Classical Civilization*, 2 vols. (New Brunswick, NJ: Rutgers UP, Vol. 1 [1987], Vol. 2 [1991]). Also note the angry response by Mary R. Lefkowitz, *Not Out of Africa: How Afrocentrism Became an Excuse to Teach Myth as History* (New York: Basic, 1996), and the even more pungent Lefkowitz and Guy MacLean Rogers, eds., *Black Athena Revisited* (Chapel Hill: U of North Carolina P, 1996). Basically, Bernal argues that Egypt in Africa may have civilized Greece. Lefkowitz will have none of this—it is mere Afrocentric claptrap.

4. See Jan Read, *The Moors in Spain and Portugal* (London: Faber and Faber, 1974), 53–59, 71–85, 92–96, 147–51, 174–80, 212–19.

5. Quite a few books have been written on Africa and the Western gaze. One of the earliest was Philip D. Curtin, ed., *Africa and the West: Intellectual Responses to European Culture* (Madison: U of Madison P, 1972). See Curtin's introduction on vii–x.

6. Note the English/english discussion first launched in Bill Ashcroft, Gareth Griffiths, and Helen Tiffin, eds., *The Empire Writes Back: Theory and Practice in Post-Colonial Literatures* (London and New York: Routledge, 1989), 121–23, 195–97.

7. Frantz Fanon, *Black Skin, White Masks: The Experiences of a Black Man in a White World* [1952], trans. Charles Lam Markmann (New York: Grove, 1967), 18.

8. CLR James always stressed to me that "Pan-Africanism" did not bring the Africans on board until relatively late. Up until the Manchester Conference, it was a New World movement led by W.E.B. Du Bois and Marcus Garvey, as well as a cohort of lesser known believers, including George Padmore and H. Sylverster Williams. A text that stresses the Caribbean contribution is Winston James, *Holding Aloft the Banner of Ethiopia: Caribbean Radicalism in Early Twentieth-century America* (London: Verso, 1998), especially 52–55, 75–76, 97–99, 118–19, 193–94.

9. Gayatri Chakravorty Spivak, *A Critique of Post-Colonial Reason: Toward a History of the Vanishing Present* (Cambridge, MA: Harvard UP, 1999), 363–64.

10. Gilles Deleuze and Félix Guattari, *Kafka: Toward a Minor Literature* [1975], trans. Dana Polan (Minneapolis: U of Minnesota P, 1986), 19; also see 16–27.

11. Spivak does not term academe a "class-making machine" but the assumption of its elitism exists throughout this text. See Gayatri Chakravorty Spivak, *Outside in the Teaching Machine* (New York: Routledge, 1993), 25–76.

12. For a good discussion on the problematics of writing in English, see Ngugi wa Thiong'O, *Decolonizing the Mind: The Politics of Language in African Literature* (London: James Currey, 1986), 5–9. The issue of language has asserted itself most prominently in the French Caribbean, where Créole as music, dance, food, race, authentic language, and lifestyle is often put forward in nationalistic terms as a realistic alternative to any one racial preference, such as négritude. See Edouard Glissant, *Caribbean Discourse: Selected Essays* [1981] Trans. Michael Dash (Charlottesville: UP of Virginia, 1989) and Patrick Chamoiseau, Raphaël Confiant and Jean Bernabé, *Éloge de la créolité* (Paris: Gallimard, 1989). Both texts were initially published in French, written by academics.

13. Concerning Onitsha literature, see the following studies: Ulli Beier, "Public Opinion on Lovers," *Black Orpheus* 14 (Feb. 1964): 4–16, is concerned with the production and some literary assessment of the writing; Donatus Nwoga, "Onitsha Market Literature," *Transition* 4 (1963): 26–33, attempts to evaluate the work in terms of literature; Nancy J. Schmidt, "Nigeria: Fiction for the Average Man," *Africa Report* 10 (Aug 1965): 39–41, is a more general account; and Harold Collins, *Onitsha Chap-Books* (Athens: Ohio UP, 1971).

14. See William Megenney, *Cuba and Brasil: Etnohistoria del Empleo Religioso del Lenguaje Afro Americano* (Miami: Ediciones Universal, 1999). This is a thoroughly researched book using language, music and religion to show parallels and similarities.

15. For flying as a trope, see Michael A. Gomez, *Exchanging Our Country Marks: The Transformation of African Identities in the Colonial and Antebellum South* (Chapel Hill: U of North Carolina P, 1998), 117–20. For actual accounts of Africans flying back to Africa, see Georgia Writers' Project, *Drums and Shadows: Survival Studies Among the Georgia Coastal Negroes* (Athens, GA: U of Georgia P, 1940). Also see Toni Morrison, *Song of Solomon* (New York: Knopf, 1978), 337.

16. Cited in "Ayuba's Return to Africa" in Philip D. Curtin, ed., *Africa Remembered: Narratives by West Africans from the Era of the Slave Trade* (Madison: U of Wisconsin P, 1967), 55, 57.

17. Jacobus Eliza Johannes Capitein delivered this oration in Latin on March 10, 1742. See Janheinz Jahn, *A History of Neo-African Literature* (New York: Grove,

1968), and Kwesi Kwaa Prah, *Jacobus Eliza Johannes Capitein,1717–1747* (Trenton, NJ: Africa World, 1992).

18. Note Leo Africanus, *A Geographical Historie of Africa* [1600], ed. John Pory (New York: De Capo, 1969). Africanus became the indigenous authority for some two hundred years of African marginalization.

19. James Boswell, *The Life of Samuel Johnson*, 3 vols. (London: Swan, Sonnenschein, 1988), 3:161–64.

20. I discussed many of these writers in O. R. Dathorne, *The Black Mind: A History of African Literature* (Minneapolis: U of Minnesota P, 1974), 73–88. For more recent studies, see Vincent Carretta, *Unchained Voices* (Lexington, KY: UP of Kentucky, 1996); Gretchen Gerzina, *Black London: Life before Emancipation* (New Brunswick, NJ: Rutgers UP, 1995); Adam Potkay and Sandra Burr ed., *Black Atlantic Writers of the Eighteenth Century* (New York: St. Martin's Press, 1995); Keith A. Sandiford, *Measuring the Moment: Strategies of Protest in Eighteenth Century Afro-English Writing* (Cranbury, NJ: Associated University Presses, 1988); Edward Scobie, *Black Britannia: A History of Blacks in Britain* (Chicago: Johnson, 1972); and Folarin Shyllon, *Black People in Britain 1555–1833* (London: Oxford UP and the Institute of Race Relations, 1977). Also see a book written in French in 1808, Henri Grégoire, *On the Cultural Achievements of Negroes*. 1808. Trans. Thomas Cassirer and Jean-François Brière. Amherst, MA: U of Massachusetts P, 1996. 75–112. An early translation in English by David Bailie Warden was published in the Untied States in 1810.

21. Kwame Anthony Appiah, *In My Father's House: Africa in the Philosophy of Culture* (New York: Oxford UP, 1992), 5–6, 13–19, 21–26.

22. For details on the Du Bois/Garvey conflict, see Robert Hill, *The Marcus Garvey and Universal Negro Improvement Association Papers*, 9 vols. (Berkeley: U of California P, 1983 to present), 6:173 and 195.

23. There is no concept of "black" in Africa as positive or negative. "Black" is a New World invention and one that endures the consequences of the concept. A major exception is in a "settler" community such as South Africa.

24. Consult *The Secret Relationship between Blacks and Jews*, vol. 1 (Boston, MA: Nation of Islam, 1991). Also note a good review by David Mills, "Half Truths and History: The Debate over Jews and the Slave Trade," *Guardian Weekly* 149.18 (Oct. 31, 1993): 18–19.

25. See Lamont D. Thomas, *Paul Cuffe: Black Entrepreneur and Pan-Africanist* (Urbana, IL: U of Illinois P, 1988), 101–6.

26. Abraham Lincoln, *Speeches and Writings: 1832–1858* (New York: Library of America, 1989), 510. Lincoln is attempting to show that his views had changed. He goes on to speak in this First Debate with Stephen A. Douglas on August 21, 1858 that "There is a physical difference between the two [races], which in my judgment will probably forever forbid their living together upon the footing of perfect equality," p.512. See his emphasis on the need for separation on p. 478. Also note Lincoln on "colonization"—in this context sending Black citizens to Africa, pp. 271, 316, 402–3.

27. See O. R. Dathorne, *Imagining the World: Mythical Belief versus Reality in Global Encounters* (Westport, CT and London: Bergin & Garvey, 1994), 63, 170–71, for a full discussion of Prester John as myth, first in Asia and later in Africa. In the New World he was replaced by Manoa del Dorado, who took his daily bath in gold dust.

28. My recollection of my clash with Malcolm X differs somewhat from his

version. See his version in Malcolm X, with the assistance of Alex Haley, *The Autobiography of Malcolm X* [1965] (New York: Ballantine, 1973), 350–51. According to Malcolm, I was chased off the campus (where incidentally I lived). See Bruce Perry, *Malcolm: The Life of a Man Who Changed Black America* (Barrytown, NY: Station Hill, 1991), 269 and 474.

Chapter 7

Africa in Europe: Binaries and Polarities

hic scriptor nec fuit orbe satus
Aethiopum terris venit qui gesta Latinus
Austriadae mira carminis arte canat.
(Juan Latino, *Austrias*, [1573] 10)

The appearance deceives: why? this black but demure being
contains the white soul of the African moor. (Brandijin Ryser
on Capitein, cited by Kwesi Kwaa Prah, *Jacobus Eliza
Johannes Capitein, 1717–1747* [1992])

Almost as soon as contact was made between Africa and Europe,
Europeans insisted on carting off specimens of the newfound oddities
back to the motherland. From the sixteenth century onwards, the
Spaniards and Portuguese were first in the field, but they were soon
followed by the British, all of whom were eager to obtain specimens of
these new found oddities. Africans began to appear in fairly sizable
numbers in major European capitals that had had some contact with
African cities. And so in England, Spain, Portugal, Italy, Holland, and
Germany, a minority presence began to establish itself side by side with
the majority. From the inception, they began to be viewed as weird and
exotic, odd and peculiar, possessing that fascination of the horrible that
has so endeared the non-English to the English. Almost as soon as initial
contact was made, the English, indeed the "West" (and I admit to a
totalization here in including most of western Europe) began to invent
the stereotypes that went into the manufacture of a distant Other. What
is even more fascinating is that these marginalized Others began to see
themselves in just this way and to pass on the heritage of a vicious
stereotype that has been both pernicious and longlasting. Any effort to
arrest this would have been manifest in race relations today.

EARLY AFRICAN DIASPORA IN THE "NEW" WORLD

Previous African arrivants to the New World had encountered an environment relatively free from European-imposed mythologies. For instance, pre-Columbian Africans would have arrived in a place that had not yet been fallaciously named "America," where "Indians" had not yet been implanted as imaginative inhabitants from a far eastern landscape, and where cannibalistic Caribs had not yet given their name to an entire region. In other words, the first Africans who arrived before the Europeans would have entered a world virtually uncorrupted by European imaginings, partly born out of their frustrated desires to implant the East on unknown territory.

According to a fourteenth-century Arab traveler, Ibn Fadl Allah Al-'Umari, the first African arrivals came from the kingdom of Mali.[1] The reigning emperor or *mansa*, Kanku Musa, gave an account of a voyage undertaken by his predecessor to what sounds very much like the New World. The emperor related how some two hundred vessels were dispatched with food, water, and gold. Only one vessel returned, but the news of lands beyond the horizon stirred up the emperor's zeal to embark on still another adventure, from which he never returned.

The importance of such a historic rendering of this early voyage is crucial, since it helps us understand at least the curiosity of Africans who lived near the ocean and were not unnaturally curious about what they imagined lay beyond. Additionally, it lends credence to a view that is sometimes advanced that Columbus may well have learned about his secrets of navigation and the importance of ocean currents from the African sailors he encountered in his early voyages to West Africa.

In any event the presence of Africans in the New World is attested to by a thoroughly researched, but frequently ignored, scholarly study of food, art, archaeology, and language among other elements, conducted by Leo Wiener in *Africa and the Discovery of America*.[2] Indeed, were it not for this mammoth publication, the better known works by populizers such as Ivan Van Sertima could hardly have been written, as Van Sertima himself acknowledges.[3] This work established the manner in which, long before the advent of Arab or European slave trading, African customs and traditions were known to the pre-Columbian inhabitants of the New World. Africa, in other words, from quite early in the period of written European history, had already established its diaspora.

The Yoruba who arrived en masse in the New World, particularly during the nineteenth century, were new authoritative Africans from the old world. Their presence made the absence of other African values even more apparent, since their authentic voices were able to introduce a different reality of Africa. They represented the final wave of Africans from Africa, or put differently, the last group of "tribe" folk not yet contaminated by exposure to the New World and the need to adapt to its syncretic formulae.[4]

AFRICAN/OTHER DIASPORA IN EUROPE

Part of the extension of the African diaspora was in Europe itself. Scholars frequently fail to make enough of the Black presence in Spain and how this influenced the rest of Europe. For the terminologies "Moor," "Berber," and "North African Arabs" often seek to obfuscate the reality of the African presence in Europe from 711 (when they named and crossed the Straits of Gibraltar) to the beginnings of their expulsion in 1492. I have attempted to show elsewhere that Africans passed on, directly or indirectly, their important influences regarding architecture, food, music, and literature to Spain and Portugal, in particular. And along with the Arabs, they helped preserve and continue certain traditions, and even invented different novelties, to which Europe became inheritor after its long night of the so-called Dark Ages.[5]

A few examples will suffice. In England we have already noted the presence of Black people and the additional fact that no less an authority than Queen Elizabeth herself wanted them expelled.[6] Yet they remained strange, otherlike, so that Ben Jonson could devote his *Masque of Blackness* to the alluring potentiality of having the court ladies become "darkies" for a day, and even if the script dictated otherwise, that is, that they sought the king's indulgence to restore them to a former state of pristine whiteness, the practical effect was that the license of the dramatist allowed them to dally with Blackness and with being Black at the very center of White power. That this was perceived as perhaps as a little more than poetic license is seen in the muted innuendoes regarding Queen Anne of Denmark's brainwave suggesting the masque and Lady Mary Wroth (with an already checkered history of incest) being banished from court.[7] Indeed Kim F. Hall sees the very presencing of the figures of the masque as "filled with references to the new state of England as the seat of a growing empire and the significance of its identity as Britannia."[8]

Lady Mary Wroth did score some limited revenge in *The First Part of the Countess of Montgomeries Urania* (1621). The long text is really an elaborate attack on court latitude, moral depravity, and folly. The lovers in the poem, as well as in a sonnet sequence suffer because they are superficial and take nothing seriously. Perhaps Wroth had in mind the court of King James where issues of skin coloration could be laughed off in an afternoon at the masques. Not that Wroth was a stalwart liberal of her time, but I suspect she felt instead the shame of the shunned, and thus sought her revenge. As a result, she was no longer welcomed back to court.

What Wroth does is to introduce the troublesome bane of color. It is particularly intriguing that the English are so concerned about difference at a time when few "others" lived near them. Granted that the Elizabethan period had seen the beginnings of imperial order, but the "blacka-moor" remained a figure of the stage, safely constructed as such by White, male, English actors.

Two instances are worth pointing out in Wroth's work. First of all, one woman is quite carried away: "Urania's maide beheld as she beleev'd Allimarlus in the second Towre, kissing and embracing a Black-moore: which so farre inraged her, being passionately in love with him, as she must goe to revenge herselfe of that injurie." Of course the "injurie" is made all the less serious since all the events take place in a dream, much like the court ladies playing at race for their enjoyment. Wroth may well have been expressing her displeasure over the easy dalliances of court life, using the outsider to underscore the point. And she does it yet again, this time by having Pamphilia swear her undying love for her lover or else, as she says, "I rather would wish to be a Black-moore, or anything more dreadfull."[9] It is curious that, at the time that Modern English is being formed, blackness is establishing itself as part dream, part insubstantiality, but in any event something undesirable.

Others such as Shylock and Volpone suffered as well. Jews, for instance remained outsiders. They too were seen as odd, strange, and undesirable because they were considered "dark-skinned" and, as James Shapiro opines, "Jews as well as other alien groups . . . were crucial to an early-modern English culture struggling to define its own national and racial distinctiveness."[10] Race and ethnicity therefore became the markers of this new imperial Other, indeed were thus defined, expressing a presumed apartness from the hegemonic Self.

I want to place all this as the necessary and harsh backdrop against which the writers and philosophers I am going to discuss had to contend. Too often by singling out the people who wrote we give the impression that they operated against a sympathetic background, or at least one that was not pernicious. I must stress that early modern England (indeed Britain) was tiny and enclosed, shut off from its European neighbors, virtually at war with its own small borders in Scotland and across the Irish Sea (a situation the English have managed to maintain until the present). Additionally, since Rome itself had withdrawn its forces and its culture, the island was left to fend for itself, cut off from the succour and nourishing elements of its neighbors. And my third point will seem odd, that is, that once the Anglo-Saxons and Normans had made their peace, there were no other fertilizing effects that came as a by-product of conquering armies. Without invaders, the island stifled in its littleness.

As noted, to maintain the purity of her island kingdom, Elizabeth went to great extremes to rid the nation of the "negars" and "blackamoors."

When her earlier efforts at rounding them up and dispatching them had failed, she resorted to some crude chicanery—she would treat them like prisoners of war and exchange them. Peter Fryer adds that

an open warrant was sent to the lord mayor of London and all vice-admirals, mayors, and other public officers, informing them that a Lübeck merchant called Caspar van Senden, who had arranged for the release of 89 prisoners in Spain and Portugal, was asking in return "lycense to take up so much blackamoores here in this realme and to transport them into Spaine and Portugall."[11]

As I have already shown, the plan still did not work. The Blackamoors remained, and the happy dwellers who now occupy Britain's shores are fond of citing this incident as proof of an early Black presence in England. They do not usually say this sets the precedent for centuries of official disdain and outright hatred, culminating in the infamous series of Immigration Acts that once and for all brought an end to the misapprehensions of former colonials taking seriously to the notion that they were British. Stringent new laws established categories of passport holders. Needless to say, the Blacks always came off the worst. They were a little like the recent Hong Kong Chinese who, lacking finances, were forced to remain at home. Britain pulled up the drawbridge and closed the gates. Those of us who had been "lucky" enough to sneak in (Homi Bhabha, Stuart Hall, and myself) were constantly enjoined by the local citizenry to "go back to Africa."[12]

I mention all this to place in context the widely celebrated settlement in England and Europe of many much diverse personalities. Always against the background of their successes, their flirtations with aristocracy, and even with royalty lies the bitter fact that British people would just as soon not have had them in the country.

EARLY AFRO EUROPEANS IN EUROPE

Soon after this time, a number of distinguished Africans first began to make their impact in Europe. They were significant, since their lives and scholarship clearly showed how adaptable African culture became for them. An early instance, as already noticed, is Leo Africanus (c. 1485–1554), born in Granada of North African stock, who after some early travels was presented as a "gift" to Pope Leo X. He took the pope's name when he was baptized, and became Europe's sole authority on Africa for many centuries. Note again the irony of the Other as Author (ity).

Africanus put forward in his *A Geographical Historie of Africa* (1600), what was essentially a European version of the world. Indeed, he probably went further than his White contemporaries in declaring that

Africans were "a vile and base people . . . born and bred to theft, deceit, and brutish manners." Not only had Africanus read Pliny, with his account of the the brutes and monsters who lived in India and Ethiopia, but he was also familiar with the lore and monsters of medieval Europe. Almost *de rigeur*, he located them in Africa as "great numbers of people who live a brutish and savage life . . . clad in skins of beasts, and [without] specific wives."[13]

Another instance is Juan Latino (c. 1516–1594), who was brought to Spain from "Ethiopia" (probably West Africa) with his mother, when he was barely twelve.[14] Enslaved by the Duke of Sesa, he became part of an early experimental process whereby European nobles attempted to demonstrate that they could train Africans in European ways, and that in turn, these Africans would show how adaptable they could become. Indeed, Latino became so Europeanized that his proficiency in Latin earned him the name "avis rara" (rare bird), and gave him his own surname. Some records attest to his becoming a professor at the University of Granada in 1556.

Latino often utilized his poetry to side with Philip II and Don Juan of Austria as they battled the Turks. The high point of his *Austriad* is the Battle of Lepanto, where the conflict between Christian Europeans and Muslim Turks is given classical proportions as one between Greeks and Trojans. What is even of greater irony is that Latino soberly asserts that the validity of Don Juan's cause lies in the expulsion of the Moors from Spain. The Turkish leader, Bassan, has little hope for he can ill compete with the might and power of Philip's brother, Don Juan. Don Juan addresses his troops in the words of Julius Caesar, and no less a personage than Christ himself sides with the Spaniards. As Bassan wryly notes when the pope speaks to King Philip, "God is rousing you to boldness."[15] A two-line couplet sums up the pathos of Bassan's defeat: "Here it is said Bassan fell and died by the sword / And that a humble soldier left his body headless."[16] Again, the Other (Latino) has authored the Other (Bassan), creating or supplementing the creation of helplessness, docility, and defeat.

However, all is not lost. There is still a very humane glance back, almost a rebellious one especially given the time and circumstances. For instance, Africanus does admit to a certain indebtedness, arguing that despite the harshness of his words, "I stand indebted [to Africa] both for my birth and also for the best part of my education."[17] Latino, in an earlier work, *Epigrammattum Liber*, says to Philip II with a touch of jauntiness: "For if our black face, O king, displeases / Your ministers, a white face does not please the men of Ethiopia."[18]

The Noble Savage à la Jean-Jacques Rousseau had indeed proclaimed to the European world the possibility of achieving Europeanity by the most circuitous of routes. Furthermore, the belief in the Noble Savage suggested that since cultural redemption might well be achieved on its own, therefore all the more easily it would be done with the aid of a well-meaning intervener. This was the part that the eighteenth-century benefactors played; earlier on, with Africanus and Latino, what is more readily apparent is the imposition of Christian values and the substitution of a Western viewpoint. The end result was the same; the assumption on the part of Europeans of the African condition as tabula rasa meant that instead of a nonracialized prince of the Enlightenment, God became the Europeanized ideal and substitute.

First, in all cases African names were changed, so that the new names either addressed a permanent link with the benefactor, or some whimsical, even surprising, connection with the metropolitan language. Second, since these were all fairly young men, it was not difficult to instill very quickly in them one view of the world, a Eurocentric one, and that way of observation confirmed in these men what their benefactors most craved—a desire to see them as bearers of a cultural viewpoint that was correct and wholesome, proclaiming the Grand Narrative.

Both Africanus and Latino, as noted, lay outside the strict reference of Rousseau's Noble Savage. But in many respects, they help us understand that if the world of *Émile* (1762) had not been described by Rousseau, it would have had to have had to be invented as a necessary conjunction of the Enlightenment. Émile is both the embodiment and representation of Rousseau's man in a state-of-nature, uncorrupted by the corrosive effects of civilization. Thus, the young child Émile is intentionally kept away from "civilization," permitted to mature only in the most natural of surroundings, thereby developing an ethical perspective more closely akin to Deism than the advocations of institutionalized Christianity. But although at first sight it might appear that Amo, Capitein, Williams, and Barber, were subjected to the reverse of what Rousseau intended, they still show that even before Rousseau the intellectual climate was rife for experimentation. Therefore, they became the earlier prototypes of Émile, indeed an Émile who may well have been brought to Europe in order to be a teacher. First, he learns the language of the audience; then his task must be to reveal something of the world from which he came.

The problem was that, even in a pre-Rousseau climate, it is not certain that even a few intensely did or could believe in the possibilities of their own cultural redemption. Therefore, what might well have started out as an experiment in learning from the Other soon became one in which the Other was reduced to an Émile, adrift in the metropolis of his day. As such, cut off from his own familiar environment in Africa or the Afro New World, he developed a natural propensity to simply imitate what was before him and, like Africanus, attacked very harshly what was scarcely remembered and certainly not known.

ENLIGHTENED BLACKS?

Since, by their own definition, Europeans of the eighteenth century were "enlightened," obviously the Other dwelt in darkness, waiting to be recovered, resuscitated and made whole by the Word and Deed of the One. European royalty played a role by adopting young Blacks into their households, and caring for them much like favorite pets. Anton Wilhelm Amo (1700–1743) of Axim, Ghana, was enslaved at the age of four, brought to Amsterdam, and later "presented" (actually given as a present to) Duke Anton Ulrich von Braunschweig-Wolfenbüttell, who passed him on to his son, Wilhelm—hence the two names he received. He was educated at the University of Halle and, according to some accounts, received a doctorate from Wittenberg in 1739, afterwards returning to Halle as a professor.

Around the same time, Jacobus Eliza Johannes Capitein (1717–1747) had the distinction of being enslaved and taken back in his master's company to Elmina Castle, a slave fortress in Ghana. After returning to Holland with a new master, he attended the University of Leyden, and was later sent back to Ghana as a missionary, where his enthusiasm proved be too much for his benefactors.[19]

Furthermore, one should note Francis Williams (1700–1770). Born the son of freed slaves in Jamaica, he was ardently taken up by the Duke of Montagu as potential evidence that an English boarding school and the University of Cambridge could whitewash him. According to Edward Long, a contemporary critic not unduly fond of Francis Williams, Williams set up a school on his return to Jamaica, where he often described himself as a "white man acting under a black skin."[20] Alongside him, should be mentioned Dr. Johnson's "servant," Francis Barber, who arrived in England in 1750, and was personally taught Latin by Dr. Johnson himself, and sent to school in England.[21]

A major point about these writers is that they were all expected to make a complete language and cultural transformation in order to prove to their various noble benefactors that they were amenable to European culture. From the fifteenth to the eighteenth century when these writers functioned, the assumption remained that post-Moorish Europe was the center of the world and Latin the learned tongue of all educated people. As noted, a great deal of Europe was involved in the experimentation towards racial "betterment," from the Vatican to Spain, Germany, Britain, and Holland. Not unnaturally, those with a greater stake in present and future colonial enterprise most definitely wanted to make sure that cultural evolution had its definite possibilities. Therefore, it is very easy to see these early Africans in Europe as people involved in a cultural grafting. In this way they became the earliest specimens of the colonial enterprise as they willingly jettisoned their own belief system for that of a European worldview they saw as more pragmatic.

EUROCENTRIC IMPULSES

Amo, according to the most recent accounts, was one individual who refused to be coopted. One of his early poems shows he recognized in a Jewish friend some of the alienation that had plagued him and that he himself must have acutely felt.[22] Written in standard Alexandrines, the poem extols the friend because "in the order of scholars / You are accepted as a star."[23] If it is a position for which Amo also wished, his espousal of African rights hardly endeared him to his fellow academicians. He seemed to have left the University of Halle rather abruptly, soon after his now lost first dissertation was published. By 1751 he had returned to Ghana, where he worked as a goldsmith until he died.

Capitein and Francis Williams, on the other hand, allowed themselves to be easily influenced by their new European world. Capitein, as pastor at Elmina in Ghana, translated the Ten Commandments into Fanti with an opening flourish that substituted the company for the deity: "I am Jan Company that brought thee out of the land of bondage."[24] And Williams, much in the manner of Latino, utilized successive governors to Jamaica as the inspiration for his Latin odes, even as he lauded them for ransacking the Caribbean: "Guadeloupe will recognize you as conqueror / And will look down on the camp of her leaders, justly destroyed." Here he extols a long forgotten scion of Britain in the manner of any good and loyal colonial subject.[25]

On the whole, however, these were not individuals who were caught up in any kind of intercultural misalliance. They obviously saw themselves as being part of the European metropolitan centers that had nurtured them, and certainly in this way we may speak of their contributions to Latin as being within the realm of what Janheinz Jahn referred to as "Black guinea-pigs in the Age of Enlightenment."[26] But their work also helped show that these Afro Europeans whose presence had foreshadowed large-scale African settlement in the New World, anticipated the malleability of a transported culture. Unlike the fictitious Émile, these very real people demonstrated that their nature altered when the sustaining element of nurture was removed. Their own situation helps explain why the presence of Africa in the New World must be scrupulously sought after in order to be detected, identified, and recognized, for it is never obviously apparent beneath the thick layers of disguise that aided in its survival.

RE-INVENTING BRITAIN

At a British Council conference on March 21, 1997, tantalizingly entitled "Re-inventing Britain," Stuart Hall and Homi Bhabha put forward some interesting views on the issue of recent change in the makeup of the British cultural fabric. They both recognized a much-needed change that had come about with what has come to be called "diversity." But Stuart Hall noted the reflexive reaction against the very ethnicity the conferees had much touted. He contended:

There is more closure of an ethnic, religious, national, quasi-national or regional kind going on around the world, as a kind of defensive movement against openness and diversity, than we would ever have ever imagined. So there is an obverse side to the more celebratory themes we have been rehearsing.[27]

And Bhabha, still as usual committed to complicating the matter, put forward his standard middle-of-the-road neither/nor theme to advocate what later he would term a "third space" where neither majority not minority culture, neither White nor Black, could lay claim to superiority.[28] Bhabha asserted at the conference:

I propose an alternative perspective that claims that culture is less about expressing a pre-given identity (whether the source is national culture or "ethnic" culture) and more about the activity of negotiating, regulating and authorizing competing, often conflicting demands for collective self-representation. So the work of culture does not exist at the level at which a community expresses a demand, but at the level at which that demand becomes articulated with other demands in order to be able to claim a value and become meaningful as a form of cultural judgement.[29]

What happened by the twentieth century is that the chief spokespersons for minority people in Britain relate (for various reasons—some to do with self-disparagement) a discomfiture about being considered as minorities. Stuart Hall, Jamaican-born, expresses his dis-ease with being called "immigrant," and Bhabha, Muslim Indian-born, is forever seeking the validation of "hybridity," a term about which Robert J. C. Young has warned us against in *Colonial Desire* (1995). As Young points out, Edward Long, Robert Knox, Count Gobineau, T. H. Huxley, and other stalwarts all saw hybridity in very racist terms, implying that the offspring of the "different races were different species."[30] Elsewhere, Young places "hybridization," along with "mimicry" and "paranoia" as "static concepts" that "could equally well apply to Bhabha himself."[31] These words are harsh but true. I always want to say to Hall and Bhabha "thou doth protest too much." I always wonder if theirs is a slightly more sophisticated argument advocating the "reality" of a common hoped-for "whiteness," shared by all, if only the English would recognize it.

NOTES

1. Ibn Fadl Allah Al-'Umari, *Masalik Al-absar fi Mamalik al-amsar* (Cairo, 1342) in J. Devisse and S. Labib, "Africa in Inter-Continental Relations," in *Africa from the Twelfth to the Sixteenth Century* [1984] ed. D. T. Niane in *General History of Africa*. 8 vols (Paris: UNESCO, 1980–1993), 4:635–72.

2. Leo Wiener, *Africa and the Discovery of America*, 3 vols. (Philadelphia: Innes and Sons, 1920, 1923).

3. Ivan Van Sertima, *They Came before Columbus* (New York: Random, 1976).

4. For the New World Yoruba, see, *inter alia*, William R. Bascom, *Shango in the New World* (Austin: U of Texas African and Afro-American Research Institute, 1972), and Melville J. Herskovits, *Myth of the Negro Past* [1941] (Boston: Beacon, 1990), two early standard works that have stood the test of time. For more recent studies, see Joseph E. Holloway, ed., *Africanisms in American Culture* (Bloomington, IN: Indiana UP, 1991), and Margarita Fernández Olmos and Lizabeth Paravisni-Gebert, eds., *Sacred Possessions: Vodou, Santeria, Obeah and the Caribbean* (New Brunswick, NJ: Rutgers UP, 1997). Also see pioneer studies in Spanish by Fernando Ortiz, *Los Negros Brujos* [1906] (Miami: Ediciones Universal, 1963), and Lydia Cabrera, *El Monte* [1954] (Miami: Ediciones Universal, 1975), and, in French, Jean Price-Mars, *So Spoke the Uncle* [1928], trans. Magdaline W. Shannon (Washington, D.C.: Three Continents, 1983).

5. Consult O. R. Dathorne, *Imagining the World: Mythical Belief versus Reality in Global Encounters* (Westport, CT, and London: Bergin & Garvey, 1994), 160–69.

6. Refer to comments by Peter Fryer, *Staying Power: The History of Black People in Britain* (London: Pluto, 1984), 10–12, and Winthrop D. Jordan, *White over Black: American Attitudes Toward the Negro , 1550–1812* (Chapel Hill: U of North Carolina P, 1968), 3 and 8.

7. Lady Mary Wroth is herself a fascinating figure in that she proclaimed a stubborn feminist independence in both her writing and her actions.

8. Kim F. Hall, *Things of Darkness: Economies of Race and Gender in Early Modern England* (Ithaca, NY: Cornell UP, 1995), 133. I treat Elizabethan and Tudor racial issues in some detail later in this text. Also see Patricia Parker, "Fantasies of 'Race' and 'Gender': Africa, *Othello*, and Bringing to the Light," in *Women, "Race" and Writing in the Early Modern Period* ed. Margo Hendricks and Patricia Parker. London: Routledge, 1994, 84–100; and Alden T. Vaughan and Virginia Mason Vaughan, "Before *Othello*: Elizabethan Representations of Sub-Saharan Africans." *The William and Mary Quarterly* 54.1 (Jan. 1997): 19–44. The pioneering work was done by Eldred D. Jones, *Othello's Countrymen: The African in English Renaissance Drama.* (Oxford: Oxford UP, 1965).

9. Lady Mary Wroth, *The First Part of the Countess of Montgomery's Urania* [1621], ed. Josephine A. Roberts (Binghamton, NY: Center for the Medieval and Early Renaissance Studies, SUNY at Binghamton, 1995), 49 and 465. Also see *The Second Part of the Countess of Montgomery's Urania* ed. Josephine Roberts, Suzanne Gossett, and Janet Mueller (Tempe, AZ: Arizona Center for Medieval and Renaissance Studies, 2000).

10. James Saphiro, "A Jew at the Globe," *The Chronicle of Higher Education* (June 26, 1998): B 4.

11. Fryer, *Stayong Power*, 11.

12. Some recent books published in Britain are relevant regarding the presence of Blacks in the United Kingdom, particularly: Jeffrey Green, *Black*

Edwardians: Black People in Britain, 1901–1914 (London: Frank Cass, 1998); David Killingray, ed., *Africans in Britain* (Ilford, U.K: Frank Cass, 1994); and Norma Myers, *Reconstructing the Black Past: Blacks in Britain 1780–1830* (London: Frank Cass, 1930). The books show how Blacks went to Britain as students, visitors, workers, seamen, and during the War years (1914–1918 and 1939–1945), as volunteers. These books also stress that there was a transatlantic passage from the United States, especially after the felonious assumption that the Lord Mansfield Judgment of 1772 had ended slavery in Britain. Note this view to the contrary in Folarin Shyllon, *Black People in Britain, 1555–1833* (London: Oxford UP for Institute of Race Relations, 1977).

13. See Leo Africanus, *A Geographical Historie of Africa* [1600], ed. John Pory (New York: De Capo, 1969), 42 and 284.

14. Latino has still not received any in-depth study. However, see Valaurez Burwell Spratlin, *Juan Latino: Slave and Humanist* (New York: Spinner, 1938), and the more recent Henry Louis Gates Jr. and Maria Wolff, "An Overview of the Sources on the Life and Work of Juan Latino, the 'Ethiopian Humanist,' " in *Research in African Literatures* (Winter 1998) 29.4: 14–51. The Gates and Wolff account devotes too much time to the gossip of Latino's contemporaries, and not enough to an analysis of his work. Spratlin gives full bibliographical details on pp. 9–17. According to him, Latino came to Spain from Guinea at twelve and was a slave with his mother at Baena, the family seat of the Duke of Sesa. He grew up with the duke's grandson and first became known as Juan de Sesa. He attended school with the duke's grandson, and at the Cathedral School in Granada first translated Horace into Castilian and later wrote original verse in Latin. Then he began to study Greek. He afterwards went to the University of Granada where he studied poetry, music, and some medicine, receiving his first degree in 1546.

Around 1549 he married Doña Ana Carlobal, the daughter of a nobleman and a former pupil of his. They had two sons and two daughters and, though Latino still nominally remained a slave, he became a professor of Classics at the University of Granada in 1556. In 1565 he delivered an oration in Latin to open the university year. He died in 1594, or according to other sources in 1597.

In his later years he became blind, and when he died he was buried in the churchyard of Santa Ana. Also see Henri Grégoire, *On the Cultural Achievements of Negroes* [1808], trans. Thomas Cassirer and Jean-François Brière (Amherst, MA: U of Massachusetts P, 1996), 75–112.

15. This is from my partial translation of *Elegy to Pius V*. The "enemy" in the poem are Christians and Turks. See my translation in "The Pope Speaks to King Philip," in O. R. Dathorne, ed., *African Poetry* (London: Macmillan, 1969), 38.

16. This poem celebrates the famous Battle of Lepanto in October 1571, when the Spaniards fought the Turks. For Latino, Don Juan is a brave leader and Bassan, a mere coward. See Dathorne, *African Poetry*, 26.

17. Africanus, *Historie*, 42.

18. I translated this in O. R. Dathorne, *The Black Mind: A History of African Literature* (Minneapolis: U of Minnesota, 1974), 69. See also my brief review of Latino on pp. 68–73.

19. Capitein studied under Johannes Phillipus Manger, who died in 1741. Capitein wrote an eighty-line eulogy for Manger, a man he greatly admired. See Kwesi Kwaa Prah, *Jacobus Eliza Johannes Capitein, 1717–1747* (Trenton, NJ: Africa World, 1992), 57.

20. Edward Long, *A History of Jamaica* (London: printed for T. Lowndes, 1774), 478.

21. Some older texts are also worth looking at: Wylie Sypher, *Guinea's Captive Kings: British Anti-Slavery Literature of the Eighteenth Century* (Chapel Hill: U of North Carolina P, 1942); Kenneth Little, *Negroes in Britain: A Study of Racial Relations In English Society* (London: Kegan Paul, 1947), Sypher adds that by 1770 there were fourteen thousand Blacks in England; N. V. MacCullough, *The Negro in English Literature* (Ilfracombe: Stockwell, 1962).

22. For background on Amo, see Norbert Lochner, "Anton Wilhelm Amo: A Ghana Scholar in Eighteenth-Century Germany," in *Transactions of the Historical Society of Ghana* 3.3 (1959): 169–79; Burchard Brentjes, "Anton Wilhelm Amo, First African Philosopher in European Universities," in *Current Anthropology* 16.3 (Sept. 1995): 443–44; and Marilyn Sephocle, "Anton Wilhelm Amo," *Journal of Black Studies* 23.2 (Dec. 1992): 182–87. Most recently, William E. Abraham has published a piece that deserves to be better known: "The Life and Times of Anton Wilhelm Amo, the First African (Black) Philosopher in Europe," in *African Intellectual Heritage: A Book of Sources,* ed. Molefi Kete Asante and Abu S. Abarry (Philadelphia: Temple UP, 1996), 424–40.

23. See Grégoire's translation of the beginning of the ode, Grégoire *Achievements*, 95–96.

24. See F. L. Bartels, *The Roots of Ghana Methodism* (London: Cambridge UP, 1965), 3 and 72.

25. My translation. See Dathorne, *The Black Mind*, 74. I avoided Edward Long's English version, since his purpose was to make Williams look as foolish as possible.

26. Janheinz Jahn, *A History of Neo-African Literature: Writing in Two Continents* (London: Faber and Faber, 1966), 24.

27. See Stuart Hall at "Re-inventing Britain" conference, <http://www.britcoun./www.britcoun.org/studies/stdsprog.htm>. Accessed October 9, 1998. This conference was held by the British Council.

28. Homi Bhabha, *The Location of Culture* (London and New York: Routledge, 1994), 36–39, 217–18.

29. Homi Bhabha at "Re-inventing Britain" conference, <http:// www.britcoun. org/studies/stdsprog.htm>. Accessed October 9, 1998.

30. Robert J. C. Young, *Colonial Desire: Hybridity in Theory, Culture and Race* (London and New York: Routledge, 1995), 6–19.

31. Robert J. C. Young, *White Mythologies: Writing History and the West* (London and New York: Routledge, 1990), 146.

Chapter 8

Inventing Diaspora: African Cultural Extensions

Despite strong mainstream interest in blues, rock 'n' roll, rap and a steady "blackening" and "browning" of its population base, the United States still largely conceives of itself as a white country. (Robin D. Moore, *Nationalizing Blackness: Afrocubanismo and Artistic Revolution in Havana, 1920–1940* [1997], 218)

In the Asian countries which are politically stable, the translation of "America" structures everyday realities. Rock and roll, hamburgers, shopping malls, television programs, computer games and tourism constitute the materiality of "culture" which is not so much about past grandeur or political resistance as it is about accommodation, collaboration, and complicity. (Rey Chow, *Writing Diaspora: Tactics of Intervention in Contemporary Cultural Studies* [1993], 141)

"Diaspora" in the New World involves a number of ethnicities; initially used for and by Jews, the term has been extended to English, Italian, Greek, Irish and other "European" groups that make up the world populace outside indigenous ethnic regions. But somewhere within the mixture that converts all the New World into a Creole society is a persistent Black strain that surfaces every now and then as religion, as music, as song, as dance, as skin coloration. So that when "America" is interpreted abroad, even revisualized by members of the initial immigrant groups from their home base, "Black" and "White" become conflated as the culture and mores, and a concept of diasporic Africa is pushed (particularly by the visual media) towards a hegemonic "White" U.S. superstructure.

The concept of Africa exists as both imagined and factual. In order to understand the manner in which Africa functions as idea and reality, on the continent itself and in the diaspora, we must begin by looking at conflicting elements.[1] A major factor here is that African culture, or the cultures of the African world, do not have any one specific vehicle of linguistic expression. Immediately, this places any consideration of Africa into a scenario that is completely different from that of China. Additionally, the presence of a multiplicity of indigenous languages, as well as the importation of European languages (particularly English, Dutch, French, Portuguese, and Spanish), are added to the cultural mix.

If we begin by asserting that the otherness of the African world initially stems from an absence of any one common language, we must also add that the result brings about a curious dilemma. How can one justify speaking of a literature that has no language? Or, put differently, how can one assert that one literature exists when there are many languages, some certainly not indigenous to Africa, and others often inimical to African aspirations—especially given the colonial past. As stated in *The Empire Writes Back*, "the concept of authenticity itself [in language] was endorsed by a centre to which they [the writers] did not belong and yet was continually contradicted by the everyday experience of marginality."[2] This is compounded by the reality of languages that have been molded from African and European, or even African and Arab experience.

Such languages vary from the Creoles of Louisiana, and the Gullah of the Carolinas, to the Krio of Freetown, Sierra Leone.[3] Additionally, when the language shift has not been so enormous as to make mutual intelligibility impossible, there arises "pidgins," such as are found in various parts of the Caribbean, Central America, and West Africa.[4] One should add that both Creoles and pidgins may use one or more of the African and European languages as a base.

If the writers utilize these types of communication, provided that they are not "standard" and do not conform to easily recognizable forms, they may find themselves concerned with the issue of who is the audience. This would not clearly have been a problem for the oral artists since they, more often than not, were concerned with specific functions arising out of the needs of the local community. As such, oral artists of necessity had to be spokespersons dealing with issues that affected their immediate society: birth, initiation, marriage, and death. Hence, even when the oral occasions tended to be more celebratory, such as during the renditions of praise songs for chiefs and kings, the artist was still required to be both a spokesperson for the group and an intermediary with the audience.

Ruth Finnegan stresses the important role that the audience plays as language is realized in the process of oral narration:

A further essential factor is the audience, which, as is not the case with written forms, is often directly involved in the actualization and creation of a piece of oral literature. According to convention, genre, and personality, the artist may be more or less receptive to his listeners' reactions—but, with few exceptions, an audience of some kind is normally an essential part of the whole literary situation. There is no escape for the oral artist from a face-to-face confrontation with his audience, and this is something which he can exploit as well as be influenced by. Sometimes he chooses to involve his listeners directly, as in story-telling situations where it is common for the narrator to open with a formula which explicitly arouses his audience's attention; he also often expects them to participate actively in the narration and, in particular, to join in the choruses of songs which he introduces into the narrative. The audience can be exploited in similar ways in the performance of poetry, particularly in sung lyrics where it is common practice for the poet to act as leader, singing and improvising the verse line, while the audience performs as a chorus keeping up the burden of the song, sometimes to the accompaniment of dancing or instrumental music. In such cases the close connection between artist and audience can almost turn into an identity, the chorus directly participating in at least certain parts of the performance.[5]

This was in the rural, precolonial setting of African life. Once dispersal occurred, through which large numbers of Africans were shifted to Europe and the New World, the functionality of the oral message did not change, although its signification was altered.

AFRICAN CULTURAL RETENTIONS

Houston Baker did make the point several years ago that with regard to written English literature by Africans, a Sotho writer, for instance, might utilize "literary strategies . . . to preserve and communicate culturally-specific meanings." And, of course, in much the same way as the language format alters to accommodate New World reality, new oral "strategies" are utilized to convey meanings that were originally "specific" to the indigenous language.[6]

For instance, the relatively innocent African narrative accounts of how Anansy, the trickster spider, outwits his enemies and undergoes change. Within a very functional reality, Anansy by any other name now came to stand for not just the weak, not merely the cunning but, in this new context, Anansy now represented the slave. Deprived of power, the slave was able to triumph through wit and words. Over and over again, the exploits of Highjohn de Conquer (Highjohn the Conqueror) as he outwits "ole Massa" synthesize the basic characteristics of the African spider, Anansy, and the New World depiction of a powerless victim caught up in the trammels of historical consequences outside his control.[7]

This type of cultural transference is only one aspect of what emerged as Africa expanded towards Europe and the New World. At the core of our understanding, there exists a definite indicator, namely that with the change of venue from Old World to New World, from African village to New World plantation, from "tribal" affinity to ethnic life, and what is most apparent is not the degree of alteration—the function—but rather the manner in which the adaptation takes place—the signification. Obviously, therefore, the very nature of a repressive society would bring about a need for a new vision of the world; but, in addition, the newly constituted African person now interacted with an equally newly constituted European, each borrowing from the other. This may be seen not only in language and oral literature, as already observed, but also in music, dance, religion, and other activities.[8]

Religion is perhaps the most obvious way in which African spiritual beliefs become New World physical representations. Cuban santería, Haitian vodún and Brazilian candomblé have all taken facets of African religion, particularly from Yoruba faith.[9] But this is only part of what occurs in the genesis of these religions in the New World. First, the Yoruba gods are actively associated with Roman Catholic saints—so that, even though they never become the saints, they are named for the saints, actively made to look like the saints, and prayed to on the saints' days. Next, the types of ritual—drumming, dancing, and possession—that accompany worship have more to do with the desire to satisfy the needs of clients, rather than the demands of some aloof god. Indeed, the music and dance have the desired effect (only in the New World) of calling down the god, of actively summoning him or her to participate at the ritual. As Joseph M. Murphy remarked in *Working the Spirit*, "the complexities of rhythms in each community's ceremonies represent a complexity of distinctions that each makes in recognizing spiritual presence."[10] In Africa, the god is seen as always present and need not be summoned. For instance, E. Bolaji Idowu demonstrates that through "liturgies" and "attributive names," the Yoruba achieve "communication with their objects of worship."[11]

Third, again within the New World context, a different set of intermediaries has arisen. The santero of Cuban santería, the houngan of Haitian vodún and the *pae/mae de santo* of Brazilian candomblé do not act in the same capacity as the African priest. They are not representative of the godhead, nor do they have hereditary functions. Instead, they are trained appointees, who after a period of apprenticeship, begin to assume the roles of their trainers. What similarity does occur between these New World priests and their African counterparts exists in the nature of their relationship with the gods: both have a secret contract with the deity, and both are able to interpret the gods' commands, as a result of this familiarity. But here the resemblance ends, since the New World priest intermediates between the client and the god in a non-African language, and is often forced to translate the mundane wishes of his client into larger terms. This is especially evident where the New World *babalawo* or interpreter of the Ifa oracle is concerned.[12]

In the Yoruba context, the Ifa oracle strictly refers to the manner in which human behavior may be historically related and the future predicted as a result of the interpretation of some 256 *odu* verses. The *babalawo* will correctly interpret the *odu* based on, for instance, the casting of cowrie shells. All of this is partly a feat of memory learned by the *babalawo* over a period of years. In Africa the client gives the *babalawo* some token of appreciation, and the *babalawo* in turn intones the verses and riddles; he may suggest a possible interpretation relevant for the person's life. In the New World, the case is slightly different in that the *babalawo* is often paid and consulted much as one would a professional advisor. His interpretation of the *odu* is based on what the client actually tells him, whereas in Africa the *babalawo* utilizes the *odu* as a pointer for the general references it may indicate about a client's life and future.[13]

Thus, we note that at least at these three levels, where language, oral literature, and religion are concerned, the idea of Africa is refashioned in the New World context. This allows us to embark on a consideration of what truly constitutes African reality as opposed to African myth, and the extent to which there is an overlapping of these, both on the African continent itself and in the diaspora. Once we are willing to admit to this possibility, what becomes most evident is that Africa as shadow and substance, as the ideal and the real, takes on a significance that goes beyond the issue of heritage and bequeathal. Certainly we have to note that in the larger social context this would help us understand something of the debate regarding Africa. In the New World, such a discourse has raged for the last two and a half centuries; few could be quite sure of what is meant by "Africa," and fewer still have ventured to attempt to interpret its reality. As motif and theme, therefore, Africa has become a conjuring board that assumes protean dimensions during various periods of diasporan existence.

Not all of this is a smooth transition, in that very often the intentional will to link Africa with the New World may be "conscripted" by decrees, governmental ones, that either support or attack the attempted linkage. In *Shango de Ima*, Pepe Carril decries those official institutions which refuse to see "racial blackness as a value beyond the limits of folklore."[14] On the other hand, when Carlos Moore uses the United States pulpit to denounce Cuba for "maintaining an Afrophobic stance domestically,"[15] this seems more than a little absurd, since Moore himself had been employed in Cuba for several years and, indeed, seemed quite content. Of course both the cold hand of censure and the warm clasp of friendship are equally detrimental if a measure of cultural veracity has to be maintained.

In order to fully comprehend the manner in which Africa functions as filter, it would be useful to examine oral literature. Interestingly enough, on both sides of the Atlantic, African oral literature shares common qualities: it is functional, often group related, and tends to be accompanied by music and dance. Here the resemblances virtually end, since with the population shift from the old world of Africa to the small and New World of the Americas, interesting phenomena take place. For, since the Christianizing process was an integral part of Westernization, this often entailed the loss of the African name, the substitution of a new Western name (often meaningless), and more importantly, a reinvention of orality, often for purposes of entertainment.[16]

DIASPORAN DISCOURSES

Within the New World context this will signify a new kind of application, whereby certain categories will no longer be utilized, since they are irrelevant to the new environment. Second, an invention will take place whereby ancient ideas of "tribe" give way to relatively new latter day concepts of race. In this process, oral literature substitutes not only racial figures for former tribal markers, but posits new altercations, whereby clever "tribal" tricksters like Anansy/Hare/Fox give way to angry racial spokespersons like Highjohn/Staggerlee/Shine. The New World heroic recreation is representative of a different kind of discourse that goes beyond mere cleverness, adroitness, or skill used to outwit power; here, in the New World context, the new representative figures become indicative of the history and cultural yearnings of the new society. A case in point is Shine on the Titanic, first confined to a segregated place below the captain in the hold of the ship, then spatially elevated to an integrated position on par with the captain, as he reasons about their common predicament in the face of imminent disaster. Third, is the act of voluntary separatism both assertive and individualistic (i.e., one completely outside the terrain of approved African thought), as he leaps overboard.[17]

Shine's actions demonstrate the reformation of the hero within the New World context and the need to create a new legend about him. For in Africa the legendary hero had to be basically monoethnic, functioning within a terrain and geography understood by the indigenous people. With the population movement outwards, there was an obvious need for change. The new legendary hero is, therefore, no longer confined to a specific place within the terrain of "tribal" life, but instead can now become the one who enacts a cycle in terms of a race. One is not more significant than the other; indeed, were it not for the African prototype, there would be no model for the African New World hero to duplicate. Similarly, if the New World hero did not encounter radically different challenges he would have been a mere reproduction of a static mold. Indeed, even on the continent of Africa itself, change is inevitable. As Steven Feserman notes, "Each of the many African narratives carries the marks of its own history, including the history of relations with Europe."[18]

Within the orbit of the New World, change is almost mandatory because of both new conditions and a different set of stimuli. Hence, the old organization of functional lore collapses or, put differently, is reassembled into a new arrangement that is more functionally relevant. The spoken and sung arts only transfer themselves once they seem meaningful within the new hierarchical patterns of slave master and enslaved. There was no need, for instance, for praise songs to kings when royalty was nonexistent. True, Obatala for instance, remains as the creator god in the pantheon of santería, but he is no longer the deity associated with the god who is the creator of hunchbacks (he was said to "ride on the hunchbacks"),[19] or the one who is able to guarantee a large progeny to soliciting women. In the New World, both in santería and candomblé, Obatala is acknowledged as the godhead but becomes almost a sect on par with the worshipers of Shango, Ogun, and others. All Yoruba gods are syncretized with New World Christian equivalents.[20] Obatala is often represented as Saint Peter and often portrayed with keys. The visual external, therefore, always could pass the approval of censoring Whites. But the nonapparent internal, the true and genuine representation of the African godhead, coexisted and remained very much a secret force through the generations.

Why European Catholic names were substituted for African ones is often a subject of heated debate. Some initiates contend that the so-called syncretic merging was never really a fact that, indeed, all worshipers knew that the African gods were very much present, alone in what was merely an elaborate deception. Others assert that since synthesis was done for preservation and perpetuation, the twin aspects retained the most important and significant forms of worship. However, this need not detain us unduly; it is very much an insiders' debate among New World worshipers.

What is much more significant is to note just how the blend manifested itself. George Eaton Simpson contends that the acculturative process

operates by means of three analytically distinctive but interrelated processes: retention, syncretization, and reinterpretation. Through these processes, a sizable number of African cultural elements have been incorporated into the belief systems and rituals of religious cults of the Caribbean and South America. These traits include the names and characteristics of African deities, "soul" concepts, ritual objects, drum rhythms, song styles, dance steps, spirit possession, the ritual use of herbs, stones, and water, seclusion and "mourning," animal sacrifices, belief in the immediacy of intervention of supernatural beings in human affairs, utilization of spirits of the dead, and ritual words. These traits have been blended with Christian elements—including the names of Catholic saints, Catholic and Protestant theological concepts, hymns, prayers, Bible verses, the cross and crucifixes, and with spiritualist doctrine—in diverse ways which are set forth in this and subsequent chapters. In addition to the intrinsic interest which these rich materials have, they show, in the case of the Neo-African cults, that Cuban sante-

ria, Haitian vodun, Brazilian candomblés and shango, and Trinidadian-
Grenadian shango developed along the same general lines in isolation from one
another.[21]

Thus the need for survivability established a common denotation on the
part of all the various religions. This neither made them similar nor
different, but it did indicate that the African presence was operating in a
very real sense, in that it was accommodating itself to change.

At another level, since African languages only survived in
fragmentary fashion, most of the language-dependent forms of New
World African orality became extinct.[22] African proverbs and riddles
which depend on the tone and structure of indigenous African
languages, could have little place in a society where the language was
lost and new languages were being created. Instead, with the
restructuring process there came about as a direct result of the
reformation of language, new proverbs, and new riddles. But these were
based on different considerations and newer concepts of the
environment and the cultural landscape. Now language could be applied
in different ways, even as it broke away from metropolitan European
languages, to articulate issues and claim territories that were relevant to
African New World experience, which as Henry Louis Gates Jr. has
shown often involved the Black speaker's "capacity to create . . . and to
derive from these rituals a complex attitude towards attempts at
domination."[23] The format of the African original was kept, but instead
of tonality (which has little place in English), rhyme would be utilized.
We note this in occasions as disparate as the so-called "dozens,"
sermons, and even political speeches.

NEW WORDS/NEW EXPERIENCE

Most of the oral transition to the New World would obviously take
the form of new words about new experiences. What is truly significant
is that the creative process very often occurs in place but often out of
time; the process, as stated before, is a continuation of its African
original, but it takes place outside the African continent and at a time
that is far removed from its own raison d'être. Therefore, the
preservation of the format often results in new types of arrangements
such as the songs and dances of John Canoe (Junkanoo) parades, Mother
Sally festivals at Christmas, and the very commercialized carnival
ceremonies throughout the New World.[24] Note how these latter
occasions bring together standard Roman Catholic holiday celebration
with both slave holiday pastime activity and African ritualized
ceremony. On these occasions, clearly African masquerades become the
obvious cultural extension into the New World; they are not even as

disguised as was found with santería, because these were occasions that were acceptable to the censoring authorities.

These are ways in which Africa and the African influence have clearly manifested themselves in the diaspora, and thus it becomes a little difficult to assert with any degree of certainty what may be termed "genuine" or "invented." It would be easy to delegate the "Afro," for instance, to the realm of mythical invention; equally, few would argue with Maulana Karenga's personal invention of Kwanzaa—a little Jewish, a little Christian, and all expressed in Swahili idiom.[25] But the problems of true and false become compounded when we realize that the shift of cultural belongingness between Africa and the New World is not one-sided. Often, when the "Afro" and Kwanza resurface, we find that they are present also in Africa; in other words, Black America invents images of Africa, then exports them to the continent, where very often they become validated.

Because of this one treads warily in categorizing Africanisms in some crude manner. What seems of more paramount importance is the realization that with the advance of Africa into the New World, a conquest takes place, whereby all people are affected by this new presence. In Brazil, every Saturday *feijoada* is solemnly eaten as "slave food" by all members of the population. In the United States, "soul food" (actually unhealthy food fed to southern slaves) is often seen as a manifestation of Black cultural pride. Yet in both these instances, the degree of belief invested the various activities goes a long way toward establishing an "authenticity" that is distinct and apart from any objective analysis.

Therefore, at the levels of language, religion, and oral literature one may perceive how Africa became an essential way of understanding the New World. In "What the Twilight Says," Derek Walcott asserts that English is a Caribbean language.[26] To this one may add French and Spanish, and in the New World environment, Dutch and Portuguese, although the contention is now being made for Creole languages. The European languages have become features of New World expression, not because of the literatures, or because they have expressed New World realities, although, to some extent, both of these are true. They are basically localized because their speakers and writers had to find ways of communicating among themselves and also to the metropolitan centers. This resulted in a language contract whereby bidialectalism became the sine qua non of everyone who sought to avoid the misinterpretation of signs, and the failure at dialogue that Stephen Greenblatt has noted as the rupture of early European/Native American contact. He alludes to Columbus's words, for instance, as "empty place-holders for the unknown and the unimaginable," since they are vacant, stripped of meaning for the other, and possessing "the virtue of at once inviting and precluding contradiction both in the present and the future."[27]

Consequently, although the languages of Africa spill over into the rituals of religious ceremonies, the various Afrocentric religions are only relevant when they address the immediate concerns of people within the immediate area, and when this can be expressed in a mutually intelligible language. And nearly always this tends to be done in a metropolitan-created language of Europe that has been localized and, in some instances, bolstered by being given the Yoruba sounds of, say, *odu*, or the Benin sounds of vodún. Thus, in all cases the base language that serves as transmitter of the message is European, even though the content of the message may be African, or African derived.[28]

In the broad terminology of oral literature, we therefore include both the way through which the literature works, that is its language, and at least one manifestation of how it operates, that is, religion. In coming together under this general rubric of oral literature, what is most apparent is that the vestiges of Africa are part carryovers, part reconstructions, but cannot be identified or classified in a specific manner. The oral literature expresses the life and culture of a new and different people who both hark back to an African past and, at the same time, attempt to define their European present. An important point worth stressing, as done by Richard Price and Sidney M. Mintz, is that in the process of culture transferral, African cultural patterns altered the dominant European cultures.[29]

For Angelina Pollak-Eltz, the Venezuelan situation was different:

The celebration of feasts in honor of St. John, St. Anthony, St. Peter and St. Benito of Palermo are still of great importance in black villages where these traditions have existed since colonial times. Certainly, these are not feasts for African divinities, but rather re-interpretations of African rites in honor of Christian saints who may or may not show some traits of African ancestral spirits. The deafricanization of the black population in Venezuela did not permit the conservation of coherent magico-religious complexes, such as Cuban Santeria of the Candomble in Brazil.[30]

Most of Pollak-Eltz's research has been done in Barlovento, but she would be the first to admit that she is both a foreigner to Venezuela, and literally lived in a house on a hill, apart from the people she relates. This does not invalidate her work, but merely situates it within the context of the observer and observed, the one and the other.

What is clear from her research is that direct African cultural transfer becomes impossible because an important non-European factor mitigates against this: I refer to the presence of other groups also contending for cultural space and, in the process, influencing one another.[31] For instance, in nearby Guyana, I recall that as a boy, I was often told of the way in which Hindu holy books, the Muslim Koran, and the Christian Bible were all considered as effective means of interpreting African ritual, locally known as obeah. It did not seem a curious phenomenon then or now. All that it suggested was that, with its expansion, Africa opened itself up to different mythologies, and that these became the new representations of African reality in the New World.

NOTES

1. For instance, Davidson Nicol (a Sierra Leonean poet) in "The Meaning of Africa" concludes "You are not a country, Africa." See John Reed and Clive Wake, eds., *A Book of African Verse* (London: Heinemann, 1964), 45. Also for a critical examination of Black writers who attempt to describe Africa from within, but fail to do so, see Ngugi wa Thiong'o, *Homecoming* (London: Heinemann, 1972), 81–95.

2. Bill Ashcroft, Gareth Griffiths, and Helen Tiffin, eds. *The Empire Writes Back: Theory and Practice in Post-Colonial Literatures* (London and New York: Routledge, 1989), 41.

3. For the African background in Louisiana, consult John Blassingame, *Black New Orleans* (Chicago: U of Chicago P, 1973), 3–6, where Blassingame deals briefly with voodoo (hoodoo) and the influence of Marie Laveau. For Gullah, the standard reference is Lorenzo Turner, *Africanisms in the Gullah Dialect* (Chicago: U of Chicago P, 1949) where, for instance, in tense usage, he compares Gullah with Ewe and Mandika (34). For Sierra Leone Krio, the authority is Eldred Jones, who has compiled a dictionary and written extensively on this subject. See especially "Krio: An English-Based Language of Sierra Leone" in *The English Language in West Africa*, ed. John Spencer (London: Longman, 1971), 66–94. Jones's view often argues for transplanted English from Jamaica rather than "African roots."

4. The Creole/dialect difference may be found in Joseph H. Greenberg, *Universals of Language* (Cambridge, MA: MIT P, 1963) and in his *Languages of West Africa* (The Hague: Mouton, 1966).

5. Ruth Finnegan, *Oral Literature in Africa* (Oxford: Clarendon, 1970), 10. Also see W. H. Whiteley, ed., *A Selection of African Prose.*, 2 vols. (Oxford: Clarendon, 1964), for the rather odd contention that audience interaction must be downplayed. He argues that "if the expression and arousing of emotion is due, not to the individual reciter but to the material itself, then one still has not got literature but only the stuff from which literature is created" (1: 6).

6. Leslie Fiedler and Houston A. Baker Jr., eds., *English Literature: Opening up the Canon* (Baltimore: Johns Hopkins UP, 1981), xiii.

7. See discussion of the African American "trickster" figure in Roger Abrahams, *Deep Down in the Jungle* (New York: Aldine, 1970), 61–85, and how the trickster alters into the Black "badman." Compare with Finnegan, *Literature* (344–53), where the African tricksters "are portrayed as thinking and acting like human beings, in a human setting" (346).

8. A particularly reliable source is Joseph E. Holloway, ed., *Africanisms in American Culture* (Bloomington: Indiana UP, 1991), 1–32 and 211–24.

9. See Holloway, *Africanisms* concerning "Voodoo" in New Orleans (34–66), and santería (119–47). A more specialized book has been written on santería in the United States by Joseph M. Murphy, *Santería: An African Religion in America* (Boston: Beacon, 1988), see especially 20–24, 26–28, 105–07, 112–13. Regarding

Haitian vodún, see the more popular Wade Davis, *The Serpent and the Rainbow* (New York: Warner, 1985), and Alfred Métraux, *Vodoo in Haiti* (London: André Deutsch, 1959). For Brazilian candomblé consult Seth Peacock and Ruth Peacock, *Spirits of the Deep* (Garden City, NY: Anchor, Doubleday, 1975). For a good overall view see Patrick J. Bellegarde-Smith, ed., *Traditional Spirituality in the African Diaspora* (Lexington, KY: Association of Caribbean Studies, 1994).

10. Joseph M. Murphy, *Working the Spirit* (Boston: Beacon, 1994), 185.

11. E. Bolaji Idowu, *Olódùmarè: God in Yoruba Belief* (London: Longman, 1962), 9.

12. Note the old world African *babalawo* or "father of secrets" as defined by Wande Abimbola, ed., *Yoruba Oral Tradition* (Ife, Nigeria: U of Ife, 1975), but especially in his shorter *Ifa: An Exposition of Ifa Literary Corpus* (Ibadan, Nigeria: Oxford UP, 1976) 13–40. Compare with the New World *babalawo* in J. M. Castill, *Oba oriate: Ifa en Tierra de Ifa* (Miami: privately printed, 1976). There is, incidentally, only a rough correlation between the printed Yoruba and Spanish versions of *odu*.

13. Italero Ernesto Pichardo (who took his defense of santería to the Supreme Court) first introduced me to santería some twenty-five years ago. He feels differently and argues that the Cuban *babalawo* has to deal directly with his client, whereas the African *babalawo* can be more indirect.

14. Pepe Carril, *Shango de Ima, a Yoruba Mystery Play* (Garden City, NY: Doubleday, 1969), 27.

15. Carlos Moore, *Castro, the Blacks and Africa* (Los Angeles: Center for Afro-American Studies, UCLA, 1918), 103.

16. For a specific study of these phenomena within a Yoruba context, consult a short pamphlet by William Bascom, *Shango in the New World* (Austin: U of Texas, African and Afro-American Research Institute, 1972), and the longer work, also by William Bascom, *Sixteen Cowries: Yoruba Divination from Africa to the New World* (Bloomington: Indiana UP, 1980). Despite its subtitle, Bascom's work deals mainly with Yoruba divination in Africa. It is particularly useful since it has both Yoruba and English texts.

17. Roger Abrahams, *Deep Down*, 120–29. Compare a milder version in Langston Hughes and Arna Bontemps, *The Book of Negro Folklore* (New York: Dodd, Mead, 1958), 366, and another in Geneva Smitherman, *Talkin' and Testifyin': The Language of Black America* (Boston: Houghton Mifflin, 1977), 224–25.

18. Steven Feserman, "African Histories and the Dissolution of World History" in *Africa and the Disciplines*, ed. Robert H. Bates, V. Y. Mudimbe, and Jean O'Barr (Chicago: U of Chicago P, 1993), 198.

19. See English version of a Yoruba *oriki* or praise-song to Obatala in *African Poetry*, ed. O. R. Dathorne (London: Macmillan, 1969), 28–29.

20. Most of the publications on synthesis are in Spanish. I specially recommend Lydia Cabrera, *El Monte* [1954] (Miami: Ediciones Universal, 1975). See also Melville Herskovits, *The Myth of the Negro Past* [1941] (Boston: Beacon, 1990), 207–60 for a general account of African crossovers into religious life. I also suggest George Eaton Simpson, *Black Religions in the New World* (New York: Columbia UP, 1978), 65–67 (for vodún), 75–78 (for Trinidadian shango), 86–91 (for santería), and 177–94 (for Brazilian candomblé). Simpson discusses the merging of African gods and Catholic saints.

21. Simpson, *Black Religions*, 61.

22. I am, of course, not arguing here that Africanisms do not survive in, say,

English in the New World. I am setting out a more obvious point that the African languages, as a whole, did not survive and with their demise went language-dependent forms of communication, such as riddles and proverbs in the original languages. In addition to Lorenzo Turner, already mentioned, also see two books concerned with the African base of not just African American, but U.S. English. I refer to Joseph E. Holloway and Winifred K. Vass, *The African Heritage of American English* (Bloomington: Indiana UP, 1993), especially 125–60; and Winifred K. Vass, *The Bantu Speaking Heritage of the United States* (Los Angeles: Center for Afro-American Studies, UCLA, 1979), especially 99–115. Also note Frederic C. Cassidy, *Jamaica Talk* (London: Macmillan, 1961), especially 19–25 and 192. And, at last, after years of extensive research, Richard Allsopp of the University of the West Indies, Cave Hill, Barbados, has published his *Dictionary of Caribbean English Usage* (Oxford: Oxford UP, 1996).

23. Henry Louis Gates Jr., *The Signifying Monkey: A Theory of African-American Literary Criticism* (Oxford: Oxford UP, 1988), 77.

24. Errol Hill, *The Jamaican Stage* (Amherst: U of Massachusetts P, 1992), 229–37 and 248–50, where Hill terms the "Jonkonnu" a masquerade of Jamaica with its music, apparel, and symbols. Concerning carnival celebrations, see *Caribbean Quarterly*, 4. 3/4 (March and June, 1956), and the more easily available, Donald R. Hill, *Calypso Calaloo: Early Carnival Music in Trinidad* (with accompanying compact disc) (Gainesville: UP of Florida, 1993), 22–63.

25. See Maulana Karenga, *The African American Holiday of Kwanza: A Celebration of Family, Community and Culture* (Los Angeles: U of Sankore P, 1988).

26. Derek Walcott, "What the Twilight Says: An Overture," in *Dream on Monkey Mountain and other Plays* (New York: Farrar, Straus and Giroux, 1970), 1–40. Contrast the Nobel lecture (1992) when, at an Indian festival, Walcott remarks on the multicultural significance of "an old, an epic vocabulary, from Asia and from Africa . . ." (p. 5 of the manuscript of the lecture given December 7, 1992).

27. Stephen Greenblatt, *Marvelous Possessions: The Wonder of the New World* (Chicago: U of Chicago P, and Oxford: Oxford UP, 1991), 60.

28. See some basic discussion of Black English forms in Robert McCrum, William Cran, and Robert McNeil, *The Story of English* (New York: Penguin, 1993), especially 190, 196–223, 342, 348.

29. Richard Price and Sidney M. Mintz introduced a methodology that is acceptable to most scholars in the field. They argue that with migration, only certain aspects of any cultural group traits will be transferred. There are basic ideas about the world, such as interpersonal ways of acting, assumptions about social relationships, and beliefs about the natural and supernatural world that are implanted through "cognitive orientation" in the New World. Price is, by the way, very opposed to creolité. See Richard Price and Sidney M. Mintz, *An Anthropological Approach to the Afro-American Past: A Caribbean Perspective* (Philadelphia: ISHU, 1976), passim.

30. Angelina Pollak-Elzt, *Black Culture and Society in Venezuela* (Caracas, Venezuela: Lagoven, 1994), 154.

31. See Antonio Benítez-Rojo, *The Repeating Island: The Caribbean and the Postmodern Perspective.* Durham, NC: Duke UP, 1996. Benítez-Rojo deals with the common nature of the cultural inheritance, all emerging from a geographical and cultural Chaos. The Caribbean, he contends, is a cultural link between North and South America, "having neither a boundary nor a center (p. 4). Compare this

with a two volume study that continues to stress Blackness in the Caribbean. See *Blackness in Latin America and the Caribbean*, ed. Norman E. Whitten Jr., and Arlene Torres. vols 1 and 2 (Bloomington, IN: Indiana UP, 1998), 1:10–15; 23–33; 34–53; 2:189–210; 345–46.

Chapter 9

When Nomads Go Home:
Inventing a Third Space

So-called erotic books (one must add of recent vintage, in order to except Sade and a few others) *represent* not so much the erotic scene as the expectation of it, the preparation for it, its ascent; that is what makes them "exciting;" and when the scene occurs, naturally there is disappointment, deflation. In other words, these are books of Desire, not of Pleasure. (Roland Barthes, *The Pleasure of the Text* [1975], 58)

The history of madness would be the history of the Other—of that which, for a given culture, is at once interior and foreign, therefore to be excluded (so as to exorcise the interior danger) but by being shut away (in order to reduce its otherness); whereas the history of the order imposed on things would be the history of the Same—of that which, for a given culture, is both dispersed and related, therefore to be distinguished by kinds and to be collected together into identities. (Michel Foucault, *The Order of Things: An Archeology of the Human Sciences* [1994], xxiv)

First of all the product of their despair could not be German literature, through outwardly it seemed to be so. They existed among three impossibilities, which I just happen to call linguistic impossibilities. . . . These are the impossibility of not writing, the impossibility of writing German, the impossibility of writing differently. One might add a fourth impossibility, the impossibility of writing. . . . Thus what resulted was a literature impossible in all respects, a gypsy literature. . . . (Letter from Franz Kafka to Max Brod, June 1921. Cited in notes of translation of chapter 3 of Gilles Deleuze and Félix Guattari, "What is a Minor Literature?" Trans. Rosere Appel et al. *Mississippi Review*, 22.3 [1983], 28, note 2)

I want to use the models of Gilles Deleuze and Félix Guattari to demonstrate ways in which some of their contentions are very relevant for the kinds of ideas that a nonmajority expresses in texts. In their major works, *Anti-Oedipus* (1972), and *A Thousand Plateaus* (1980), they express their interest in both Foucauldian thinking and postmodernism. In between they produced *Kafka: Toward a Minor Literature* (1973), where Kafka is a perfect choice to discuss the ramifications of state macro controls, and how they relate to the individual. Deleuze and Guattari are concerned with the intrusion of the state, and the manner in which the state exerts its enormous (often perverse) influence on both private and public spheres. The state apparatus is actually arboresque, complete with roots and branches, symbolic of a system that is vertical and hierarchical, not horizontal and egalitarian. We are trapped into this, unless we seek to break out, and the writers provide us with other models that will enable us to free ourselves and establish our own parallel kind of development, quite independent of previous models of dependency.

The three ways in which Deleuze and Guattari see this breakaway occurring is in the manner that schizos, nomads, and rhizomes operate. All three threaten the system of apparent established hierarchical order, but all three also offer the possibility of breaking apart from a fairly ordinary run-of-the-mill existence toward the establishment of new paths that *may* really lead somewhere. Therefore, even at the risk of incurring the wrath of the dominant norm of the Western majority society and being considered schizoid (a meaning allied with insanity that Foucault recognized shifted with time), or finding ourselves banished to the outer spaces like a nomad, or living partly under and partly above ground like a rhizome, there is still more than a degree of hope in our existence, once we break free from controls (territorialized flows) into establishing our own priorities (deterritorialization), even finally setting this up as a new norm (reterritorialization). I shall discuss this as laid out by Deleuze and Guattari, and then attempt to establish its relevance for the issues with which we have been concerned.

ANTI-OEDIPUS: SCHIZOS IN RETERRITORIALIZED FLOWS

For instance, take the case of "schizophrenia." This would merely suggest an almost necessary way of looking at the world as divided between two types of reality—one manufactured for us at home, and another that we ourselves have made abroad—that best satisfies and appeases us. Almost a century ago W.E.B. DuBois had recognized schizophrenia as a necessary prerequisite for the "negro." This was "normalcy" as Du Bois defined it, if Blacks had to live in a White society, to which they only partly belonged. As he put it in 1903 in one of his more famous references in *The Souls of Black Folk:*

the Negro is a sort of seventh son, born with a veil, and gifted with a second sight in this American world,—a world which yields him no true self-consciousness, but only lets him see himself through the revelation of the other world. It is a peculiar sensation, this double consciousness, this sense of always looking at one's self through the eyes of others, of measuring one's soul by the tape of a world that looks on in amused contempt and pity. One ever feels his two-ness,—an American, a Negro; two souls, two thoughts, two unreconciled strivings; two warring ideals in one dark body, whose dogged strength alone keeps it from being torn asunder.[1]

Du Bois would continue in this vein, hammering away at the domestic concoction of "race" until he finally took up Marcus Garvey's advice and moved abroad to Ghana.

On the level of race then, at least as applied to living within the "norms" of Westernized U.S. society, duality regarding the West and the non-West supposedly brought on the condition that was both "normal," necessary, and typical. Add to this the actualization of "difference," and it became even more *de rigeur* to assume the characteristics of the persons torn between themselves and their environment, forever perched on the edge of the tightrope between one type of local consciousness and another foreign alien perception of the world. Several novels, such as Nella Larsen's *Passing* (1929), or short stories such as Jean Toomer's *Cane* (1923) attest to this New World condition. This is called by different names—biracialism, biculturalism, and hybridity, but never normalcy.

"Schizoanalysis" in *Anti-Oedipus* will later be termed "nomadology" in *A Thousand Plateaus*. These are ways of describing the healthy multiplicities into which the subject is split. Desire works through a kind of machinelike "body without organs" (as a force, not because of "lack") enabling it to be no longer operating from a neurotic standpoint, but becoming something productive. Indeed, the major difference between the Freud/Lacanian and Guattari-Deleuzean concept of desire is that, in the former instance, desire is individually driven, depending on a concept as irrelevant as childhood, and working through the linguistic unconscious. With Deleuze and Guattari, desire is socially and politically driven ("machine" is their word), depending on adults, and operating through the mechanized unconscious (which the writers insist is no metaphor). Even as this occurs, capitalism attempts to control all processes through its method of deterritorialization. But minorities, nomads, and outsiders resist the controlling force of the state, living on the fringes of existence beyond the policing controls of what may be described as a race-enforcing, class-ordering, and gender-maintaining system.

What Deleuze and Guattari urge is that we set the nomadic instinct loose, so that we can, as individuals and people, recapture the territorial spaces taken from us by (colonized/ghettoized) urges that are controlled and circumscribed within the neat parameters of the (colonizer's) belief system—his language, his religion, his family. Oedipus is a case in point: he is a small variant of the *pater familias*. Indeed, when looked at from a more global perspective, Oedipus can represent nothing other than a rather parochial, Euro-family, complete with mother, father and child. Deleuze and Guattari see our fixation on the child as a basic error of Freudian psychoanalysis. This reliance on the child to understand the adult is one of the major fantasies of the discipline. Further, the assumptions always exist that the father had sole will and control, that the mother was non-threatening, merely existing at the whim of the father, and that the child (of course the son) could do nothing other than follow a tradition that had been already laid out. This is why Deleuze and Guattari urge us to break free from these established little ridges, into new flows, into fragmented and even random multiplicities that will establish new fields of representation. Hence desire can never represent just lack or absence, but must be less personal and more "machinic," and hence a desiring machine.

In the words of Steven Best and Douglas Kellner there had formerly existed, a "poststructuralist characterization of desire as incessant flux [that] echoes Nietzsche's theory of will to power, Lacan's emphasis on libidinal instability, Derrida's idea of dissemination, and Foucault's conception of productive power."[2] We are no longer inherently confined to old areas of demarcation, as such, we are now able to mark out new spaces that need not have a pattern, but may simply indicate directions in which we wish to go.

Deleuze and Guattari argue for a revolution of instinct. However, the primacy of the signifier in describing desire, whether from the viewpoint of Nietzsche, Freud/Lacan, Derrida, or even Foucault (who they especially admire) is that desire depends on our understanding the verbal signifiers. Deleuze and Guattari seek to free up desire then, not just from the familiar family unit within which we usually enclose it, but from the strictures of language—indeed psychoanalysis—itself. According to Jessica Munns and Gita Rajan:

Deleuze and Guattari systematically unravel the truth claims of psychoanalysis as a whole, which in an attempt to make meaning of the text/culture braids together metaphors of Oedipus, castration, and repression, all of which are signs of absence and trauma. They argue that the values in these terms are vested in bourgeois interests of masculine presence, heterosexual, familial, and control/monitored libidinal expressions. While they agree with Freud on the crucial role of the unconscious, they do not read it in idealistic or mythic terms.[3]

Additionally, I should add that Oedipus can be no kin to me for two reasons. First, as every stalwart, heterosexual Black footballer will attest, his momma is next to God, and always revered (as the "dozens" testify) as a sacrosanct irreproachable member of the extended human family. Second, Deleuze and Guattari cite Lacan approvingly in *Anti-Oedipus*, arguing that "Lacan has demonstrated in a profound way the link between Oedipus and segregation," and conclude that "the segregative use is a precondition of Oedipus, to the extent that *the social field is not reduced to the familial tie except by presupposing an enormous archaism, an incarnation of the race in person or in spirit*" (emphasis added).[4] Oedipus is a White guy wandering in a world of Whites closely related to each other. Derek Walcott would do well to remember this, when moved to pen another variant of *Omeros*!

The impact of the "body without organs" (or the body without organization) is most helpful in the model that Deleuze and Guattari construct, for it (the body of a person, an institution, a thing) can no longer be the subject, whole, and unfractured. Instead, this body has now become broken up, disorganized, and thus able to be re-assembled in new ways. This is where the concepts of "deterritorialization" and "reterritorialization" of a mind, a body, a culture, and a country are most appropriately understood. Deterritorialization is of course the condition most feared by the arboresque status quo with its Europeanized normative practices, its established hierarchy, its firm roots and branches of knowledge, belief, ideology, model, and fixed race. Thus *creolité* borrows from the shifting and pliable interpretation that is rendered here. No longer does race have the nineteenth-century fixity, but it now shows a new fluidity, as does class, gender and nationhood.

Schizoanalysis is a method that shows how decentering and fragmentation had taken place. Schizoanalysis also shows what had gone wrong, how in a way, a person, a thing, an organization, a subject, a culture worked best when it felt assured that it was repressed, indeed may have even desired its own repression to sustain itself. Whereas psychoanalysis seeks to find a way to establish "norms" that will help a "deviant" subject return to the acceptable, "schizophrenia" assumes that there is no norm and tries to validate the behavior of a person or a society, categorically moving away from old conforming hierarchies and social controls to new explosive linkages and individual assertions.

The centered subject, the group in common, usually sets up and moves along rigid "molar" lines of hierarchy and agreement; the decentered subject, the person/group at variance with normalcy easily travels along "molecular" lines. The "molar" establishes a gigantic macrostructure; the "molecular" concerns itself with the more microphysical. However, in the final analysis, in politics micro is macro and macro is micro. Deleuze and Guattari warn us to be wary of those revolutionaries who lurk within, fomenting opposition, ready to strike and become the oppressor of the oppressed.

KAFKA AS MINORITY WRITER IN AFRICA

Much of the theory explicated by Deleuze and Guattari in *Anti-Oedipus*, is very relevant for them and us, as they show when they seek to apply it to the works of Franz Kafka (1883–1924), particularly *The Trial* (1925), *The Castle* (1926), and *Amerika* (1927). Deleuze and Guattari make a point of looking at Kafka as a Jew, outside the majority German literature, yet one who is writing in the German language. Second, we know that Kafka did not have a very "normal" relationship with his patriarchal father, and that much of the sovereign model of the autocratic state, its aloof, bullying representation probably had its origin in the distant, estranged father with whom Kafka did not get along. Yet there was no standard Freudian compensation that provided an obliging blame-taking mother, as Freud would have it, complete with Freudian Oedipal attachments. Third, Kafka had declared himself opposed to many of the accepted "isms" of his time, such as the Church and capitalism. He was barely luke-warm toward Zionism and socialism, although a chance encounter would restore his interest in Judaism in the latter years of his short life.

Yet Kafka is enormously meaningful for us today. The sparseness of the prose makes him very relevant at a time of "the disappeared," in Africa, Bosnia, Serbia, and the Americas; at a time of the U.S. penchant for bombing Iraq, or the Chinese insistence that Tibet is China, as is Taiwan; as well as the period of a decreasing, shrinking world, and an increasing, swelling, and hegemonic center of power, answerable to no one.

In *The Trial*, nothing is explained, perhaps because nothing can be. In the first sentence of the text, Joseph K states something about his inability to understand cause in the modern world, "for without having done anything wrong he was arrested one fine morning."[5] Only the supposedly schizoid can react in just such a way, for the majority society has fuelled his "schizophrenia," bringing about what might seem like "neurosis," but is actually quite normal within the circumstances of a schizophrenic life. Likewise, *The Castle* extends the image of neurosis, of sickness, of being ill at ease in the so-called normalcy of the society. Against a dark and wintry background, K arrives. He seeks recognition from the Count, from the castellan, from those people high up on the hill in the castle that he is someone, the Land Surveyor. And just as Joseph K proclaimed his innocence, K asserted his experience. Joseph K wished to metamorphose, and at the end of the novel, when he is executed, perhaps this is the irony of his situation. And with K, at the "end" there is still the unfinished gaze back at himself: "he was a nonentity. . . . He was a Land Surveyor."[6]

Kafka stresses the process of decodification or deterritorialization that we easily notice in the literatures of Africa in French or Portuguese, and the literature of the Caribbean in English, Dutch, French, and Spanish. The "interpreter," that is, the critic, teacher, explicator, reviewer, and so on may well be "an agent of a dominant social code." However, this does not apply to the reader whose reading, according to Jean-François Lyotard, "becomes a nomadic of intensities," thus helping to maintain that the literature and culture of minorities "affirm another space of a patchwork of laws and customs . . . without a center." As Deleuze and Guattari readily conclude this is "what Blacks today can do with the American tongue."[7] Update this with "nomads" from India, Pakistan, and the Caribbean in England, Algerians in France, and Turks in Germany. Deterritorialization in Europe is proceeding apace, although I do not see the hopeful impact that some recent commentators suggest that the border has on the center. I think the periphery is merely condemned to a new "Third World" status and left to suffer as best they can.

Deleuze and Guattari relate a complete historical development to all of this. First, territorialization or codification, through which the master narrative encoded its authenticity on the language, the custom, and the text of existence. Second, in order to bring about some kind of indigenous authenticity, the struggle occurred for political and cultural freedom, through which the deterritorialization or decodification of the majority culture, the *grands récits*, took place, leaving a kind of open space for nomadic urges to flow free. We can assert that at this stage of the model, from what might appear like chaos—anomie is another word—that a kind of recombinant effect takes place. The majority culture at this stage is fragmented, distributed in parts, existing only in pieces. Third, the new claim is staked, a differing authenticity will be now established, a reterritorialization or recodification of former patterns and values. Perhaps the renewal process will begin all over again.

MINORITY TEXTS

At this stage, we would hardly need to argue about the validity of the new texts that have challenged and usurped the old grand narratives. Instead, I would surmise that the process can hardly be complete, since it must always renew itself over and over again. This is what will happen in the case of Wole Soyinka, Chinua Achebe, Ngugi wa Thiong'o, Wilson Harris, and Salman Rushdie, even as they continue to share commonalities from Africa, the Caribbean, and India. For what did not exist between them and the master discourse still survives at the minority discourse level, where in a new way (different from before) "native" perspectives showed new characteristics. Interestingly, these various characteristics—the writer as spokesperson, the relevance of orality, the communal nature of all composition, and the novel as oral narrative—cross over into the new Europeanized texts from the indigenous cultures, and thus establish a greater relationship between one African text and author, than between varieties of European genres.

Obviously, at least one African writer clearly noticed the relevance of Kafka. In *Radiance of the King*, Camara Laye moved sharply away from the realism of his earlier work to engage in a new kind of discourse.[8] There has been much talk that Laye did not compose the text, that it was probably the work of a European, and that it draws too heavily on Kafka, and there may be something in all of this, but I am going to regard it as his work for purposes of this discussion. The text is, among various possibilities, a quest for an African god/king, and a search for the indigenous self. An additional note subverts the idea of the minority; Clarence, the seeker, is White in Black Africa. As he journeys from north to south, he meets in no particular order of significance, a beggar, a eunuch, a blacksmith, and a fortune-teller. And if he reminds us of K and Joseph K in their endless searches, he is also the African folktale hero (like Amos Tutuola's palm wine Drinkard) seeking a boon for his ethnic group—here one is tempted to proffer one interpretation among many possibilities—the boon as a saving device for the majority/White race.

There is more to *Radiance of the King*. Laye had experimented in his first novel, *The African Child*, with growing up African in a French possession. Although Laye had been criticized locally for revealing some of the "secrets" associated with male initiation rites, his argument at the time was that the colonial gaze had exposed what few "secrets" had been still part of Africa. One could go further and agree with Michael Gomez's contention in *Exchanging Our Country Marks* (1998) that these forbidden areas of African knowledge were no different from that possessed by Western health providers or government agencies, and they all (African and Western) maintain a constant secretive front because they seek "impenetrability or resistance to explication along conventional lines of analysis."[9]

COLONIAL (CON)TEXTS

One can indeed argue that the entire colonial process of "education" was a method by which the emancipated would freely give up these secrets (since they were considered irrelevant or barbaric) and, in this respect, Western anthropology is the major plunderer, but no European discipline is entirely innocent of raiding and plagiarizing African borders. The "native," the "barbarian," plays a major but unattributed role in the accumulation of European knowledge, indeed is the sole authentic source in such places as the Commonwealth Center, appropriate parts of the British Museum, La Musée de l'Homme, the School of Oriental and African Studies, University of London, and similar equivalent places of purloined knowledge in France, Germany, Scandinavia, Holland, Belgium, Spain, Portugal, Italy, and so on. I shall cite three specific instances within British, French, and White South African hegemonic control.

First, let me mention a British example which I recall from the 1950s at the Nigerian College of Arts, Science and Technology, Zaria, where I taught. One of the conditions for obtaining a much-coveted diploma meant that students were required to write a minithesis. This was done on a topic such as circumcision, "fattening ceremonies" for young brides, the "divided-man" culture, and so on—in other words anything that would give the colonial authorities a peep into the forbidden past, when the gaze of the authority had been absent, and when such a past could only have been seen through the authentic confessionals of these newly converted "informants."

Second, a French instance: L'École William Ponty also utilized the school pupils of the then French West and French Equatorial Africa as willing guinea pigs in that they wrote and acted out plays. Situated in St. Louis, Senegal, from the 1930s onward during their school vacations, the school had students work on various projects associated with their own lives and traditions. At the end of the academic year, they presented plays. For instance, at the end of the 1932–1933 session, Dahomeyan pupils put on a play whose theme and subject-matter set the stage for many that would follow until 1947. What emerged was a generalized concept that one could make not of tribal societies, but of évolués in the process of change from the "native" to the "French."

The extent to which this is most relevant is that it takes us back to the Deleuze/Guattari model. At this point of alteration, what is most noticeable is the territorialization of space and environment, the manner in which French culture is beginning to be inscribed on the African continent. The plays are performed in French, and nearly always, as with the references cited by Bakary Traoré, we note the outright intergenerational clash as the pupil-writers assume the role of the French and show the superiority of the new "civilization." As with the student texts I helped supervise in the fifties at the college in Nigeria, the important point was to constantly affirm the rightness of the European lifestyle and the wrongness of the African. This was not a clash, as would occur later on, but a level-headed assertion of the wisdom of Europeanness.

Third, in South Africa, apartheid, colonialism, and Europeanization went hand in hand, for there, just as with the British and French models I cited, the Western authorities (here the Church) used writing and literature as the barter of exchange. The logic went something like this: the students would receive licenses to work as teachers, in exchange for passing on information about their groups. In South Africa it took a dangerous turn, whereby the barter of information often meant a complete surrender of the native self. Robert Ross contends in "The Self-Image of Jacob Adams" that regarding the Khoisan, from as early as 1792, "Moravian tradition encouraged the recording of life histories by its adepts." He cites one Jacob Adams, who on July 25, 1808, admitted to his own savageness. Adams told the missionary that formerly they (the people to whom the missionary referred as "Bushmen") "were a quiet and well-disposed people," but deprived of their land and cattle by European colonists, they "became, in their turn, savage, and given to plunder."[10] Thus, Jacob Adams is made to construct himself as the barbarous binary, the other as defined by the One. This is no mean feat of propaganda.

One issue that intentionally confounds us is that no longer can Europeanity be identified solely in terms of race. In *The European Tribe* (1987), for instance, Caryl Phillips has noted that the contemporary White "tribe" is close to anarchy and possible self-annihilation, because within it there are people like himself, born in St. Kitts, and only a White tribal member by default and happenstance. He writes:

The crisis of a second generation black British community, with no viable alternative to offer in either language or religion, will deepen in direct proportion to the vigour with which Britain tries to ignore the gross inequity of opportunity. . . . *I cannot write in Yoruba or Kikuyu*, anymore than a black youth born in Peckham or Middlesborough can hope to feel at home in Addis Ababa or Kingston, Jamaica. . . . *I fear the prolonged wandering of the displaced*, who inevitably become the victims of handy theories, particularly if the host country is in trouble. (Emphasis added)[11]

This is yet another aspect to the incorporation of the minority, only slightly different from the students at École William Ponty, but yet all very much part of the effects of colonialism. Two points here are worth stressing: First, how socioeconomic conditions continue to manufacture minorities and their literature, which Deleuze and Guattari remind us, "is not the literature of a minor language but the literature a minority makes in a major language." To this we should add that we are specifically conscious of Salman Rushdie, V.S. Naipaul, Chinua Achebe, even Toni Morrison. Second, they assert quite clearly an important point that "[o]rdinarily a tongue compensates for its deterritorialization through a reterritorialization in meaning."[12] This is the effect of the "wandering of the displaced." In this the meaning of such French African novels as *Radiance of the King* becomes clearer, since the journey to meet the king and to ultimately embrace him is that of the nomad rearranging territorial space into a new order.

Clarence in *The Radiance of the King*, and the real life Caryl Phillips are not Bhabhaesque figures, lying quite neutral on the edge of the European master text, but are indeed willfully employed in composing their own discourses, with its own logic. And a particular logic here is that we have to see Clarence as a leftover from colonialism, desperately trying to move across the space from his reliance on privilege to his acceptance of powerlessness. Laye dramatically stages the encounter as he has Clarence strip naked and sum up enough courage to walk across the square to the waiting arms of the African god/king.

Clarence lacks the attributes of the conqueror—power, success, money, and contacts. Not only is he the isolated and lonely K figures of Kafka, but his added dimension of whiteness helps stress the role reversal. He makes his way humbly to the African king in the company of a beggar. Where Europeans had been representatives of kings and queens, Clarence stands as an abject, pitiful peasant. Where Europeans had enslaved, Clarence is enslaved. Whereas Europeans settlers had come clothed, Clarence's own clothes were stolen from him and he can only enter the king's service naked and without material gain. He is only worth a little, when he is worth less. This is the conundrum of K in Africa.

AUTHOR(ITY) AND AUTHOR(SHIP): *A THOUSAND PLATEAUS*

K as nomad, as itinerant, as one caught up in the flow of deterritorialization is replaced in *A Thousand Plateaus* by other terms that deny us the opportunity to have ready access to the castle. There is already a hint of multifaceted meanings and interpretations about Kafka in *Kafka: Toward a Minor Literature*; "It is a rhizome, a burrow. The castle has many entrances,"[13] they write about interpreting Kafka. One possible way to understand what is taking place is to note that, "The three characteristics of minor literature are the deterritorialization of the language, the connection of the individual and the political, [and] the collective arrangement of utterance."[14]

It seems fair to conclude, then, that the idea of group collectivity seeps into the new form that is being developed—call it novel, poetry, or drama. Equally, with the assumption of the new metropolitan language comes the shift, the removal, the unwriting of the former modes of agreement that had been accepted as part and parcel of the established language of author(ity), but obviously not author(ship). What Deleuze and Guattari term the "political" may have been true for a Czech and Jew like Kafka, but does not seem to be a conscious choice for writers in Africa, India, and the New World. In these places, it is inconceivable that writing could exist without a function—after all, no other art form ever did.

Anti-Oedipus had attacked and expelled Freud because he had mobilized "all the resources of myth, of tragedy, of dreams, in order to re-enslave desire, this time from within: an intimate theater," and had noted that schizophrenia was "the absolute limit of every society" since "it sets in motion decoded and deterritorialized flows that it restores to desiring machines." Hence, the storehouse of the imaginative had been hijacked by a false belief, and in the West at least, many writers had been left without the social supports for what they envisioned, since sexuality and sexual impulses had been locked up within the family, reduced to "daddy, mommy, and me."[15]

It is possible to recognize that the West had trapped itself into a false formulation where the child is blamed for the sins of the adult world. But read aright, "desire can be made to desire its own repression" and break free of the race, class, and gender superiority that the Oedipus myth invokes. We can substitute the "reactionary unconscious investment" for a "revolutionary unconscious investment" that will show how this same "desire, still in its own mode, cuts across the interest of the dominated, exploited classes, and causes flows that are capable of breaking apart both the segregations and their Oedipal applications—flows capable of hallucinating history, of reanimating the races in delirium, of setting continents ablaze." Here the language explodes with the joy of the moment when the true revolution of the spirit and the flesh will open up the world and its history, bringing a new social and economic egalitarianism that the authors feel will banish racism. They continue with powerful and moving lines, "No, I am not of your kind, I am the outsider and the deterritorialized," and conclude this stunningly moving paragraph with a "sampling" from Arthur Rimbaud's "Une saison en Enfer," "I am of a race inferior for all eternity. . . . I am a beast, a Negro."[16]

RIMBAUD AS MINORITY

The Rimbaud reference is most appropriate, because if you seek a minority, he was definitely one. Or, put differently, he certainly was no mainstream adherent. Poet, Bohemian, homosexual, slave trader, and wanderer, Rimbaud embodied in this midmodern period the epitome of deterritorialization. His love affair with the older Paul Verlaine brought out all that was both noble and mean spirited in him. He clearly saw himself as the supreme outsider—perhaps there might have even been a dash of an artificial and somewhat wild élan in his flair, his spontaneity, his style.

In 1871, when Rimbaud was only seventeen, Paul Verlaine had invited the younger poet to Paris. Rimbaud had sent him some of his verse, and Verlaine was most impressed. However, perhaps Verlaine was not quite ready for what happened next: he fell in love with Rimbaud, so much so that it broke up his own shaky marriage. Together the two poets began the lives of nomads, travelling from France, to London and Brussels. The film *Total Eclipse* captures the angst of these years as well as the fear of being caught as practicing homosexuals. Finally, in 1873, after one of their more violent quarrels, Verlaine shot Rimbaud. This landed Verlaine in prison, and Rimbaud had an opportunity to rethink their rather tempestuous life together. He however continued the wanderlust, to Cyprus, Java, Aden, and finally to Harar in then Abyssinia as a gunrunner, a trader, and possibly a slave-dealer. After several years, illness drove him back to France where he finally died.

Rimbaud makes an interesting case in that he represents two affiliations. He is "other" in two senses—certainly gender-wise, although I suspect that his earlier public demonstration of his homosexuality with Verlaine subsided in his later years. And though there is much talk about an Ethiopian female lover, there is less about a servant for whom he left a fairly sizable sum of money. Kwame Anthony Appiah, himself a homosexual and the son of a Ghanaian and English parentage, had this to say in the context of "ethical" gender and "ethical" race:

I am asserting here, therefore, a contrast between our attitudes to (ethical) gender and (ethical) "race;" I suggest that we standardly hold it open to someone to believe that the replacement of the characteristic morphology of their sex with a (facsimile) of that of the other (major) one would produce someone other than themselves, a new ethical person; while the replacement of the characteristic morphology of their ethical "race" by that of another would not leave them free to disclaim the new person. "Racial" ethical identities are for us—and that means something like us in the modern West—apparently less conceptually central to who one is than gender ethical identities.[17]

Beyond the personal point that Appiah is making lies a new appropriation; the construct of a new ethnicity of race and gender, one that is not "bi," but certainly whole and wholesome. He erases the boundaries that the straight world would set up around accepted polarities of straight/gay and Black/White, and furthermore delegitimizes the entire issue of racial and gender norms.

Within the new discursive space we can easily fit Rimbaud, both as one who has enunciated a new race and gender and one whose gendering and ethnic-making radically engender a new and different kind of being. I wish to suggest that Rimbaud escaped to the ends of the world until the end of his life, because he was this new "ethnicity"—neither Black nor White, neither heterosexual nor homosexual. In other words, Rimbaud had dispensed with the monological voice in the production of a new narrative space. He was somebody else, an other.

Although he stopped writing poetry when he was relatively young, Rimbaud's life is still partly captured in the significance of prose. He wrote letters to his mother and sister; he drafted a report about a journey to Ogaden, south of Harar, for the Société de Géographie in February 1884. He was always ill, and in between bouts of recovery, he would write up his travel, as he did in *Le Bosphore Egyptien* in 1877. However, a major problem remains in that his sister Isabelle, seeking to save him from a fate worse than death, and to "guard" his reputation, went through the process of altering and changing some of his letters. She wanted them to fit the notion she had bandied about that Rimbaud had returned to the safe bosom of the Roman Catholic Church, and while one might commend her for caring that much about Rimbaud's soul, many others cared even more about the authenticity of his work. For what it is worth, we are left now with bits and pieces from this final period of the poet's life, as seen in Wallace Fowlie's *Rimbaud: Complete Works, Selected Letters* (1966), the letters from Egypt, Arabia and Ethiopia published in 1989, and Jean Voellmy's more recent correspondence edited in 1965.[18]

Deleuze and Guattari adored Rimbaud's cultivation of studied irresponsibility. He was the nomad par excellence, moving to what was then termed Abyssinia in the last ten years of his life, perhaps to seek the possibility of momentary fulfillment that might almost mirror the visions he always had of otherness, of different spaces, which we might well have mistakingly called his metaphors of alterity. Perhaps in a way these were metonymies of his larger self, the other, inscribing itself over and over again in little visions, before the final reality that drove the nomad Rimbaud "home" to Africa.

Africa silenced him. Perhaps voice and words were all already there, already marked out in elaborate signifiers, so that a puny mortal could hope to say little, reproduce less from the gigantic text that was the landscape, the sea, and the desert. Perhaps, in another way, Africa had the effect of silencing him because he who had paraded his rich bold images since he was a teenager, might well have been overcome by the awesome and overpowering sight of a whole continent ablaze with heat and light, and moreover, one (he had gone to Abyssinia) where the weight of its history lay heavily on it. Perhaps in truly overcoming a feeling, there is a point of silence, when there is nothing left to do except to listen to the sound of your own voice echoing, in a hollow manner, next to the mighty roar of God's chamber. Perhaps this is what wakes you up to a new life outside you, beyond the sound of hearing and the purview of eyes, where dreams reside. Perhaps Rimbaud had finally met his own younger dreamer, and he had taken back the poet's words.

SEXUALITY AND SADE

The general approach to desire as a "desiring machine" reminds me of the Marquis de Sade. For him, in the most extreme sexual encounters, he also depersonalized sex by introducing the whipping machine and the raping machine. For Sade, this also made much sense, since he always had to keep at least two steps ahead of the law, having endured much for the excesses he constantly sought to experience. Indeed, I venture to suggest that were he not an aristocrat with connections, he would have been locked away long before the French Revolution of 1789.

I think that he would, however, have to represent the ultimate in a life liberated, totally without the slightest concessions to everyday norms and beliefs. But Sade's irony must surely be that even as the ultimate decentering, the mother of all deterritorializations descended on him, despite his truly revolutionary zeal and ardors (at least in the sexual department) he could hardly have been totally accepted by a movement that sought economical, physical, and spiritual liberation from the thralldom of aristocratic excesses. The revolution did not send Sade back to a prison, it dispatched him to a mental hospital instead.

In Peter Weiss's *Marat/Sade*, first performed in 1964, Sade conducts the inmates of the asylum to reveal the bedlam that is present within and without the walls of the sanatorium.[19] Above all, Weiss indicates that Sade is involved in total pleasure, so that though the confrontation with Marat is deadly serious in one sense, it is pleasurable in another. As Barthes put it, hedonism is "[a]n old, a very old tradition. . . . [which] has been repressed by nearly every philosophy; we find it defended only by marginal figures . . . ," of which Roland Barthes names Sade as one of the few.[20]

Therefore, when Deleuze and Guattari specifically mention Kafka, Rimbaud, and Sade, they are indicating/indicting persons/personae/ personalities and authors/authorship, or perhaps the point at which any linkage between these conceptualizations is impossible to fracture. Kafka, Rimbaud, and Sade are "fringe" figures who, by exceeding, manage to normalize, to maintain a special kind of equilibrium between action and intention, wish and achievement of desire. They either ignore or shunt aside the superego, by pretending that it does not exist, is totally irrelevant, and in any case, cannot affect final outcomes. Indeed, Kafka as Jew, Rimbaud as homosexual, and Sade as jailed pervert, share with Camara Laye and Caryl Phillips an intention to deterritorialize the European cultural map, so that they might codify it anew. It is this recodification that evokes memories of "home," where truly for Laye (France and Guinea), and for Phillips (Britain and the Caribbean) provide a true "third space" for their nomadic wanderlust—a space only imagined by Kafka, Rimbaud and Sade.

NOTES

1. W.E.B. Du Bois, *The Souls of Black Folk* [1903] (Boston: Bedford, 1997), 38.
2. Steven Best and Douglas Kellner, *Postmodern Theory: Critical Interrogations* (New York: Guilford, 1991), 87.

3. Jessica Munns and Gita Rajan, eds., *A Cultural Studies Reader: History, Theory, Practice* (London and New York: Longman, 1995), 85–86.

4. Gilles Deleuze and Félix Guattari, *Anti-Oedipus: Capitalism and Schizophrenia* [1972] (Minneapolis: U of Minnesota P, 1983), 104.

5. Franz Kafka, *The Trial* [1925] (Harmondsworth, U.K.: Penguin, 1953), 8.

6. Franz Kafka, *The Castle* [1926] (Harmondsworth,U.K.: Penguin, 1930), 280.

7. Gilles Deleuze and Félix Guattari, "What is a Minor Literature?," *Mississippi Review*. Trans. Rosere Appel et al., 22.3. (1983): 13–14, 16.

8. Camara Laye, *The Radiance of the King* [1956] (New York: Collier, 1971).

9. Michael A. Gomez, *Exchanging Our Country Marks: The Transformation of African Identities in the Colonial and Antebellum South* (Chapel Hill, NC.: U of North Carolina P, 1998), 94–95.

10. Robert Ross, "The Self-Image of Jacob Adams," in *Miscast: Negotiating the Presence of the Bushmen* ed. Pippa Skotnes (Cape Town: U of Cape Town P, 1996), 62–63.

11. Caryl Phillips, *The European Tribe* (London: Faber and Faber, 1987), 125–26.

12. Deleuze and Guattari, "What is a Minor Literature?," 16.

13. Gilles Deleuze and Félix Guattari, *Kafka: Toward a Minor Literature* [1975], trans. Dana Polan (Minneapolis: U of Minnesota P, 1986), 13.

14. Deleuze and Guattari, "What is a Minor Literature?," 18.

15. Deleuze and Guattari, *Anti-Oedipus*, 271, 266, 285.

16. Ibid. 105.

17. Kwame Anthony Appiah, " 'But Would That Still Be Me?': Notes on Gender, 'Race,' Ethnicity, as Sources of 'Identity,' " in *Race/Sex: Their Sameness, Difference and Interplay* ed. Naomi Zack (London and New York: Routledge, 1997), 78–79.

18. See Charles Nicoll, *Somebody Else: Arthur Rimbaud in Africa, 1880–91* (London: Jonathan Cape, 1997); Arthur Rimbaud, *Correspondance, 1888–1891*, ed. Jean Voellmy (Paris: Gallimard, 1965); and Arthur Rimbaud, *Rimbaud: Complete Works, Selected Letters.*, trans. Wallace Fowlie (Chicago: U of Chicago P, 1966).

19. Peter Weiss, *The Persecution and Assassination of Jean-Paul Marat as Performed by the Inmates of the Asylum of Charenton under the Direction of the Marquis de Sade* [performed 1964] (New York: Highgate, 1966).

20. Roland Barthes, *The Pleasure of the Text* [1973] (New York: Hill and Wang, 1975), 57.

Chapter 10

Interacting at the Margins:
When Race is Class is Gender

> Thus, for contemporary man the representation of reality by the film is incomparably more significant than that of the painter, since it offers, precisely because of the thoroughgoing permeation of reality with mechanical equipment, an aspect of reality which is free of all equipment. (Walter Benjamin, *Illuminations: Essays and Reflections* [1968], 234)

> The bourgeoisie has no relish for language, which it no longer regards even as a luxury, an element of the art of living (death of "great" literature), but merely as an instrument of decor (phraseology). (Roland Barthes, *The Pleasure of the Text* [1975], 38).

I want to look at the manner in which people who inhabited what Homi Bhabha terms the "interstices"[1] have responded to their environments. In this regard, I ought, of course, to be concerned with those who are marginalized, with regard to European culture—women, Africans, Asians, Native Americans, and people from the Caribbean—but this is only a partial list of a great part of the world, and could not be satisfactorily pursued within the limitations of a short presentation. Additionally, I also wish to consider Europeans themselves who have ventured into this neutral space, beyond their own norms of discourse, to see the extent to which I can identify both their sense of "home" and the acquisition and assumption of foreign values. In so doing, I am conscious that I shall very often be venturing beyond the parameters of the culture to which some of these texts belong, and for which they were very often inscribed. Furthermore, I shall more often than not be applying readings that derive from my own sense of selfhood as only partly former colonial, still tethered to the language and cultural trappings of the very metropolitan ventures I wish to relate.

From the beginning, therefore, I can lay claim to scant "objectivity," since I am merely able to assert my own curiosity as the reason why I probed in the first place. I am an Empsonian-trained child of the New Criticism, and so in many respects I am intentionally going against the grain in order to set my scalpel against works that have been given over the past seventy years or so laudatory treatments by people who adhere to these schools. However, in many respects, I am seeking some type of antidote to deal with much that has remained unwritten, unspoken, and unsaid, either because it was not deemed relevant by those who spoke, or simply omitted because it seemed to lack relevance within the power contexts of what was being said.

There are specific issues with which I have not tried to concern myself. These include the extent to which non-English cultures, even those as close as Greece and Egypt, became the prime location for booty seekers. In this context, note how Lord Elgin in Greece, Richard Burton and John Henning Speke in Africa, or Hiram Bingham in Mexico attempted to use this new license to obtain a new currency (at times literal, at times not) for themselves. I wish to note in passing how "travellers" across Asia, "explorers" in Africa, and "discoverers" of the New World, all exported concepts of themselves and their original master worlds to the margins, how the peripheral areas in the process altered and changed, and how the travellers themselves underwent processes of change that they bore back with them to their homes at the center. This is why when one speaks of a so-called colonial society, one secure in its "culture," one is not only describing a polarity between center and periphery, but also admitting to a cultural confluence in which influence flowed both ways—not as much as it has become fashionable to assert, but nevertheless a two-way outcome is marked.

I wish also to consider women in the context that I have suggested, certainly as what Anne McClintock has termed "boundary markers,"[2] but also to extend the term even beyond the male imposition of such a role on women. I should like to see ways in which women first enter the European orbit as a kind of trope (and here I would be mindful of Elizabethan and Jacobean drama, as well as Victorian novel forms by women themselves). Additionally, surely the question must be asked whether women such as Florence von Sass Baker or Mary Kingsley operated within the same format as their male explorer counterparts, or whether we could reasonably argue that their gender provided a kind of gentle dispensation?

MOVING AWAY FROM EUROPEAN TEXTMAKING

A major interest in this enterprise is to attempt two considerations. First, to note the way in which Africa, Asia, Native America, Latin

America, and the Caribbean, as presences, have always been part of the European cultural continuum. And second, to see how indigenous writers manipulate what is basically a European format in order to define themselves away from and beyond the given assumptions of European textmaking. In doing this, we should note that such a discourse would be concerned with two important issues: how is "non-Europe" seen within the context of European arts, and how do these disparate areas see themselves, within their own terms of reference.

The problem in trying to obtain reasonable answers to this lies in the lacuna between the reflections of area writers, on the part of both Europeans and Africans, and the refraction of locale, again on the part of Europeans and non-Europeans. From the onset, therefore, we must concede that this can be no easy search for truth, veracity, authenticity, or even some neat balancing act between a fictive "imaginary" and an equally fictitious "real." For the purposes of this debate I wish to suggest that not only are both elusive to the point where perhaps neither really exists, but also both tend to be confusing, since by establishing a false hierarchy they bring about an assumption that in some way indigenous writers (despite the colonizing process and the influence of an educational system of hundreds of years that centered on the West) nevertheless possess a monopolization of something integral termed the "truth."

Therefore, such a task—the search for objective "truth"—cannot really be a worthwhile endeavor, since if truth had ever existed, it perished a long time ago. And since we must relay on the cultural translations and transformations of experts, anthropologists, folklorists, and authors, what has to remain dubious is the extent to which we can ever honestly say that beyond the page there is some kind of supertext that we could identify. Indeed, the culture may affirm for us a degree of "authenticity," but where do we begin? Against what do we hold up some aspect of a supraculture, in a futile effort to compare apples and bananas?

In a consideration of New World "discovery," for instance, what emerges first and foremost is that once contact had been made, there occurred definite degrees of transformation on the part of both Native Americans and Europeans. For the Europeans, their own world and its view had dramatically altered in that no longer was the West confined within the Pillars of Hercules, with a *mappa mundi* centered on Jerusalem, and an earth circumscribed by the Ocean Sea.[3] Now not only was the world larger, but it offered enormous imaginative possibilities—true enough unreal speculations that had their origin in Europe itself—but also the journeyings to the New World freed up the imagination to attempt to take this bold leap: to seek for the famed cities of Antilla, St. Brendan's Island, Amazon women, the Fountain of Eternal Youth, even the physical presence of Prester John himself, who would once and for all slay the Muslims and restore Jerusalem to the European Christians.[4]

It was a desperate hope, one that had been cultivated for two centuries. Even as late as the opening years of the sixteenth century, the presence of such a savior had been widely touted—Ismail Savavi (born c. 1487) from Azerbaijan had conquered Tabriz, and ten years later Baghdad. Soon he would proclaim a Muslim hegemony in the area, and although he did not accomplish this in his lifetime, Europeans who knew little about him had transformed him into "a warrior-king of mythic proportion . . . a Christian-like holy man . . . a warrior endowed with divine qualities . . . the long-awaited savior who would free Europe from the scourge of the Ottoman Turks."[5] New World ventures, like Asian and African acts that had preceded them, were really attempts to satisfy these wild imaginings, which, incidentally, in the process, became curbed.

This phantom imagining, indeed what can only be imagined but never realized, has been lauded by Guyanese writer Wilson Harris in "History, Fable and Myth" (1970) as a "limbo imagination" that can free the New World artist from the very trap of history—he calls it a "prison house"—that the Old World had imposed on it. He links this with the "limbo imagination," no mere song or dance meant for tourist consumption, but instead a recollection of the need to rehearse the historical encounters on slave ships, when the body had to be small and contorted to fit into its allotted space.[6] Here, as Wilson Harris once suggested to me, is not only the birth of limbo, but the active enactment of the historical embodiment of Anancy, the spider trickster, as dark bodies lay below deck, their outstretched legs dangling like spiders. It seemed far-fetched then as it still does now, but it is worth our consideration.

This leap of the imagination is what supremely permits Africans from their Old World and Native Americans from their New World to seek common territory on soil that is differently experienced, one from the other, as well as from Europe. For Europeans, the land could be owned, traded, settled, mined, and sold; for Africans and Native Americans, the saturation of the soil with the memory of ancestral blood both renews and forever keeps it close, bound to a community, not a person.

WOMAN AND LIMINALITY

This attachment to the land, the sky, and the feel of place does not exist with the early "dicoverers." Both Christopher Columbus and Amerigo Vespucci see the land and its people as observers from a distance. There is no smell, no touch, only the visual sense, as they relate what is perhaps the most obvious of what they encounter—they *see* the trees, the sea, the naked "Indians." "Discovery" can then only have meaning in the pragmatic utilization of a tree, sea, and Indian, or the yoking of landscape to labor.

In early settlement in the United States, at Roanoke and Jamestown, the motives were no different, and the result the same. The settlers do not feel the spirit of the place, or bear witness to its presence as real. Again, the New World is translated into tropes, in this instance, a place of abundance, where Europeans could be fed, free from the harassment of overpopulation. This is precisely why Pocahontas is so important at this juncture of history; she is a nurturer for the transition, one who through her own marriage to John Rolf, will graphically open up both land and woman to the conquering European. She is whore/betrayer/ gatekeeper, both in the sense in which Homi Bhabha noted a presencing at the interstices, and also in the manner in which she perches, liminally, at the border as an inviting and threatening symbol that must be despoiled and robbed, expelled and extirpated, even as the conqueror .1ar-rativizes these experiences of her death and demise in a primordial ritual of threshold-crossing and initiation. With the arrival of the Pilgrims/ Puritans, still another narratavized version explains her. She is the land, the "New Eden," the "New Jerusalem," an empty space to accommodate the phallus of half-impotent men who had used up Europe.[7]

In the process of *contact* (the sexual reverberations of the sound of the word are important), the Native American viewpoint is naturally altered. Obviously, at one level for instance, when the French fur trappers provide the eager Native Americans of Canada with dried food and guns in exchange for fur, hunting ceased to be of prime importance. But even more important Native Americans began to inhabit a new synthetic world, since the French moved upcountry and lived with them, and this became a world where not merely goods were exchanged, but new alliances were built. Here human met human, and as they ate together and cohabited, they learnt each other's language. It is out of this cosmopolitan mix that Squanto emerges. As far as the Pilgrims were concerned, God had sent him to them, complete with his knowledge of Europe and the English tongue. But here, in this person, I think more effectively than in any other case, we begin to see the early indications of a hybridity that would constitute what is after all a creole culture in all the Americas.

These interactions whether between Europeans and New World Native Americans, or Europeans and Asians, or Europeans and Africans represent ways of threshold crossing, whereby all enter into a kind of neutral zone. Take for instance the Spanish contact with the Calusa people of early Florida, or Hernando de Soto's mad rush through northern Florida and the American southwest.[8] Both are examples certainly of conquest and unspeakable (at times unintended) cruelty, but both through representative figures like Fernando d'Escalante Fontesada and Alvar Núñez Cabeza de Vaca as well as Soto show ways in which both peoples became hybridized (not totally) in the process of contact.[9]

The Spaniards may well have entered with the lust for gold and women, and concomittantly, the fervent belief in the righteousness of their cause, but after years among the Native Americans, both Escalante and Cabeza de Vaca would see for themselves how the local people fished, ate, clothed themselves, and worshipped their gods. And, even though the Spaniards might have set down strong reservations against what they claimed was the stubborn paganism of the indigenous people, nevertheless, in the process, even these parochial conquistadors came to understand the nature of dependency, since the Native Americans fed, clothed, and housed them, and the nature of interdependency, since the Europeans lived apart, far from their own language and culture contacts.

CLASS AT HOME AND RACE ABROAD: SHAKESPEARE AND DICKENS

The crossing of thresholds to another world is also observable in the manner in which fictionalized characters move in and out of situations over which they have little or no control. An early example may be found in *Macbeth*, performed 1606, especially when we note the manner in which Macbeth comes into contact with the unnatural, supernatural world of the dark witches on the heath, a domain that he, in turn, imports back to the castle and the banquethall, since, in effect, the witches have not only prophesied the inevitability of his fate, but have directed his subsequent actions. Instances multiply in Elizabethan and Jacobean drama as a changing people and an altering English language swing erratically between polarities of race(ism) and class(ism).

A later example occurs in Charles Dickens's *Great Expectations* (1860–1861).[10] The atmosphere and smell of the graveyard, much like Macbeth's heath, remains with Pip, whether he is an apprentice blacksmith, in Miss Havisham's employ, or partaking of gentlemanly delights in London. The physical presence of death and life, his old ancestors and his new self, dramatically come together with Abel Magwitch (a first name that has strong Victorian associations with their Jewish anti-Semitism, and a surname that reminds us of *Macbeth* and both "hag" and "witch"). Magwitch's promises have helped groom an English gentleman, and are like Macbeth's prophecies from the witches in the fen that had seemingly promised to exalt a thane into a king.

Of course both Shakespeare and Dickens were addressing the iron-clad social system in Britain that would never have permitted any such easy ride up the class ladder, but in the process we are also seeing how interactions are occurring between the barn and the boudoir, the hovel and the house, country and city, outside and inside. In working this out, both Macbeth and Pip share much in common. First, they have aspired to what we suspect quite rightly is a futile enterprise, but in the process, they have been able to internalize aspects of the hybrid worlds that mask their aspirations. Both are excellent examples of the effect of gentrification. In Macbeth's case, he fails to understand the riddle of the field, the street talk, that would have been essential to his survival as a victorious warrior king. In Pip's case, he also does not quite understand the experience of the graveyard, where humans go a-begging for sustenance, can be suddenly cut down, and indeed "transported," carried off to another land "down under" at the bottom of the world, where roles may be reversed.

Hence, the confrontation between Magwitch and Pip moves beyond mere assertions that class cannot be bought; it clearly shows the interchangeability of roles, whereby the convict literally enters into the domain of the gentleman, reminding Pip that a criminal/colonial has purchased his clothes, food, and lodging, indeed his books, that is even the very "magic" that Prospero once solely possessed. The territory shared by Pip and Magwich, Macbeth and the witches is one that stresses polarities and banishes perhaps for just a fleeting moment, the absurd independence over which they would claim to have some degree of supervision.

Likewise, in the cases earlier cited—Columbus and Vespucci, Sir Walter Raleigh, John White, Pocahontas, the Pilgrims, John Cabot and Jacques Cartier, and Cabeza de Vaca and Hernando de Soto—were all negotiating to occupy new spaces. Often this might involve the surrender of the compelling visions with which they came, such as God, glory, everlasting youth, gold, and perpetual hope for the assumption of a new kind of polarized beliefs, such as evil, failure, omnipresent death, poverty, and total disillusionment. Perhaps they did not even take on these new burdens lightly, but it is factual that the conquistadors from Columbus onward gained little reward or even recognition for what they had so glibly penned as heroic stances. Perhaps the reversal was intentional.

As Trinh T. Minh-ha has correctly stated:

Depending on who is looking, the exotic is the other, or it is me. For the one who is off and outside the culture is not the one over there, whose familiar culture I am still part of, or whose unfamiliar culture I come to learn from. I am the one making a detour with myself, having left upon my departure from over there not only a place but also one of my selves. The itinerary displaces the foundation, the background of my identity, and what it necessarily unfolds is the very encounter of self with the other—other than myself, and my other self.[11]

In this way, because the exchange is always taking place, always being freshly negotiated, there can be no static "self" or "other" but only protean dimensions to being that constantly shift, are always in flux, alteration, and change. Perhaps Shakespeare's Othello is one of the best literary examples in that he is both Moor and Venetian, "savage" and "civilized," pagan and Christian, destroying victor on the battlefield and destroyed/destructive victim in the bedroom.

Once the untamed moor/Moor entered the serene palace, the rigid distinction between field and house, campground and palace, and battlefield and battlement became artificial. Once Macbeth's heath or Pip's graveyard came indoors, they would constantly interact with each other and the interior, and thus bring about a rupture between space and person. Once Columbus, Raleigh, Cabot, and Soto had been exposed to the outdoors of the New World, they would forever alter the indoors of the Old World. Such alterations would come about through (ex)changes of food and language, and music and dress. More importantly, the alterations would result in the consequent inability to distinguish between the essential self and other. Therefore, what occurs is actually a breakdown in rigid class hierarchies at home, and strict ethnic constructions abroad. Of course these continued to exist, but they had been seriously threatened.

THE HORROR, WHOSE HORROR?: CONRAD IN AFRICA

In Joseph Conrad's *Heart of Darkness* (1902),[12] despite his harsh press of late, one could reasonably argue, therefore, that the "lie" that Marlow brings back to the Intended about Kurtz and his vision of the world, regarding the last words he supposedly spoke, are not really lies at all. Marlow had himself seen the horror, the real truth, but this is not something that he can share with anyone in the capital of one of the leading colonial world powers—it is too distant, too far beyond its rigid regimentation, the white drapes, the neat room in Brussels where he finds himself. He cannot tell the truth about Kurtz, because Kurtz had made a headlong fling into the "wilderness" that was Africa, had "gone native" (and in the process had been driven mad). In any event Kurtz is another example of a more obvious ethnic hybridity, regardless of whatever may have been Conrad's presuppositions about his own Britishness as an adopted ward of the British crown.

It is a dualism I wish to stress, which lies at the core of the matter, and whereby the text often betrays itself, as a too ardent supporter of British (not French or Belgian) imperialism. But there is an additional problem, as if Conrad may have had second thoughts. Note that in *Heart of Darkness*, what the British term "inverted commas" strategically placed throughout the account lend not merely the idea of a second-hand notion to what is being stated, but also help to subvert (invert) the truth of the page, by reminding the *reader* that this is something *narrated, recounted, spoken, not written*, perhaps a sailor's yarn, possibly not even true. And the visual effect of Marlow's inverted commas is to act like an anchor, securely placing the narrative in Marlow's telling, not the author's veracity.

Kurtz, far from being the embodiment of a lusty colonialist, seems to be far less. He is, most assuredly, someone who had gazed out at the wilderness, as the text reminds us in almost biblical phraseology, and saw "The horror! The horror!" His famous last words that so deeply disturbed T. S. Eliot, Chinua Achebe, and a host of other writers, have seemed to me very indicative, under the circumstances, of a man's final understanding that there was no glory in death in the service of king and country. Perhaps Kurtz's attempt at becoming God could best be understood as a European wish for self-deification, in keeping with Columbus, Vespucci, Hernando Cortés, Francisco Pizarro, and James Cook, as well as the archetypal Prospero and Crusoe. Or perhaps we could look at all these would-be gods as still other examples of ways in which these unfamiliar spaces could not be negotiated by European males. If so, Kurtz takes a rightful place with every would-be conqueror, every adventurer, who attempted to see how best he could be accepted into the new environment. Being a god was a very good way of negotiating acceptance and acceptability, but it does not happen here. Kurtz is a little frightened human.

PLAYING AT RACE AND CLASS AT HOME: MASSA AND MAID

Class, race, and gender roles were clearly dictated in Victorian Britain, separating "ladies" from working-class women, whites from nonwhites, "gentlemen" from laboring men, and those with few pretensions to humanity (the Celts, Irish, Welsh, Blacks, Hottentots and a host of "others") from English males. Race affected the condition of humans, although gender and class often intruded into and invaded racial categories. The extent to which race impinged on class and gender, and how more often than not it could be utilized in verbal gamesmanship is particularly evident in the instance of Hannah Cullwick and Arthur Joseph Munby.

In real life, Arthur Joseph Munby (1828–1910),[13] poet, lawyer, and diarist, had also attempted to negotiate two worlds—in his instance that of the Victorian gentleman and man of letters, and that of the the working-class husband totally intoxicated with the smell and sweat of working-class life. Much of his verse, and particularly his romance *Susan* (1893), stressed his preoccupation with straddling the class barrier, which he translated into a trope of race and gender. Munby had found his ideal in Hannah Cullwick (1833–1909), having met her in 1854 and secretly married her some nineteen years later. Munby kept a meticulous diary of his experiences with her, their playacting, since few knew that their relationship was anything other than gentleman and "maid of all work." In Derek Huson's *Munby: Man of Two Worlds* (1972), what is stressed is the uneasy way in which Munby sought to tread a thin line between the two social extremes, and how, in effect, his very caginess demonstrated his failure.

Munby tells us something important though about the threshold, namely that the point about the early conquistadors and Kurtz is very valid—a European male could become a cultural doppelgänger, but only on his own terms. This means that the world at large had, of necessity, to be accommodated to his Whiteness, his whimsies. Therefore, even at home, at the center, where the boundary was social, not racial, the terms seemed to have been the same. Munby played out a colonial fancy complete with "slave" and master, dark bodies in subjection, and Munby as supreme lord and master. He too was a compulsive writer, so he penned it all, and had his serf do the same. The polarization was scripted: He as man, master, White, demanding; she was the obliging opposite. His response to first contact is patronizing and remotely curious, like the gaze of the colonizer on the "native." Munby sees Cullwick as: "A robust hardworking lass, with the marks of labour and servitude upon her everywhere: yet endowed with a grace and beauty, an obvious intelligence, that would have become a lady of the highest."[14]

Cullwick, the potential lady-in-making, agreed to be his pretend-maid, and even wore a slave band, sported a blackened face, and called him "Massa" to indicate her lowly status, as she saw it. Although she violently refused to remove her symbol of servitude, even on his direct orders and threat of dismissal, there seems little to suggest that Munby would have wished for a relationship that did not permit him more than this awesome degree of superiority. From her point of view, Hannah transcended race, class, and gender constructs by role-playing and cross-dressing. The role-playing would last their entire lives.

Munby was not admitted to the Bar to practice Law until 1855. Law, however, was not of great interest to him; instead, he taught Latin for most of his life at the Working Men's College, and later at the Working Women's College. He was on friendly terms with (among others) John Ruskin, Dante Gabriel Rossetti, and Robert Browning—sometimes leaving poor Cullwick outside while he visited. Additionally, for good measure he did court at least two members of his middle-class friends, but nothing came of it.

Munby, in his work and life, attempted to bestraddle the world. But he was no colossus; instead, he was a rather mild-mannered Victorian pervert who, I suspect, found greater degrees of fortitude and fortification by moving outside his social circle. He had "gone native" (like Kurtz), clearly recognizing in his surreptitious meetings with pit lasses and female chimney sweeps the extent to which the lower classes in Victorian Britain were much like the colonized—outside his reach, yet within his desire. They could even be introduced into the palace, as indeed even Queen Victoria had done with two Indians from the subcontinent.[15] And, in this way at least, not only had they altered themselves, but also the palace itself must have been altered. Munby's complete fascination with working-class women changed him from being a mere peeping Tom, at first with a sketchbook and later with a camera, into an active participant.

In his relationship with Cullwick, Munby mirrors, in all instances, one between a White master and a Black servant. It drives home the point that is made time and time again in the class-conscious literature of Victorian England, that more often than not working-class people were not just treated as, but were often seen as, the equivalent and mirror-images of inferior colonial people. In a way, then, the "diary" that Cullwick was ordered to keep, and which she faithfully maintained until her "emancipation" from Munby by marriage, reads like a slave narrative. There are all the elements—solecisms, misspellings, the constant soulful urge to change the condition of servitude, accompanied by the equally paradoxical notion that Massa was special and godlike.

Cullwick does free herself when she retires by moving into a cottage on her own. She died on July 9, 1909, in Shifnal at the age of seventy-six. Munby died a year later at Wheeler's Farm on January 29, 1910. The reading of his will made headlines at the time, since he was at last able to lamely confess to an everlasting love for her, and to leave her a small annuity—a trifle too late. Theirs is no romantic love story, but a typical instance of "colonial desire," whereby lust and disgust are intermingled in a relationship that could never be made whole. In this instance they were married, but I would be hardpressed to say that even the most careful reading of their diaries reveals even a smatter of sexual delight.

One can easily translate some of Cullwick's sentiments. Take, for instance, her refrain that she would at all times prefer to be a nobody to a "gentleman" than to be the love of any mere working-class man. This is echoed in response, if not in words, in the actions of female slave narrators who quite clearly saw the contradictions around them. They may have wanted the situation to be different, but could not have willed it into being. Consider also Cullwick's humility, which we often mistake for her accommodation of Munby's perversities. But the requirement does not exist that she has to be so good at fawning, at bowing and scraping to Massa, since more often than not, she anticipates his obsessions. Quite independently, for instance, one day she surprised a missionary newly back from India with the request to wash his feet. And she writes quite blithely of carrying out Munby's peculiar requests.

These apparent assertions of humility are accompanied by outbursts of anger, so that she and Munby do not just live one pleasant life of unending repose, but often engage in serious bouts of anger, the personal equivalent of a slave revolt. Eventually, her break with him, especially after their marriage, is a true declaration of her independence.

She resumed working as a maid, until it was time for her to retire. And she continued to live on her own. Reasons could be given for this that differ from mine—the most obvious being that Munby was afraid of the censure of his professional friends. However, it is just as likely that Cullwick, strongwilled as ever, had decided that she would prefer to live alone, apart from Munby, and not have to bother herself with the rules and regulations that came with the previous bondage.

NÉGRITUDE AND ANGRY YOUNG MEN

Perhaps this is why we need to acknowledge the similarity of two parallel situations, at home and abroad, although as far as I know they have not been comparatively studied. Colonialism was the impetus for the new articulation of the Black writers of the *négritude* movement, and, two decades later, European classism was the drive for the new formulation by working-class writers of the so-called "kitchen-sink" school of drama. In the 1930s, *négritude* writers like Léopold Sédar Senghor of Senegal, Léon Damas of French Guiana, and Aimé Césaire of Martinique (who gave the movement its name) spoke out against the injustices of a system that would deny them their rights. In the 1950s, British writers like Kingsley Amis in *Lucky Jim* (1953)[16] and John Osborne in *Look Back in Anger* (performed 1956)[17] did exactly the same. Both were reacting against an all-embracing, suffocative culture that sought to define them in ways that seemed different from their originary predispositioning. They were not just colonial natives nor merely working-class denizens. Perhaps the point had come when some subalterns at home and abroad felt the need for self-articulation.

The angry young men from home and overseas had more in common than seems at first likely—and I wish to go beyond the denunciations that they levelled at the system that had seemingly boxed them in. Like Senghor, Damas, and Césaire, Amis received public accolades from the very system he sought to villify. All of them had learned to speak in the trusted measures of their master's voice. When Senghor was a young man in Paris, as Damas told me, he was a very African young man, and I have suggested elsewhere that his contact with overseas Africans awakened impulses in him about an Africa of the mind that he had never before entertained. When Amis was young, and a lecturer at Swansea, before his success, he had still not acquired the hallmark accent of British nobility that later became his trademark, like Senghor's French that made him an official watchdog of the French language.

When I met Senghor, Damas, and Césaire later in life, I did not encounter fierce revolutionaries.[18] What they mostly shared in common is that they had all spoken against a system into which they craved acceptability, and into which they were eventually welcomed. Like Amis and Osborne, the *négritude* writers were the least suspect in the system, since they were products of its own backdoor educational process (the space where class and colony meet) and would later be rewarded not for compliance, but for their abilities to fit in so well, while denouncing the system. Then later occurred the irony of ironies: as an established figure Amis taught for years at Swansea and Oxford, and Senghor became a member of the august body of the Academie Française, where he continues to help keep at bay any and all marginal influences from corrupting the sacred French tongue.

If my tone seems a trifle acerbic, I intend these as *ad hominem* arguments. I wish to illustrate as dramatically as possible that nowadays when we glibly speak of "hybridity," in whatever context, colonial or domestic, race or class, we have to be sure that we note that it is very often accompanied with more than a small degree of the painful surrender of a former (Black/Indian) working-class "other" to a larger, more powerful, European capital(ized) "Self." The smaller other, at home in the provinces, or abroad in the colony, did not possess the degree of sameness—across race and class—to make dialogue mutually comprehensible. If a real discourse were to take place, there must surely be a level of mutual comprehensibility, whether for purposes of consensus or dissensus. The much berated middle class must read Amis, attend Osborne's plays, and recognize in Césaire (as André Breton did) good fodder for a Surrealist manifesto, providing the society's consonance to even its voices of dissonance.[19]

Interestingly, what has occurred is that issues of gender, class, and race do not and did not interact at a horizontal level. There was never a recognition, in he manner of Marx, that there was a greater, more monstrous bugbear out there. Instead, at the vertical level, within the same established rigidities of the society's proclamations, issues of gender, class and race were absorbed. "Black" *négritude* in the 1930s and "White" anger in the 1950s were fused, not with each other, but within a larger societal concern. Thus it posed no threat to the hegemonic White, male, heterosexual order.

OTHER/ODDER/OUTER/OUTERMOST

For the marginalized text to become acceptable, it must therefore bear some kind of recognizable imaging that European hierarchical control might find at first threatening, but is also easily able to absorb at a later time. Thus, the nature of the text as a mongrel creature assumes a posture that, in a crude way, harks back to the self-glorification of Columbus and those that followed him. There could be no truck with Carib man-eating cannibals—they were too alien as both Columbus and Vespucci averred, even if they failed to recognize the phantoms if not the substance of their own post-Medieval selves. But the Arawaks were not that odder; they could speak and gesture, offer to trade, were even supposedly willing to be kidnapped and taken back to Europe, as Africans had first been, and later people from the South Pacific would be.

Thus, there occurs again and again degrees of increasing marginalization, whereby we note a pattern of recidivism that seeks to distinguish between one type of contempt and still another, degrees that make the signifiers shift and float endlessly toward some most distant and horrific spectacle—other/odder/outer/outermost. The furthest removed is the last to be conscripted into the European theater of observation (although Gayatri Chakravorty Spivak's latest Native Informant would disagree); I would suspect that this is the real *sub-altern,* the one beneath every other alterity.

"The Wild Man from Borneo" (neither wild nor from Borneo) could be easily fitted into P. T. Barnum's circus, because he represented an extreme that made the norm seem more real and acceptable, even bearable.[20] Equally, the art of the Noble Savage could be admitted to Europe's galleries, when they first made their way via painters like Pablo Picasso and Henri Matisse. And the Wild Man's art could also find a place at the various fairs and expositions that rounded out the nineteenth century, and sounded in the twentieth. The Wild Man and his art, his music, dance, and sex, indeed every projection of him, could be seen by the less sophisticated as deviations away from European normalcy, and by the more sophisticated as proof positive that here was the Missing Link that could bolster clearly understood notions about a rather pernicious branch of Nietzscheanism, plus a more perverted conceptualization of popular Darwinism.

COLONIZER AS GOD

Any such discussion leads us back to the god-concept—the way in which class on the homefront and skin pigmentation in the colonial backyard reestablished that most sacred of archetypes—the making of God. God was now exported; he (and it was he, although his wife could lay some petty claims to godlike status [21]) would now be addressed in the third person, given the power of life and death over unfortunate "natives," but above all elevated to the status of deity by those he served, among whom he walked. Therefore, the role of godhead was the only term on which *the colonizer abroad* and *aristocrat at home* were prepared to negotiate their participatory space. This could not have been done without the active consent, zeal, encouragement, and eager support of the underlings.

On the other hand, I am also conscious that the place beyond provided a space for critical self-appraisal. There in the desert and jungle, rigid

European guidelines did not seem to matter and the taboos of sex and speech wore down. Mick Gidley writes in his essay on Conrad:

The imaginative function of the African landscape and its inhabitants as exotic Other (thoroughly exploited in the voluminous travel literature of the period) was twofold. On the one hand it represented an impulse of flight from aspects of the dominant European bourgeois culture could be criticised. On the other hand, confronting the strange and the unfamiliar held out the promise of self-discovery.[22]

Gidley concludes that through the savage Other abroad, the West could lay claim to the freedom it desired in the One at home.

Two fairly contemporary works continue to further illustrate the way in which Europeans must need become gods if they were to negotiate spaces for themselves in unfamiliar terrains. In a way, it is a natural and almost *de rigeur* transformation from class to caste, as we observed with Munby. Let us briefly look at E. M. Forster's *A Passage to India* (1924)[23] and Joyce Cary's *Mr. Johnson* (1939).[24] Forster had worked in India and Cary in Nigeria. What they attempt to do is a little different from Conrad; they try to portray the "native." But Forster's Aziz, supposedly a medical doctor with a knowledge of several Indian languages and the scion of early Moghuls who had invaded the Indian state, is a servile man, seemingly intent only on pleasing Fielding, a local schoolmaster from England. The less Westernized Mr. Johnson is equally as incredulous; the pidgin English in which he banters with the district officer, Mr. Rudbeck, should not let us forget that he spoke not only his own language (probably Igbo), but also that, as Rudbeck's pointsman, he would have been also very familiar with Hausa, the language of Northern Nigeria. So why then do we remember Aziz and Mr. Johnson mainly as victims?

The reason lies in the lens through which we view them; Forster/ Fielding and Cary/Rudbeck are godlike figures, and receive the adulation that seems to be properly theirs. It is Fielding's thoughts at the end of the novel that sum up Aziz's predicament as a marginalized man. As he and Aziz gallop together, in a scene that evokes strong homoerotic overtones, it is Fielding's final judgment that is conclusive, arguing that the time is not yet right for a friendship between the two men. Similarly, Mr. Johson's downfall and death occur because he has this apelike faith in Rudbeck's goodness. He willingly dies so that Rudbeck can exercise his bureaucratic responsibilities.

Yet, we are bound to say that, even as they go through their daily drills, even as they intentionally wear the slave band of Hannah Cull-wick, the major purpose of Aziz and Mr. Johnson is to demonstrate how God, the Englishman, functions in the world at large. It comes as no surprise, therefore, that despite the fact that no one has ever accused Hinduism of suffering from a paucity of gods, Indians zealously proclaim the deceased Englishwoman Mrs. Moore as a new and important god in their canon.

If therefore we say, as Homi Bhabha does, that colonial peoples negotiated hybridities, then we must add that it was not done on their own terms, as it best suited them. And we have also seen how the contemporary god-figure harks back to the first encounters, much as if European males were in fact saying that this was the only way they could interact, and the only terms that they were prepared to interact with their colonial underlings. "Make-me-a-God-and-we'll-talk" is at the heart of the encounters between the powerful and the powerless, whether they were both located in the same metropolitan place, and spoke to each other across social and gender boundaries, or whether they were positioned in a foreign place, and addressed each other over an ethnic chasm. Race and class confrontation and conquest were initiated on these terms, and still retain the same familiar echoes today.

NOTES

1. Homi K. Bhabha, *The Location of Culture* (London and New York: Routledge, 1994), 3–4, 7, 9, 15, 17, 24–25, 127, 174, 217, 219, 227, 230.

2. Anne McClintock, *Imperial Leather: Race, Gender and Sexuality in the Colonial Context* (London and New York: Routledge, 1995), 24–25.

3. For more on the Ocean Sea and the Pillars of Hercules, indeed the general circumscription and containment of Europe, see my discussion in O. R. Dathorne, *Imagining the World: Mythical Belief Versus Reality in Global Encounters* (Westport, CT, and London: Bergin & Garvey, 1994), 27–29.

4. For discussion of some of this as medieval myths that survived into the Age of Exploration, see my discussion of Amazon, Antilla, Cibola, El Dorado, Hy Brasil, Island of Seven Cities, Quivira, St. Brendan's Island, Three Indias, and Prester John, among others, in my previously cited, *Imagining the World*, passim.

5. Palmira Brummett, "The Myth of Shah Ismail Safavi: Political Rhetoric and 'Divine' Kingship," in *Medieval Christian Perceptions of Islam: A Book of Essays*, ed. John Victor Tolan (New York: Garland, 1996), 331–32. Also see details of Ismail in *The Cambridge History of Iran* ed. Peter Jackson and Laurence Lockhart, (Cambridge: Cambridge UP, 1991), 6: 249–340.

6. Wilson Harris, "History, Fable and Myth in the Caribbean and Guianas," *Caribbean Quarterly* 16 (June 1970), 6.

7. Pocahontas suffers from being a fairy-tale princess, as seen in the Disney cartoon, and traitor in the manner of Doña Marina/Malinche, the companion/ translator/childbearer of Hernando Cortés. Regarding Doña Marina/Malinche, her Hispanicized name suggests almost a near link with the Virgin; the other name, indigenous, almost a nickname, hints at a dangerous familiarity, with the possible ramifications of "whore." In any event her two names indicate that there is still dispute about her presence and her role. See Sandra Messinger Cypess, *La Malinche in Mexican Literature: From History to Myth* (Austin: U of Texas P, 1991), and Donna J. Kessler, *The Making of Sacagawea: A Euro-American Legend*

(Tuscaloosa, AL: U of Alabama P, 1996). Both writers see large degrees of insubstantiality in La Malinche and Sacagawea, in that they are both European constructs, having little to do with a living reality. I see the same in Pocahontas. In the Disney cartoon, she has a teenage romance with John Smith; in reality, she was a child when she met Smith. And the issue of color, which could have been boldly tackled, is saved from causing offense by having Pocahontas *painted* brown, and John Smith *painted* white, so that their color does not represent race, but are only neat tinctures and veneers that blend with their smiles and the scenery.

8. Concerning Soto, see *The De Soto Chronicles: The Expedition of Hernando de Soto to North America in 1539–1543*, 2 vols, ed. Lawrence A. Clayton, Vernon James Knight Jr., and Edward C. Moore (Tuscaloosa, AL: U of Alabama P, 1993).

9. Concerning Cabeza de Vaca, see a recent translation, Alvar Núñez Cabeza de Vaca, *Castaways,1528–1536*, ed. Enrique Pupo-Walker, trans. Frances M. López-Morillas (Berkeley: U of California P, 1993).

10. Edward Said treats the subject of the interaction between margin and center, periphery and metropolis, and colonial hinterland and capital in *Culture and Imperialism* (New York: Vintage, 1994). See consideration of *Great Expectations* on xiv–xvi, 62–63. Said also identifies Sir Thomas Bertram's West Indian possessions in Jane Austen's *Mansfield Park;* Bertha Mason in *Jane Eyre;* characters in William Thackeray, Charles Kingsley, Benjamin Disraeli, and George Eliot, as well as the usual imperialist suspects, Rudyard Kipling, Joseph Conrad, H. Rider Haggard, Joyce Cary, E. M. Forster, and T. E. Lawrence (see pp. 62–63). I am not quite certain how much the mere mention of place can supposedly demonstrate the impact of colonialism.

11. George Robertson, Melinda Mash et al., eds., *Travellers' Tales: Narratives of Home and Displacement* (New York: Routledge, 1994), 23.

12. See Chinua Achebe's famous essay, "An Image of Africa: Racism in Conrad's *Heart of Darkness*," in *Hopes and Impediments: Selected Essays* (New York: Doubleday, 1988), 1–20.

13. Both the diaries of Arthur J. Munby and Hannah Cullwick have been published in edited form. See Derek Hudson, ed., *Munby, Man of Two Worlds: The Life and Diaries of Arthur J. Munby, 1812–1910*(Cambridge: Gambit, 1974); and Liz Stanley, ed., *The Diaries of Hannah Cullwick: Victorian Maidservan*t (New Brunswick, NJ: Rutgers UP, 1984).

14. Hudson, *Munby*, 15.

15. Queen Victoria became quite fascinated with the idea of her being "Empress" of India, and since she traveled little, she did the next best thing by importing from India Indians who were subsequently employed in the Royal Household. Abdul Karim, aged twenty-four, seemed to be particularly endearing to her at her rather advanced age of seventy. He introduced her to curry and to daily lessons in Hindi—strange, considering that he was Muslim, and probably spoke Urdu much better. She confided in him about matters of state, about which "Munshi" or "Teacher," as she called him, could have known very little. She heaped him with honors, as well of gifts of land and houses, much to the consternation of her domestic entourage. See Sushila Anand, *Indian Sahib: Queen Victoria's Dear Abdul* (London: Duckworth, 1996). See the account about Abdul Karim and other Indian servants given by Sir James Reid, a rather staid personal physician to the queen in Michaela Reid, *Ask Sir James* [1987] (London: Eland, 1996), 102, 118, 128–133, 143–156. Sir James's biographer mentions the closeness

between Queen Victoria and Abdul Karim, and the latter's unpleasantness and quarrelsomeness. To me, as an uncaring and casual observer a century later, it merely seems surprising that the margin had moved that close to the center of centers!

16. Kingsley Amis, *Lucky Jim* (New York: Viking, 1953). I am aware that critics have been lambasted for desperately attempting to fit Amis into any school—"anger" or "Beat." The argument goes that this has detracted from serious consideration of his work. Amis's dates are 1922–1995.

17. John Osborne, *Look Back in Anger* [performed London 1956] (New York: Criterion, 1957). The film version from Warner Brothers appeared in 1959, starring Richard Burton, Mary Ure, and Claire Bloom. Osborne's dates are 1929–1995. Of course, the very approach I am using has been heavily criticized as a biographical fallacy that has prevented the more detailed evaluation of Osborne's plays. For an almost contemporary book that includes work by Osborne and Amis and other contemporaries, see Michael Skovmand and Steffen Skovmand, eds., *The Angry Young Men: Osborne, Sillitoe, Wain, Braine, Amis* (Copenhagen: Akademisk Forlag, 1975).

18. I interviewed Léon Damas (1912–1978) and published this in the first issue of the *Journal of Caribbean Studies*, 1.1 (Winter 1980), 63–73.

19. André Breton saw Césaire's poetry as surrealist verse, and wrote the introduction for the 1944 publication that came out with Présence Africaine. Therefore, the introduction fit it in neatly with the European avant-garde, although the publisher pinpointed its very relevant significance as a *négritude* text. See Gregson Davis, *Aimé Césaire* (Cambridge: Cambridge UP, 1997). Consult Jody Blake, *Le Tumulte Noir: Modernist Art and Popular Entertainment in Jazz-Age Paris, 1900–1930* (University Park, PA: Pennsylvania State UP, 1999), who argues that this early part of the century was a period of "Primitivism" when Europeans sought out what they wanted from the discourses of the Other. In this connection Jody Blake contends that there was no distinction in the European mind between African sculpture and African American music and dance—they were all part of a savage fetish called "L'Art nègre." Also see Sieglinde Lenke, *Primitivist Modernism: Black Culture and the Origin of Transatlantic Modernism* (Oxford: Oxford UP, 1998).

20. Concerning Barnum, see two of his self-promoting biographies: P. T. Barnum, *Struggles and Triumphs: Or, Forty Years' Recollections of P. T. Barnum Written by Himself* [1869] (New York: Arno, 1970); and P. T. Barnum, *Struggles and Triumphs: Or, Sixty Years' Recollections of P. T. Barnum, Including His Golden Rules for Money-Making* (Buffalo: Courier, 1889). See also Bluford Adams, " 'A Stupendous Mirror of Departed Empires': The Barnum Hippodrome and Circuses, 1874–1891," *American Literary History*, 8:1 (Spring 1996), 34–56. Also, I recommend very highly the three part series *P. T. Barnum: Prince of Showmen*, broadcast in 1995 by The Discovery Channel, as well as another documentary of more than tangential interest, *Freak Shows*, broadcast by the The Learning Channel in 1996. The former documentary was supported by an accompanying book by Philip B. Kunhardt Jr., Philip B. Kunhardt III, and Peter W. Kunhardt, *Barnum: Prince of Showmen* (New York: Random, 1995).

21. This recurrent theme of White women is being discussed more and more by several (White) male writers who have carved a niche for themselves in the burgeoning study of "whiteness." See for instance, Theodore W. Allen, *The Invention of the White Race: The Origin of Racial Oppression in Anglo-America*, 2

vols. (London and New York: Verso, 1997). Note the instance of Elizabeth Key, which quite early established a *de facto* if not *de iure* difference between a White female free person and others (1:194–99); Richard Dyer, *White* (London: Routledge, 1997), thoroughly discusses the issues of whiteness and womanhood. See especially 70–81, 122–42, 222–23; and David R. Roediger, *The Wages of Whiteness: Race and the Making of the American Working Class* (London and New York: Verso, 1991), 69–71.

22. Mick Gidley, ed., *Representing Others: White Views of Indigenous Peoples* (Exeter: U of Exeter P, 1992), 49.

23. E. M. Forster, *A Passage to India* [1924] (San Diego: Harcourt Brace Jovanovich, 1952). The book is dedicated to Syed Ross Masood and "to the seventeen years of our friendship." As the horses turn away from each other, perhaps they are suggesting for Fielding/Aziz as well as Forster/Masood that not merely the ethnic association would provide a problem, but the homoerotic link as well. Until late into the modern period, homosexuality carried a gaol sentence in Britain. Also see the David Lean film with Alec Guinness, Peggy Ashcroft, and Victor Bannerjee. Note that the film version deals more with race and sex than with homosexuality, although there are subtle homosexual references in the film. Indeed, the publication of *Maurice* was withheld until 1971, a year after Forster's death.

24. Joyce Cary, *Mister Johnson* [1935] (New York: New Directions, 1989). The film version settles for presenting Mr. Johnson as an ardent and servile devotee of Empire, dealing very superficially with his own (Igbo?) world, even in the limited manner that Cary had attempted in the novel. Indeed, the film world seems stuck between the majesty of Lex Barker or Cornel Wilde striding across African savannahs, or the belittling spectacle of crouching, dancing, barbaric natives. Recent attempts have not improved the situation, as witness *A Good Man in Africa* or Eddie Murphy's *Coming to America*. Despite the impoverished squalor and superstition of the former and the sumptuous overdone simplicity of the latter, they both point to the same thing—Africans are really damn funny!

Afterword

> Given the mixed history of the word *primitive*, the urge to jettison it is understandable. . . . [Various Western peoples] take the West as norm and define the rest as inferior, different, deviant, subordinate, and subordinatable. (Marianna Torgovnick, *Gone Primitive: Savage Intellect, Modern Lives* [1990], 21)

The problem with attempting any kind of conclusion after such a study is that one cannot really be absolutely conclusive. At this stage, I wish to review what we discussed and then, hopefully, try to assert the directions in which I perceive the movement of ideas and beliefs. For instance, when we discussed orality we anticipated a later development in this work in which I contend that the non-West makes constant use of "spoken images" as opposed to written words. In this way, Otherness can be easily defined as only a half sign, since the signifier-word often takes the place of something that is either never written, or at least never regarded as significant by the West. The modern writers who mine the linguistic trough, seeking to find the equivalents to their local experiences, must make do with whatever comes to hand. Therefore, what they use may often not be very relevant to the experiences they describe or the cultures they relate.

We noted the introduction of "race" from the advent of the first European explorers to the New World, but, interestingly, before Columbus and before the Vikings, for some strange reason Europe at least was still preoccupied with skin coloration and its possible meaning. Take the instance of the Ethiopian boy who appears as a figure of evil in the travels of St. Brendan, and before that, following Pliny and Alexander, the account of Black people described in *"Wonders of the East"* as monstrous and evil.[1]

The point I wish to stress is that long before the physical advent of

Blacks in Europe, particularly in England, they feature over and over again in literature as marginalized Others. When Blacks did arrive, even in small numbers, not only were they drawn by renowned artists such as Albrecht Dürer, but they were even beatified by the Roman Catholic Church—the examples of St. Maurice and the plethora of Black Virgins testify to this.[2] But rarely do we note the presence of real Blacks in the continued interest in race, and in the presence of stereotypical Blackamoors and Negroes on the Elizabethan and Jacobean stage.

I cannot concur with those who argue that English racism does not begin until the eighteenth century. Instead, I agree with Kim F. Hall and her denunciation of Kwame Anthony Appiah, when she argues that she would have expected him to take a more objective view of race as it developed among the English.[3] Certainly one of the most obvious points is that even as English developed as a language, race would sneak into the evolution of the signifiers, so that words like "darkness," "blackness," and so on became heavily charged with negative connotations.

There is an instance of how clumsily this operates. In the plays of John Marston, Richard Broome, and John Webster, we often see the Black person playing the part of the fool. Anthony Gerard Barthelemy demonstrates in *Black Face, Maligned Race*, that any dark-skinned person could be essentialized into a familiar stage Black, and adds that

the words *Turk, Saracen, Oriental*, and *Indian*, [like] *Moor* [are] difficult to define precisely. In the fifteenth, sixteenth, and seventeenth centuries, the words meant different things to different people. All these words, however, shared a common connotation: alien, or foreigner. Because these words were used so imprecisely— frequently they were used simply to identify any non-Christian—they came to denote a rather general category of alien.[4]

This is exactly how the negative elements surrounding Blackness were transferred to Native Americans, to Indians, to South Pacific islanders, and others.

Therefore, my attempt at looking at Native American narration is a way of reconstructing another alien Other in the New World. Perhaps the best example of this (mis)construction should be noted in Aphra Behn's *Oroonoko*, where the English invent a mythology and then extend it to people about whom they knew very little.[5] Oroonoko is both the Native American name of a river (Orinoco) and a supposed prince from Africa. The confusion is further compounded when Imoinda mysteriously becomes white in subsequent editions of the plays based on the novel.[6] Here we note ethnic and racial confusion that would continue to add to the misunderstanding of race in the world.

This is why Linnaeus and his "Apostles" felt perfectly justified in Latinizing every flora and fauna within sight, and why he also approved of the importation of European mythologies into his model. Race, therefore, now appears as *objective Science*, required by every "educated" person. Latin was neutral because none of the colonial powers spoke it, and those of the Enlightenment could easily romanticize the language as the source of all thought.

My problem is that, when I view Africa or its diaspora, an enormous problem occurs. In a way, it is a trifle complimentary to agree with Georg Hegel, Karl Marx or Sigmund Freud that not only did Africa lack history, but it seemed to exist out of time. For me this merely means that we are returning over and over again to a specific meaning of racing Blackness, as savage, uncivilized, and monstrous.

However, to seek to explore the areas where Gilles Deleuze and Félix Guattari have led us means that we need to approve of the role of the "nomad" who is "deterritorializing" the old cultural space in order to bring about much-needed change. In a way, we can contend that so-called primitivism from the early part of the twentieth century was a means by which the West and the Rest enter into an alliance that constitutes the Bhabhaesque "Third Space." But primitivism is still distorted, certainly not on equal terms with what European artists saw as delightful and Romantic exoticism.

I disapprove of the word "primitivism," since it broke free from its Latin roots, of "first," "original," perhaps even "innocent," and began to mean "simplistic," "untutored," and even a trifle "barbaric." But if we are truly to understand the origins and significance of the high modern White interest in a Black self, whether dubbed the Harlem Renaissance, *négritude,* or *negrismo,* we must explore its origins in the rather murky waters of that modern European movement dubbed "primitivism."

If truth be told, primitivism actually can be traced not to Africa or the Black United States, but to a mythical Judeo-Christian past in the Garden of Eden, or to one that is Greek European where the rites of Minos in Crete, never very clearly understood, suggested sacrifice, bloodletting, and pre-Christian initiation rites. It became most convenient to latch primitivism on to *la race nègre* since from the beginning of the twentieth century an African American and African influence began to assert itself particularly in Paris.[7] Most likely, the interest had come about in response to the long nineteenth century with its feverish speculations concerning Black people and their simian equivalences.

As Europeans saw it, there was no distinction between Black America and Africa regarding Blackness, the jungle, savagery, and brutality. Africa itself came to Europe at first indirectly, through Fang sculptures from Africa, and through the folklore collections of Leo Frobenius. In this way the European artists and artistes were free to make whatever they wanted of primitivism.

With the African American presence, there was some difference in that Black people from the United States represented themselves. Blacks had not been unknown in Europe before, and as late as the nineteenth century, "push" factors of U.S. slavery and discrimination drove many African Americans to visit England on their own. Witness William Wells Brown who spent some time in Europe and observed the unfortunate plight of other Blacks.[8]

From the beginning of the twentieth century, African Americans were not merely tourists, but were dancers, drummers, and singers who introduced the blackbottom dance and the Charleston to eager Europeans. Later would come jazz through the persons of James Reese Europe, who entertained audiences in Germany, Britain, France, and Belgium, and Sydney Bechet, who was better known in Paris.

Europeans thought this much—*nègre* was *nègre*. They made no distinctions between the rhythms of what they fondly referred to as the "tam-tam" and the dancing routine of a comparatively Westernized African American group such as "les petits Walkers." Furthermore, as various French galleries exhibited African sculpture, and full houses accommodated musicals such as *Blackbirds* and *La Revue nègre*, Black primitivism was expressing itself more and more independently, and divorcing itself still more from the general "oriental" exoticism of Sergei Diaghilev and "Les Ballets Russes."

Before Clive Bell, English art-critic and Virginia Woolf's one time brother-in law, would issue his almost martial "Call to Order" against the excessive influence of *l'art nègre*, so-called African primitivism had made a definite dent in the fabric of French culture. As is well known, Picasso and Matisse experimented with the forms of what little sculpture they could observe; Igor Stravinsky in "Rite of Spring" (1913) introduced jazz elements into what was supposedly classical European musical composition for ballet; and each new French government-sponsored exposition from 1889 onwards stressed otherness, often with an emphasis on the abnormality of the non-Western people.

In addition to its presence in France, we note African primitivism in, of all places, the works of Euro Americans. Four instances stand out: First, there is Vachel Lindsay's "Congo" with its drum-like rhythm, and its association of common rituals shared by both African Americans and Africans—neither of whom Lindsday knew well.[9] Second, there is Gertrude Stein's attempt at constructing a Black character in *Three Lives*—actually her character is biracial.[10] Third, there is Brutus Jones in Eugene O'Neill's "The Emperor Jones," a brutish man who has no conscience (happily played by Paul Robeson), and is content with exploiting fellow Black people.[11] And finally, there is the novel that launches the Negro Movement (what later would be called the Harlem Renaissance), *Nigger Heaven* by Carl Van Vechten.[12] In other words, we have noted that the influences from Africa and the Black United States are blended and conflated both in Europe and the United States. Yet intriguingly what emerges from this will be a model that Black writers will copy over and over again. Europe had created its Other, and the Other had not revolted at the apparition but quietly acquiesced at the horror.

Ironically, therefore, when the Other sees the self created by the West, (s)he does not merely recoil. Instead the Lacanian mirror-image confirms a certain authenticity, albeit counterfeit, that supposedly represents the colonial object in whom unwanted images of the One are still permanently situated. Were this not so, we could hardly have had the uproarious laughter that V. S. Naipaul directed at himself and his society from his earliest books—the silly, misfit of a rogue noted in *The Mystic Masseur,* and the many comical snapshots of streetlife of unreal people seen in *Miguel Street.* Add to these depictions of make-believe representations created by willing accomplices of the Negro Movement, and we note contemporary poet Countee Cullen's doubts about the sanity of a god that could construct this paradox: a human who was Black, yet a person who could still be an artist. Or see the way in which Langston Hughes and Claude McKay exult in an indecent exoticization of their own skins, their dance, their music. I want to stress that for me they are all spinoffs of primitivism.

The result from this that continued to demarcate the endless stretches of Black primitivism was to be observed both in *négritude* in French and *negrismo* in Spanish. In *négritude,* the woman exists as ideal mother, but in *negrismo* as part whore she must die as a consumptive dancer. Therefore, even as Léopold Sédar Senghor (now under heavy attack from those with newer issues, advocating Créolité) celebrated and romanticized the Black woman as life and night, wife and mother, Marcelino Arozarena from Cuba and Luis Palés Matos from Puerto Rico as well as others from various parts of the Spanish-speaking New World saw the Black man and Black woman as compulsive dancers, and the woman at least doomed to an early death. To be truthful, it was all a bit silly and simplistic.

Europe therefore bequeathed its superficial primitivism to us, and we bought it, temporarily feeling that it flattered us with the numerous stereotypes it offered. The problem was the extent to which we mimicked the single-minded concerns of the master narrative. Could we not inject a modicum of common sense into our art? Would we be always bound up within the tentacles of the romanticization of skin color? Would we remain forever doomed in this song of racial self-heraldry? Or can we break away?

NOTES

1. Paul Allen Gibb, "*Wonders of the East*: A Critical Edition and Commentary" (Ph.D. diss., Duke University, 1977).

2. See Ladislas Bugner, ed., *The Image of the Black in the Western Art*, 5 vols. to date (Cambridge, MA: Harvard UP, 1976–1989). For Black Virgins, consult Ean Begg, *The Cult of the Black Virgin* (London: Penguin, 1996).

3. Kim F. Hall, *Things of Darkness: Economies of Race and Gender in Early Modern England* (Ithaca, NY: Cornell UP, 1995), 3–4, n. 7.

4. Anthony Gerard Barthelemy, *Black Face, Maligned Race: The Representation of Blacks in English Drama from Shakespeare to Southerne* (Baton Rouge: Louisiana State UP, 1987), 6.

5. Aphra Behn, *Oroonoko* [1688], in *Oroonoko, The Rover and Other Works* (London and New York: Penguin, 1992). For the English background to this mythmaking that persists a century later, see Angus Ross, ed., *Selections from The Tatler and The Spectator* (Harmondsworth, U.K.: Penguin, 1982), 465–66.

6. Joyce Green McDonald, ed., "Introduction" to *Race, Ethnicity and Power in the Renaissance* (Cranbury, NJ: Associated U Presses, 1997), 7–16.

7. Some of the information regarding primitivism is taken from the following texts: Jody Blake, *Le Tumulte noir: Modernist Art and Popular Entertainment in Jazz-Age Paris, 1900–1930* (University Park, PA: Pennsylvania State UP, 1999); Sieglinde Lemke, *Primitivist Modernism.: Black Culture and the Origins of Transatlantic Modernism* (Oxford: Oxford UP, 1998); and T. Denean Sharpley-Whiting, *Sexualized Savages, Primal Fears, and Primitive Narratives in French* (Durham, NC: Duke UP, 1999).

8. William Wells Brown, *The Travels of William Wells Brown*, ed. Paul Jefferson (Princeton, NJ: Markus Wiener, 1991).

9. Vachel Lindsay, *The Congo and Other Poems* (New York: Macmillan, 1914).

10. Gertrude Stein, *Three Lives* [1909] (New York: Vintage, 1936). See the story entitled "Melanchta," 86–236.

11. Eugene O'Neill, "The Emperor Jones," in *Nine Plays* (New York: Random, 1932), 2–35.

12. Carl Van Vechten, *Nigger Heaven* (New York: Knopf, 1926).

Bibliography

Abarca, Meredith E., "The Ambiguity of Three Mexican Archetypes: La Malinche, La Virgen de Guadalupe, and La Llorona," in *genre* 16/1995:65–77.

Abimbola, Wande, ed. *Ifa: An Exposition of Ifa Literary Corpus*. Ibadan, Nigeria: Oxford UP, 1976.

———. *Yoruba Oral Tradition*. Ife, Nigeria: U of Ife, 1975.

Abraham, William E. "The Life and Times of Anton Wilhelm Amo, the First African (Black) Philosopher in Europe." In *African Intellectual Heritage: A Book of Sources*. Ed. Molefi Kete Asante and Abu S. Abarry. Philadelphia: Temple UP, 1996.

Abrahams, Roger. *Deep Down in the Jungle*. New York: Aldine, 1970.

Achebe, Chinua. *Hopes and Impediments: Selected Essays*. New York: Doubleday, 1988.

———. *Things Fall Apart*. London: Heinemann, 1958.

Adams, Bluford. " 'A Stupendous Mirror of Departed Empires': The Barnum Hippodrome and Circuses, 1874–1891." *American Literary History* 8.1 (Spring 1996): 34–56.

Africanus, Leo. *A Geographical Historie of Africa*. 1600. Ed. John Pory. New York: De Capo, 1969.

Allen, Theodore W. *The Invention of the White Race: The Origin of Racial Oppression in Anglo-America*. 2 vols. London and New York: Verso, 1997.

Allsopp, Richard. *Dictionary of Caribbean English*. Oxford: Oxford UP, 1996.

Amis, Kingsley. *Lucky Jim*. New York: Viking, 1953.

Anand, Sushila. *Indian Sahib: Queen Victoria's Dear Abdul*. London: Duckworth, 1996.

Appiah, Kwame Anthony. " 'But Would That Still Be Me?': Notes on Gender, 'Race,' Ethnicity, as Sources of 'Identity.' " In *Race/Sex: Their Sameness, Difference and Interplay*. Ed. Naomi Zack. London and New York: Routledge, 1997.

———. *In My Father's House: Africa in the Philosophy of Culture*. New York: Oxford UP, 1992.

Arber, Edward, ed. *The First Three English Books on America [?1511]-1555 A.D.* 1555. Trans. Richard Eden. Birmingham, U.K: n.p., 1885.

Armstrong, Samuel C. *The Indian Question*. Hampton, VA: Normal School Steam P, 1883.

Ashcroft, Bill, Gareth Griffiths, and Helen Tiffin, eds. *The Empire Writes Back: Theory and Practice in Post-Colonial Literatures*. London and New York: Routledge, 1989.

Barnum, P. T. *Struggles and Triumphs: Or, Forty Years' Recollections of P. T. Barnum Written by Himself*. 1869. New York: Arno, 1970.

————. *Struggles and Triumphs: Or, Sixty Years' Recollections of P. T. Barnum, Including His Golden Rules for Money-Making*. Buffalo: Courier, 1889.

Baron, Robert C., ed. *America: One Land, One People*. Golden, CO: Fulcrum, 1987.

Bartels, F. L. *The Roots of Ghana Methodism*. London: Cambridge UP, 1965.

Barthelemy, Anthony Gerard. *Black Face Maligned Race: The Representation of Blacks in English Drama from Shakespeare to Southerne*. Baton Rouge: Louisiana State UP, 1987.

Barthes, Roland. *The Pleasure of the Text*. 1973. New York: Hill and Wang, 1975.

————. *S/Z: An Essay*. 1970. Trans. Richard Miller. New York: Hill and Wang, 1974.

Bascom, William R. *Shango in the New World*. Austin: U of Texas, African and Afro-American Research Institute, 1972.

————. *Sixteen Cowries: Yoruba Divination from Africa to the New World*. Bloomington: Indiana UP, 1980.

Bataille, Gretchen M. and Charles L.P. Silet, *The Pretend Indians: Images of Native Americans in the Movies*. Ames, IA: Iowa State UP, 1980.

Bates, Robert H., V. Y. Mudimbe, and Jean O'Barr, eds. *Africa and the Disciplines*. Chicago: U of Chicago P, 1993.

Bedini, Silvio A., ed. *Christopher Columbus and the Age of Exploration: An Encyclopedia*. New York: De Capo, 1998.

Begg, Ean. *The Cult of the Black Virgin*. London: Penguin, 1996.

Behn, Aphra. *Oroonoko*. 1688. In *Oroonoko, The Rover and other Works*. London and New York: Penguin, 1992.

Beier, Ulli. "Naive Nigerian Art." *Black Orpheus* 19 (March 1966): 31–32, followed by eight unnumbered pages of illustrations, then p. 39.

————. "Public Opinion on Lovers." *Black Orpheus* 14 (February 1964): 4–16.

Bell, Diane. "An Accidental Australian Tourist: Or a Feminist Anthropologist at Sea and on Land." In *Implicit Understandings: Observing, Reporting, and Reflecting on the Encounters between Europeans and other Peoples in the Early Modern Era*. Ed. Stuart B. Schwartz. Cambridge: Cambridge UP, 1994, 502–55.

Bellegarde-Smith, Patrick J., ed. *Traditional Spirituality in the African Diaspora*. Lexington, KY: Association of Caribbean Studies, 1994.

Benítez-Rojo, Antonio. *The Repeating Island: The Caribbean and the Postmodern Perspective*. Durham, NC: Duke UP, 1996.

Benjamin, Walter. *Illuminations: Essays and Reflections*. 1955. Trans. Harry Zohn. New York: Schocken, 1968.

Ben-Jochannan, Yosef A. A. *Africa, Mother of Western Civilization*. 1971. Baltimore, MD: Black Classic, 1988.

————. *Black Man of the Nile and His Family*. Baltimore, MD: Alkebu-lan, 1989.

Bergon, Frank ed., *The Journals of Lewis and Clark* [1904–1905]. New York: Penguin, 1989.

Berkhofer, Robert F. Jr. *Salvation and the Savage: An Analysis of Protestant Missions and American Indian Response 1787–1862*. Lexington: U of Kentucky P, 1965.

————. *The White Man's Indian*. New York: Vintage, 1979.

Bernal, Martin. *Black Athena: The Afroasiatic Roots of Classical Civilization*. Vol. 1. "The Fabrication of Ancient Greece 1785–1985." New Brunswick, NJ: Rutgers UP, 1987.

————. *Black Athena: The Afroasiatic Roots of Classical Civilization*. Vol. 2. "The Archaeological and Documentary Evidence." New Brunswick, N.J: Rutgers UP, 1991.

————. Review of *Black Athena Revisited*. ed. Mary Lefkowitz and Guy MacLean Rogers, and *Not Out of Africa*. By Mary Lefkowitz in *London Review of Books* 18.24 (Dec. 12, 1996): 17–18.

Best, George. "A true discourse of the three voyages of discoverie, for the finding of a passage to Cathaya, by the Northwest, under the conduct of Martin Frobisher Generall; . . ." *The Principal Navigations, Voyages, Traffiques and Discoveries of the English Nation*. Ed. Richard Hakluyt. 1598. 12 vols. Glasgow: James MacLehose and Sons, 1903–1905. Vol. 7, 250–83.

Best, Steven, and Douglas Kellner. *Postmodern Theory: Critical Interrogations*. New York: Guilford, 1991.

Bewell, Alan. "On the Banks of the South Sea." In *Visions of Empire: Voyages, Botany, and Representations of Nature*. Ed. David Philip Miller and Peter Hannis Reill. Cambridge and New York: Cambridge UP, 1996. 173–93.

Bhabha, Homi K. *The Location of Culture*. London and New York: Routledge, 1994.

Bird, Elizabeth S. ed., *Dressing in Feathers: The Construction of the Indian in American Popular Culture*. Boulder, CO: Westview, 1996.

Blackburn, Julia. *Daisy Bates: A Woman's Life among the Aborigines*. New York: Pantheon, 1994.

Blake, Jody. *Le Tumulte noir: Modernist Art and Popular Entertainment in Jazz-Age Paris, 1900–1930*. University Park, PA: Pennsylvania State UP, 1999.

Blassingame, John. *Black New Orleans*. Chicago: U of Chicago P, 1973.

Blunt, Wilfrid. *The Complete Naturalist: A Life of Linnaeus*. London: Collins, 1971.

Boorstin, Daniel. *The Discoverers: A History of Man's Search to Know His World and Himself*. New York: Vintage, 1983.

Boswell, James. *The Life of Samuel Johnson*. 3 vols. London: Swan, Sonnenschein, 1988.

Bradford, Gamaliel. *Elizabethan Women*. Cambridge, MA: Riverside, 1936.

Brathwaite, Edward. *The Arrivants: A New World Trilogy*. Oxford: Oxford UP, 1978.

————. *Roots*. Havana: Casa de las Américas, 1986.

————. "Timeheri." In *Is Massa Day Dead?* ed. Orde Coombs. Garden City, NY: Anchor/Doubleday, 1974. 29–45.

Brentjes, Burchard. "Anton Wilhelm Amo, First African Philosopher in European Universities." *Current Anthropology* 16.3 (Sept. 1995): 443–44.

Brown, Dee. *The American West*. New York: Scribner's, 1994.

Brown, William Wells. *The Travels of William Wells Brown*. Ed. Paul Jefferson. Princeton, NJ:Markus Wiener, 1991.

Brummett, Palmira. "The Myth of Shah Ismail Safavi: Political Rhetoric and 'Divine' Kingship." In *Medieval Christian Perceptions of Islam: A Book of Essays*. Ed. John Victor Tolan. New York: Garland, 1996.

Buckmaster, Henrietta. *The Seminole Wars*. New York: Collier, 1966.

Bugner, Ladislas, ed. *The Image of the Black in the Western Art*. 5 vols. to date. Cambridge, MA: Harvard UP, 1976–1989.

Burg, B. R. *Sodomy and the Pirate Tradition*. New York: New York UP, 1984.

Cabeza de Vaca, Alvar Núñez. *Castaways*. 1528–1536. Ed. Enrique Pupo-Walker. Trans. Frances M. López-Morillas. Berkeley: U of California P, 1993.

Cabrera, Lydia. *El Monte*. 1954. Miami: Universal, 1975.

Cambridge History of Iran. 7 vols. Ed. Peter Jackson and Laurence Lockhart. Cambridge: Cambridge UP, 1991.

Cambridge History of Latin American Literature. 3 vols. Ed. Roberto González Echevarría and Enrique Pupo-Walker. Cambridge: Cambridge UP, 1996.

Campbell, Mary B. *The Witness and the other World: Exotic European Travel Writing, 400–1600*. Ithaca, NY: Cornell UP, 1988.

Carretta, Vincent. *Unchained Voices*. Lexington, KY: UP of Kentucky, 1996.

Carril, Pepe. *Shango de Ima, a Yoruba Mystery Play*. Garden City, NY: Doubleday, 1969.

Cary, Joyce. *Mister Johnson*. 1935. New York: New Directions, 1989.

Cassidy, Frederic C. *Jamaica Talk*. London: Macmillan, 1961.

Castillo, J. M. *Oba oriate: Ifa en Tierra de Ifa*. Miami: privately printed, 1976.

Chambers, Iain, and Linda Curti. *The Post-Colonial Question*. London and New York: Routledge, 1996.

Chamoiseau, Patrick, Raphaël Confiant and Jean Bernabé, *Éloge de la créolité*. Paris: Gallimard, 1989.

Chidester, David. "Bushman Religion: Open, Closed, and New Frontiers." In *Miscast: Negotiating the Presence of the Bushman*. Ed. Pippa Skotnes. U of Cape Town P, 1996. 51–59.

Chow, Rey. *Writing Diaspora: Tactics of Intervention in Contemporary Cultural Studies*. Bloomington, IN: Indiana UP, 1993.

Clarke, John Henrik. "African Warrior Queens." In *Black Women in Antiquity*. Ed. Ivan Van Sertima. New Brunswick, NJ: Transaction, 1984. 126–7.

Clifton, James, ed. *The Invented Indian: Cultural Fictions and Government Policies*. New Brunswick, NJ: Transaction, 1994.

Collins, Harold. *Onitsha Chap-Books*. Athens: Ohio UP, 1971.

Columbus, Christopher. *The Journal of Christopher Columbus*. Trans. Cecil Jane. New York: Bonanza, 1960.

———. *Select Documents Illustrating the Four Voyages of Columbus*. Trans. and ed. Cecil Jane. 2vols. London: Hakluyt Society, 1929 and 1932.

———. *The Book of Privileges Issued to Christopher Columbus by King Fernando and Queen Isabel, 1492–1502*. Ed. and trans. Helen Nader. Berkeley: U of California P, 1996.

———. *The Book of Prophecies Edited by Christopher Columbus*. Ed. Roberto Rusconi. Berkeley: U of California P, 1997.

Cook, James. *The Journals of Captain Cook on his Voyage of Discovery*. 3 vols. Ed. J. C. Beaglehole. Cambridge: Hakluyt, 1961 (vol. 1), 1967 (vols. 2 & 3).

Coombs, Orde ed. *Is Massa Day Dead?* Garden City, NY: Anchor/Doubleday, 1974.

Cortés, Fernando. *Fernando Cortés: Five Letters, 1519–1526*. Trans. J. Baynard Morris. New York: Norton, 1969.

Cortés, Fernando. *His Five Letters of Relation to the Emperor Charles V, 1519–1526.*. Trans. and ed. Francis Augustus MacNutt. 2 vols. Glorieta, NM: Rio Grande Press, 1977.

Cortés, Hernan. *Letters from Mexico*. Trans and ed. A. R. Pagden. New York: Grossman, 1971.

Culler, Jonathan. "De Man's Rhetoric." In *Framing the Sign: Criticism and Its Institutions*. Ed. Jonathan Culler. Oxford: Basil Blackwell, 1988. 107–35.

Cunard, Nancy, ed. *Negro: An Anthology*. 1934. New York: Continuum, 1996. A reprint of the 1970 edition with an introduction by Hugh Ford.

Curtin, Philip D., ed. *Africa and the West: Intellectual Responses to European Culture*. Madison: U of Madison P, 1972.

———. *Africa Remembered: Narratives by West Africans from the Era of the Slave Trade*. Madison: U of Wisconsin P, 1967.

Cypess, Sandra Messinger. *La Malinche in Mexican Literature: From History to Myth*. Austin: U of Texas P, 1991.

Damas, Léon. "Interview." *Journal of Caribbean Studies* 1.1 (Winter 1980): 63–73.

Dampier, William. *Dampier's Voyages*. 2 vols. London: E. Grant Richards, 1906.

Daston, Lorraine and Katherine Park, *Wonders and the Order of Nature, 1150–1750*. New York: Zone Books, 1998.

Dathorne, O. R., ed. *African Poetry*. London: Macmillan, 1969.

———. ed. *Journal of Caribbean Studies*. 1.1 (1980).

Dathorne, O. R., *Asian Voyages: Two Thousand Years of Constructing the Other*. Westport, CT, and London: Bergin & Garvey, 1996.

———. *The Black Mind: A History of African Literature*. Minneapolis: U of Minnesota P, 1974.

———. *Imagining the World: Mythical Belief versus Reality in Global Encounters*. Westport, CT, and London: Bergin & Garvey, 1994.

———. *In Europe's Image: The Need for American Multiculturalism*. Westport, CT, and London: Bergin & Garvey, 1994.

Davis, Gregson. *Aimé Césaire*. Cambridge: Cambridge UP, 1997.

Davis, Wade. *The Serpent and the Rainbow*. New York: Warner, 1985.

Debrunner, Hans Werner. *Presence and Prestige: Africans in Europe: A History of Africans in Europe before 1918*. Basel: Basler Afrika Bibliographien, 1979.

De Bry, Theodor. *América (1590–1634)*. Madrid: Siruela, 1995.

———. *Discovering the New World*. Ed. Michael Alexander. New York: Harper & Row, 1976.

Deleuze, Gilles, and Félix Guattari. *Anti-Oedipus: Capitalism and Schizophrenia*. 1972. Minneapolis: U of Minnesota P, 1983.

———. *Kafka: Toward a Minor Literature*. 1975. Trans. Dana Polan. Minneapolis: U of Minnesota P, 1986.

———. *A Thousand Plateaus: Capitalism and Schizophrenia*. 1980. Minneapolis: U of Minnesota P, 1987.

———. "What is a Minor Literature?" Trans. Rosere Appel et al. *Mississippi Review* 22.3 (1983): 13–33.

Dening, Greg. "The Theatricality of Observing and Being Observed: Eighteenth-Century Europe 'Discovers' the ? century 'Pacific.' " In *Implicit Understandings: Observing, Reporting, and Reflecting on the Encounters between European and other Peoples in the Early Modern Era*. Ed. Stuart B. Schwartz. Cambridge: Cambridge UP, 1994. 451–83.

Derrida, Jacques. *Margins of Philosophy*. Trans. Alan Bass. Chicago: U of Chicago P, 1982.

Diallo, Ayuba Suleiman [Job ben Solomon]. "Ayuba's Return to Africa." In *Africa Remembered: Narratives by West Africans from the Era of the Slave Trade*. Ed. Philip D. Curtin. Madison: U of Wisconsin P, 1967.

Díaz del Castillo, Bernal. *The Conquest of New Spain* [1632]. Trans. and ed. J. M.

Cohen. Harmondsworth, U.K: Penguin, 1965.

———.*The Discovery and Conquest of Mexico, 1517–1521.* [1632]. Trans. A. P. Maudslay and ed. Irving A. Leonard. New York: Farrar, Straus and Cudahy, 1956.

———. *The True History of the Conquest of New Spain.* [1632. Trans Alfred Maudslay and ed. Genaro García. 5 vols. London: Hakluyt Society, 1908–1916.

Diop, Cheikh Anta. *The African Origin of Civilization: Myth or Reality?* Trans. Mercer Cook. Westport, CT: Lawrence Hill, 1974.

———. *Civilization or Barbarism: An Authentic Anthropology.* 1981. Trans. Yaa-Lengi Meema Ngemi. Ed. H. J. Salemson and M. de Jager. New York: Lawrence Hill/Chicago Review, 1991.

Donald, James, and Ali Rattansi, ed. *"Race," Culture and Difference.* London: Sage, 1992.

Du Bois, W.E.B. *The Souls of Black Folk.* 1903. Boston: Bedford, 1997.

Dyer, Richard. *White.* London: Routledge, 1997.

Elenes, C. Alejandra, "Malinche, Guadalupe, and La Llorona: Patriarchy and the Formation of Mexican National Consciousness," in *Latin America: An Interdisciplinary Approach* ed. Julio López-Arias and Gladys M. Varona-Lacey. New York: Peter Lang, 1999, 87–99.

Erdoes, Richard, and Alfonso Ortiz. *American Indian Myths and Legends.* New York: Pantheon, 1984.

Eze, Emmanuel Chukwudi, ed. *Race and the Enlightenment: A Reader.* Cambridge, MA: Blackwell, 1997.

Faery, Rebecca Blevins. *Cartographies of Desire: Captivity, Race, and Sex in the Shaping of an American Nation .* Norman, OK: U of Oklahoma P, 1999.

Fanon, Frantz. *Black Skin, White Masks: The Experiences of a Black Man in a White World.* 1952. Trans. Charles Lam Markmann. New York: Grove, 1967.

———. *The Wretched of the Earth: A Negro Psychoanalyst's Study of the Problem of Racism and Colonialism in the World Today.* 1961. Trans. Constance Farrington. New York: Grove, 1966.

Feest, Christian F. "Europe's Indians." In *The Invented Indian: Cultural Fictions and Government Policies.* Ed. James Clifton. New Brunswick, NJ: Transaction, 1994, 313–32.

Fernández Olmos, Margarita, and Lizabeth Paravisni-Gebert, eds. *Sacred Possessions: Vodou, Santeria, Obeah and the Caribbean.* New Brunswick, NJ: Rutgers UP, 1997.

Feserman, Steven. "African Histories and the Dissolution of World History." In *Africa and the Disciplines.* Ed. Robert H. Bates, V. Y. Mudimbe, and Jean O'Barr. Chicago: U of Chicago P, 1993.

Fiedler, Leslie, and Houston A. Baker Jr., eds. *English Literature: Opening up the Canon.* Baltimore: Johns Hopkins UP, 1981.

Fielding. Henry. *An Apology for the Life of Mrs. Shamela Andrews. . . .* London: Printed for R. Dodd, 1741.

———. *The History of the Adventures of Joseph Andrews.* Dublin: Printed by S. Powell, 1742.

———.*The History of Tom Jones, a Foundling.* London: Printed for A. Millar, 1749.

Finnegan, Ruth. *Oral Literature in Africa.* Oxford: Clarendon, 1970.

Finney, Ben. *Voyage of Rediscovery: A Cultural Odyssey through Polynesia.* Berkeley: U of California P, 1994.

The First Three English Books on America [?1511]–1555 A.D. 1555. Trans. Richard

Eden. Ed. Edward Arber. Birmingham, U.K.: n.p., 1885.

Fish, Stanley. *Is There a Text in This Class? The Authority of Interpretive Communities.* Cambridge, MA: Harvard UP, 1980.

500 Nations . Parts 1–4. TV documentary and accompanying book. Columbia Broadcasting System, 1995.

Florescano, Enrique. *Memory, Myth and Time in Mexico: From the Aztecs to Independence.* Austin: U of Texas P, 1994.

Foote, Shelby. *The Civil War: A Narrative.* 3 vols. New York: Random, 1958 (vol. 1), 1963 (vol. 2), 1974 (vol. 3).

Forster, E. M. *A Passage to India.* 1924. San Diego: Harcourt Brace Jovanovich, 1952.

Foucault, Michel. *Language, Counter-memory, Practice: Selected Interviews and Essays.* Ed. D. F. Bouchard. New York: Cornell UP, 1977.

———. *The Order of Things: An Archaeology of the Human Sciences.* 1966. New York: Vintage, 1994.

———. *Power/Knowledge: Selected Interviews & Other Writings, 1972–1977.* New York: Pantheon, 1980.

Fraser, Walter H. *The First Landing Place of Juan Ponce de León.* St Augustine, FL: Walter H. Fraser, 1956.

Freak Shows. The Learning Channel, 1996.

Friede, Juan, and Benjamin Keen, eds. *Bartolomé de Las Casas in History: Toward an Understanding of the Man and His Work.* De Kalb, IL: Northern Illinois UP, 1971.

Friedman, John Block. *The Monstrous Races in Medieval Art and Thought.* Cambridge, MA: Harvard UP, 1981.

Fryer, Peter. *Staying Power: The History of Black People in Britain.* London: Pluto, 1984.

Fugard, Athol. *Master Harold and the Boys.* New York: Penguin, 1982.

———. *Sizwe Bansi is Dead.* Produced 1972.

Funkhouser, Erica. "Who was Sacagawea and How Did She Aid the Expedition?"<http://www.pbs.org/lewisandclark> Accessed October 26, 1999.

Garcilaso de la Vega. *The Florida of the Inca.* 1605. Trans. and ed. John Grier Varner and Jeannette Johnson Varner. Austin: U of Texas P, 1962.

Garvey, Marcus. *The Marcus Garvey and Universal Negro Improvement Association Papers.* Vol. 1, 1826–August 1919; vol. 2, August 1919–31 August 1920; vol. 3, September 1920–August 1921; vol. 4, September 1921–September 1922; vol. 5, September 1922–August 1924; vol. 6, September 1924–December 1927; vol. 7, November 1927–August 1940; vol. 8, March 1917–June 1921; vol. 9, June 1921–December 1922. Ed. Robert R. Hill. Berkeley: U of California P, 1983– .

Gates Jr., Henry Louis, ed. *"Race," Writing and Difference.* Chicago: U of Chicago P, 1986.

———. *The Signifying Monkey: A Theory of African-American Literary Criticism.* Oxford: Oxford UP, 1988.

Gates Jr., Henry Louis, and Maria Wolff. "An Overview of the Sources on the Life and Work of Juan Latino, the 'Ethiopian Humanist.' " *Research in African Literatures* 29.4: 14–51.

Georgia Writers' Project. *Drums and Shadows: Survival Studies among the Georgia Coastal Negroes.* Athens, GA: U of Georgia P, 1940.

Gerzina, Gretchen. *Black London: Life before Emancipation.* New Brunswick, NJ: Rutgers UP, 1995.

Gibb, Paul Allen."*Wonders of the East:* A Critical Edition and Commentary." Ph.D. diss., Duke University, 1977.

Gidley, Mick, ed. *Representing Others: White Views of Indigenous Peoples.* Exeter: U of Exeter P, 1992.

Gilman, Sander. "Black Bodies, White Bodies." In *"Race," Culture and Difference.* Ed. James Donald and Ali Rattansi. London: Sage, 1992.

Gleach Frederic W. *Powhatan's World and Colonial Virginia: A Conflict of Cultures* . Lincoln, NE: U of Nebraska P, 1997.

Glissant, Edouard. *Caribbean Discourse: Selected Essays* [1981] Trans. Michael Dash Charlottesville: UP of Virginia, 1989.

Goerke, Heinz. *Linnaeus.* Trans. Denver Lindley. New York: Scribner's, 1973.

Gomez, Michael A. *Exchanging Our Country Marks: The Transformation of African Identities in the Colonial and Antebellum South.* Chapel Hill, NC: U of North Carolina P, 1998.

The Great Indian Wars 1840–1890. Video documentary. Simitar Entertainment, 1991.

Gramsci, Antonio. *Prison Notebooks.* Ed. Joseph A. Buttigieg. Trans. Joseph A. Buttigieg and Antonio Callari. New York: Columbia UP, 1992–1996.

Green, Jeffrey. *Black Edwardians: Black People in Britain, 1901–1914.* London: Frank Cass, 1998.

Greenberg, Joseph H. *Languages of West Africa.* The Hague: Mouton, 1966.

———. *Universals of Language.* Cambridge, MA: MITP, 1963.

Greenblatt, Stephen. *Marvelous Possessions: The Wonder of the New World.* Chicago: U of Chicago P and Oxford: Oxford UP, 1991.

Grégoire, Henri. *On the Cultural Achievements of Negroes.* 1808. Trans. Thomas Cassirer and Jean-François Brière. Amherst, MA: U of Massachusetts P, 1996. 75–112.

Grossberg, Lawrence, Cary Nelson, and Paula A. Treichler, eds. *Cultural Studies.* New York: Routledge, 1992.

Gyeke, Kwame. *Tradition and Modernity: Philosophical Reflections on the African Experience.* New York: Oxford UP, 1997.

Hakluyt, Richard. *The Principal Navigations, Voyages, Traffiques and Discoveries of the English Nation.* 1598. 12 vols. Glasgow: James MacLehose and Sons, 1903–1905.

Hall, Hubert. *Society in the Elizabethan Age.* London: Swan Sonnenschein, 1902.

Hall, Kim F. *Things of Darkness: Economies of Race and Gender in Early Modern England.* Ithaca, NY: Cornell UP, 1995.

Hall, Stuart. "New Ethnicities." In *I. C. A Documents 7: Black Film, British Cinema.* Ed. Kobena Mercer. London: Institute of Contemporary Arts, 1988. 27–30. There is "revision" of this essay in *Stuart Hall: Critical Dialogues in Cultural Studies.* Ed. David Morley and Kuan-Hsing Chen. London and New York: Routledge, 1996, 441–9.

Hanke, Lewis. *All Mankind is One: A Study of the Disputation between Bartolomé de Las Casas and Juan Ginés de Sepúlveda in 1550 on the Intellectual and Religious Capacity of the American Indians.* De Kalb, IL: Northern Illinois UP, 1974.

———. *Bartolomé de Las Casas, Historian: An Essay in Spanish Historiography.* Gainesville, FL: U of Florida P, 1952.

Haraway, Donna. *Primate Visions: Gender, Race, and Nature in the World of Modern Science.* New York and London: Routledge, 1989.

Harris, Wilson. "History, Fable and Myth in the Caribbean and Guianas."

Caribbean Quarterly 16 (June 1970): 1–32.

Harvey, Paul, ed. *The Oxford Companion to Literature.* Oxford: Clarendon, 1960.

Hendricks, Margo and Patricia Parker eds. *Women, "Race," and Writing in the Early Modern Period.* London: Routledge, 1994.

Herodotus. *The Histories.* London: Penguin, 1954.

Herskovits, Melville. *The Myth of the Negro Past.* 1941. Boston: Beacon, 1990.

Hilger, Michael.*From Savage to Nobleman: Images of Native Americans in Film.* Lanham, MD: Scarecrow, 1995.

Hill, Donald R. *Calypso Calaloo: Early Carnival Music in Trinidad.* Gainesville: UP of Florida, 1993.

Hill, Errol. *The Jamaican Stage.* Amherst: U of Massachusetts P, 1992.

Hill, Robert. *The Marcus Garvey and Universal Negro Improvement Association Papers.* 9 vols. to date. Berkeley: U of California P, 1983– .

Holloway, Joseph E., ed. *Africanisms in American Culture.* Bloomington: Indiana UP, 1991.

Holloway, Joseph E., and Winifred K. Vass. *The African Heritage of American English.* Bloomington: Indiana UP, 1993.

How the West Was Lost. The Discovery Channel, 1994.

How the West Was Won. The Discovery Channel, 1993.

Hudson, Derek, ed. *Munby, Man of Two Worlds: The Life and Diaries of Arthur J. Munby, 1812–1910.* Cambridge: Gambit, 1974.

Hughes, Langston. *The Big Sea.* New York: Knopf, 1940.

Hughes, Langston, and Arna Bontemps. *The Book of Negro Folklore.* New York: Dodd, Mead, 1958.

Hulme, Peter. *Colonial Encounters: Europe and the Native Caribbean, 1492–1797* . London: Routledge, 1992.

———. "Tales of Distinction: European Ethnography and the Caribbean." *Implicit Understandings: Observing, Reporting, and Reflecting on the Encounters between European and other Peoples in the Early Modern Era.* Ed. Stuart B. Schwartz. 157–97.

Hurston, Zora Neale. *Dust Tracks on a Road: An Autobiography.* Philadelphia: Lippincott, 1942.

Hutgren, M. L., and P. Molin. *To Lead and Serve: American Indian Education at Hampton Institute.* Virginia Beach, VA: Virginia Foundation for the Humanities and Public Policy, 1989.

Ibn Fadl Allah Al-'Umari. *Masalik Al-absar fi Mamalik al-amsar.* Cairo, 1342. In "Africa in Inter-Continental Relations." Ed. J. Devisse and S. Labib. *Africa from the Twelfth to the Sixteenth Century.* Vol. 4 of 8 vols. In *General History of Africa.* Ed. D. T. Niane. Paris: UNESCO, 1984. 635–72.

Idowu, E. Bolaji. *Olódùmarè: God in Yoruba Belief.* London: Longmans, 1962.

Image of the Black in Western Art. Ed. Ladislas Bugner. 5 vols. to date. Cambridge, MA: Harvard UP, 1976– .

Jahn, Janheinz. *A History of Neo-African Literature: Writing in Two Continents* . London: Faber and Faber, 1966.

James, Winston. *Holding Aloft the Banner of Ethiopia: Caribbean Radicalism in Early Twentieth-Century America.* London: Verso, 1998.

Jefferson, Thomas. "Notes on the State of Virginia." 1785. *Writings.* New York: Library of America, 1984.

Jones, Eldred D. "Krio: An English-Based Language of Sierra Leone." *The English Language in West Africa.* Ed. John Spencer. London: Longman, 1971. 66–94.

————. *Othello's Countrymen: The African in English Renaissance Drama.* Oxford: Oxford UP, 1965.

Jones, Eldred D. and Clifford N. Fyle. *The Krio-English Dictionary.* Oxford: Oxford UP, 1980.

Jonson, Ben. *Timber: or Discoveries.* 1641. In *English Critical Essays.* Ed. Edmund D. Jones. London: Oxford UP, 1956.

————. *The Works of Ben Jonson.* Ed. William Gifford. London: Edward Moxon, 1853.

Jordan, Winthrop.*White over Black: American Attitudes Toward the Negro, 1550–1812.* Chapel Hill: U of North Carolina P, 1968.

Kafka, Franz. *The Castle.* 1926. Harmondsworth, U.K: Penguin, 1930.

————. *The Trial.* 1925. Harmondsworth, U.K: Penguin, 1953.

Karenga, Maulana. *The African American Holiday of Kwanza: A Celebration of Family, Community and Culture.* Los Angeles: U of Sankore P, 1988.

Kessler, Donna J. *The Making of Sacagawea: A Euro-American Legend.* Tuscaloosa, AL: U of Alabama P, 1996.

Killingray, David, ed. *Africans in Britain.* Ilford, U.K: Frank Cass, 1994.

Kilpatrick, Jacquelyn. *Celluloid Indians: Native Americans and Film.* Lincoln, NE: U of Nebraska P, 1999.

Koerner, Lisbet. "Purposes of Linnaean Travel: A Preliminary Research Report." In *Visions of Empire: Voyages, Botany, and Representations of Nature.* Ed. David Philip Miller and Peter Hannis Reill. Cambridge and New York: Cambridge UP, 1996. 117–52.

Kunhardt, Peter W., Philip B. Kunhardt Jr., and Philip B. Kunhardt III. *Barnum: Prince of Showmen.* New York: Random, 1995.

Lacan, Jacques. *Écrits: A Selection.* 1966. New York: Norton, 1977.

La Guma, Alex. *A Walk in the Night.* 1962. Evanston, IL: Northwestern UP, 1967.

Las Casas, Bartolomé de. *The Devastation of the Indies: A Brief Account.* 1552. Trans. Herma Briffault. Baltimore, MD: Johns Hopkins UP, 1992.

————. *In Defense of the Indians: The Defense of the Most Reverend Lord Don Fray Bartolomé de Las Casas of the Order of Preachers, Last Bishop of Chiapa, against the Persecutors and Slanderers of the People of the New World Discovered across the Seas.* De Kalb, IL: Northern Illinois UP, 1974.

Latino, Juan. *Ad Catholicum (pariter et invictissimum) Philippum dei gratia Hispaniarum regem, de foelicissima serenissimi Fernandi principis navitate. Epigrammatum Liber.* Garnatas [Granada], 1573. 9–25 [British Library].

————. *Austrias. Carmen de excellentissimi domini. D. Ioannis ab Austria, Caroli Quinti filii, ac Philippi invictissimi fratis, re bene gesta, in victoria mirabili eius dem Philippi adversus perfidos Turcas parta, ad illustrissimum. Pariter & reverendissimum D. D. Petrum a deza prassidem, ac pro Philippo militiae preafectu per Magistrum Ioannem Latinum garnatae studiosae adolescentiae moderatorem. Libri Duo.* Garnatas [Granada], 1573. Book 1, 1–15. Book 2, 16–36 [British Lib.].

————. *Deque sanctissimi Pii Quinti Romanae ecclesiae pontificis summi rebus & affectibus erga Phillipum regem Christianissimum. Liber Unus.* Garnatas [Granada], 1573. 26–45 [British Lib.].

Latour, Bruno.*We Have Never Been Modern.* New York: Harvester Wheatsheaf, 1993.

Latour, Bruno and Steve Woolgar, *Laboratory Life: The Social Construction of Scientific Facts.* Beverly Hills, CA: Sage, 1979.

Laye, Camara. *The Radiance of the King.* 1956. New York: Collier, 1971.

Leed, Eric. *Shores of Discovery: How Expeditionaries Have Constructed the World*. New York: Basic, 1995.

Lefkowitz, Mary R. *Not out of Africa: How Afrocentrism Became an Excuse to Teach Myth as History*. New York: Basic, 1996.

Lefkowitz, Mary R., and Guy MacLean Rogers, eds. *Black Athena Revisited*. Chapel Hill, NC: U of North Carolina, 1996.

Lemke, Sieglinde. *Primitivist Modernism: Black Culture and the Origin of Transatlantic Modernism*. Oxford: Oxford UP, 1998.

Lévi-Strauss, Claude. *The Savage Mind*. 1962. Chicago: U of Chicago P, 1966.

Lewis, David Levering. *When Harlem was in Vogue*. New York: Knopf, 1981.

Lindsay, Vachel. *The Congo and other Poems*. New York: Macmillan, 1914.

Little, Kenneth. *Negroes in Britain: A Study of Racial Relations In English Society*. London: Kegan Paul, 1947.

Lochner, Norbert. "Anton Wilhelm Amo: A Ghana Scholar in Eighteenth-century Germany." *Transactions of the Historical Society of Ghana* (c.1959) 3.3: 169–79.

Locke, Gladys E. *Queen Elizabeth*. Boston: Sherman, French and Company, 1913.

Lockhart, James. "Sightings: Initial Nahua Reactions to Spanish Culture." In *Implicit Understandings: Observing, Reporting, and Reflecting on the Encounters between European and other Peoples in the Early Modern Era*. Ed. Stuart B. Schwartz. Cambridge: Cambridge UP, 218–48.

Lomawaima, K. Tsianina. *They Called It Prairie Light*. Lincoln: U of Nebraska P, 1994.

Long, Edward. *A History of Jamaica*. London: printed for T. Lowndes, 1774.

MacCullough, N. V. *The Negro in English Literature*. Ilfracombe: Stockwell, 1962.

MacInnes, Colin. *City of Spades*. 1957. New York: Farrar, Straus and Giroux, 1969.

Malcolm X, with the assistance of Alex Haley. *The Autobiography of Malcolm X*. 1965. New York: Ballantine, 1973.

Marinelli, Peter V. *Aristo and Boiardo: The Origins of* Orlando Furioso. Columbia: U of Missouri P, 1987.

Marlowe, Christopher. "Tamburlaine the Great" Part II in *The Works of Christopher Marlowe*. Ed. Francis Cunningham. London: Chatto and Windus, 1889.

Martyr, Peter D'Anghera. *De Orbe Novo: The Eight Decades of Peter Martyr D'Anghera*. 2 vols. Trans. Francis Augustus MacNutt. New York: Burt Franklin, 1970.

Massing, Jean Michel. "Early European Images of America: The Ethnographic Approach." In *Circa 1492: Art in the Age of Exploration*. Ed. Jay A. Levinson. Washington, D.C.: National Gallery of Art, 1991. 515–20.

Mazrui, Ali. *The Africans: A Triple Heritage*. Boston: Little, Brown, 1986.

McClintock, Anne. *Imperial Leather: Race, Gender and Sexuality in the Colonial Context*. New York and London: Routledge, 1995.

McCrum, Robert, William Cran, and Robert McNeil. *The Story of English*. New York: Penguin, 1993.

McDonald, Joyce Green, ed. "Introduction" to *Race, Ethnicity and Power in the Renaissance*. Cranbury, NJ: Associated U Presses, 1997.

McDonnell, Janet A. *The Dispossession of the American Indian*. Bloomington: Indiana UP, 1991.

Megenney, William. *Cuba and Brasil: Etnohistoria del Empleo Religioso del Lenguaje Afro Americano*. Miami: Ediciones Universal, 1999.

Métraux, Alfred. *Voodoo in Haiti*. London: Andre Deutsch, 1959.

Miller, David Philip, and Peter Hannis Reill, eds. *Visions of Empire: Voyages, Botany, and Representations of Nature.* Cambridge and New York: Cambridge UP, 1996.

Mills, David. "Half Truths and History: The Debate over Jews and the Slave Trade." *Guardian Weekly* 149.18 (Oct. 31, 1993): 18–19.

Moore, Carlos. *Castro, the Blacks and Africa.* Los Angeles: Center for Afro-American Studies, UCLA, 1918.

Moore, Gerald, and Ulli Beier, eds. *The Penguin Book of Modern African Poetry.* London: Penguin, 1984.

Moore, Robin D. *Nationalizing Blackness: Afrocubanismo and Artistic Revolution in Havana, 1920–1940.* Pittsburgh: U of Pittsburgh P, 1997.

Morison, Samuel Eliot. *The European Discovery of America: Southern Voyages, 1492–1616.* New York: Oxford UP, 1974.

Morley, David, and Kuan-Hsing Chen, eds. *Stuart Hall: Critical Dialogues in Cultural Studies.* London and New York: Routledge, 1996.

Morrison, Toni. *Beloved.* New York: Knopf, 1987.

———. *Song of Solomon.* New York: Knopf, 1978.

Muir, Kenneth, ed. *Elizabethan and Jacobean Prose, 1550–1620.* London: Penguin, 1956

Munns, Jessica, and Gita Rajan, eds. *A Cultural Studies Reader: History, Theory, Practice.* London and New York: Longman, 1995.

Münster, Sebastian. *Cosmographiae Universalis.* 1550. Readex Microprint Corporation, 1966.

Murphy, Joseph M. *Santería: An African Religion in America.* Boston: Beacon, 1988.

———. *Working the Spirit.* Boston: Beacon Press, 1994.

Myers, Norma. *Reconstructing the Black Past: Blacks in Britain, 1780–1830.* London: Frank Cass, 1930.

Nabokov, Peter, ed. *Native American Testimony.* New York: Penguin, 1978.

Naipaul, V. S. *A House for Mr. Biswas.* London: Andre Deutsch, 1961.

The Native Americans. TV documentary and accompanying book. Turner Broadcasting System, 1994.

Ngugi wa Thiong'o. *Decolonising the Mind: The Politics of Language in African Literature.* London: James Currey, 1986.

———. *Homecoming.* London: Heinemann, 1972.

———. *Moving the Center: The Struggle for Cultural Freedoms.* London: James Currey, 1993.

Nicoll, Charles. *Somebody Else: Arthur Rimbaud in Africa, 1880–91.* London: Jonathan Cape, 1997.

Nketia, J. H. Kwabena. *Folk Songs of Ghana.* Legon, Ghana: U of Ghana, 1963.

———. *Funeral Dirges of the Akan People.* Achimota, Ghana: n.p., 1955.

Nwoga, Donatus. "Onitsha Market Literature." *Transition* 4 (1963): 26–33.

Obeyesekere, Gananath. *The Apotheosis of Captain Cook.* Princeton: Princeton UP, 1992.

O'Neill, Eugene. "The Emperor Jones." In *Nine Plays.* New York: Random, 1932. 2–35.

Ortiz, Fernando. *Los Negros Brujos.* 1906. Miami: Ediciones Universal, 1963.

Osborne, John. *Look Back in Anger.* Performed London 1956. New York: Criterion, 1957.

Parker, Patricia. "Fantasies of 'Race' and 'Gender': Africa, *Othello,* and Bringing to the Light," in *Women, "Race" and Writing in the Early Modern Period* ed.

Margo Hendricks and Patricia Parker. London: Routledge, 1994, 84–100.

Paton, Alan. *Cry, The Beloved Country.* 1948. New York: Scribner's, 1968.

Peacock, Seth, and Ruth Peacock. *Spirits of the Deep.* Garden City, NY: Anchor, Doubleday, 1975.

Perry, Bruce. *Malcolm: The Life of a Man Who Changed Black America.* Barrytown, NY: Station Hill, 1991.

Phillips, Caryl. *The European Tribe.* London: Faber and Faber, 1987.

Pollak-Elzt, Angelina. *Black Culture and Society in Venezuela.* Caracas, Venezuela: Lagoven, 1994.

Potkay, Adam and Sandra Burr. *Black Atlantic Writers of the Eighteenth Century.* New York: St. Martin's Press, 1995.

Prah, Kwesi Kwaa. *Jacobus Eliza Johannes Capitein, 1717–1747.* Trenton, NJ: Africa World, 1992.

Pratt, Mary Louise. *Imperial Eyes: Travel Writing and Transculturation.* London and New York: Routledge, 1992.

Price, Richard, and Sidney M. Mintz. *An Anthropological Approach to the Afro-American Past: A Caribbean Perspective.* Philadelphia: ISHU, 1976.

Price-Mars, Jean. *So Spoke the Uncle.* 1928. Trans. Magdaline W. Shannon. Washington, D.C.: Three Continents, 1983.

Prince, Gerald. "Introduction to the Study of the Narratee." In *Reader Response Criticism.* Ed. Jane P. Tompkins. Baltimore: Johns Hopkins UP, 1980. 7–25.

P. T. Barnum: Prince of Showmen. 3 parts. The Discovery Channel, 1995.

Quinn, David Beers. *The Roanoke Voyages, 1584–1590.* 2 vols. London: The Hakluyt Society, 1955.

Rampersad, Arnold. *The Life of Langston Hughes.* 2 vols. New York: Oxford UP, 1986.

Read, Jan. *The Moors in Spain and Portugal.* London: Faber and Faber, 1974.

Reed, John, and Clive Wake, eds. *A Book of African Verse.* London: Heinemann, 1964.

Reid, Michaela. *Ask Sir James.* 1987. London: Eland, 1996.

"Re-inventing Britain Conference." British Council, March 2, 1997. <http://www.britcoun.org/studies/stdsprog.htm>. Accessed Oct. 9, 1998.

Report of the U.S. Senate Committee on Labor and Public Welfare, Special Sub Committee on Indian Education. [Senate Report #91–501]. Washington, D.C.: U.S. Government Printing Office, 1969.

Richardson, Samuel, *Pamela: or, Virtue Rewarded. . . .* London: Printed for C. Rivington, . . . and J. Osborn . . . ,1741.

Rimbaud, Arthur. *Rimbaud: Complete Works, Selected Letters.* Trans. Wallace Fowlie. Chicago: U of Chicago P, 1966.

———. *Correspondance, 1888–1891.* Ed. Jean Voellmy. Paris: Gallimard, 1965.

Robertson, George, Melinda Mash et al., eds. *Travellers' Tales: Narratives of Home and Displacement.* New York: Routledge, 1994.

Roediger, David R. *The Wages of Whiteness: Race and the Making of the American Working Class.* London and New York: Verso, 1991.

Rogers, J. A. *World's Great Men of Color.* New York: J. A. Rogers, 1946.

Roger, Jacques. *Buffon: A Life in Natural History.* Ithaca, NY: Cornell UP, 1997.

Rollins, Peter C. and John E. O'Connor eds., *Hollywood's Indian: The Portrayal of the Native American in Film.* Lexington, KY: U P of Kentucky, 1998.

Ross, Angus, ed. *Selections from* The Tatler *and* The Spectator. Harmondsworth, U.K.: Penguin, 1982.

Ross, Robert. "The Self-Image of Jacob Adams." In *Miscast: Negotiating the Presence of the Bushmen.* Ed. Pippa Skotnes. Cape Town: U of Cape Town P, 1996. 61–65.

Roumain, Jacques. *Masters of the Dew.* 1947. Trans. Langston Hughes and Mercer Cook. New York: Collier, 1971.

Rowse, A. L. *The Expansion of Elizabethan England.* London: Macmillan, 1955.

Sahagún, Fray Bernardino de. *Florentine Codex, General History of the Things of New Spain.* 12 vols. Ed. Arthur J. O. Anderson and Charles Dibble. Salt Lake City: School of American Research and U of Utah, 1950–1982.

Said, Edward W. *Beginnings: Intention and Method.* New York: Columbia UP, 1985.

———.*Culture and Imperialism.* New York: Vintage, 1994.

Sandiford Keith A. *Measuring the Moment: Strategies of Protest in Eighteenth Century Afro-English Writing.* Cranbury, NJ: Associated University Presses, 1988.

Saussure, Ferdinand de. *Course in General Linguistics.* Ed. Charles Bally and Albert Sechehaye. Trans. Roy Harris. La Salle, IL: Open Court, 1986.

Scobie, Edward. *Black Britannia: A History of Blacks in Britain.* Chicago: Johnson, 1972.

Schiebinger, Londa L. *Nature's Body: Gender in the Making of Modern Science.* Boston: Beacon Press, 1993.

Schmidt, Nancy J. "Nigeria: Fiction for the Average Man." *Africa Report* 10 (August 1965): 39–41.

Schwartz, Stuart B., ed. *Implicit Understandings: Observing, Reporting, and Reflecting on the Encounters between European and other Peoples in the Early Modern Era.* Cambridge: Cambridge UP, 1994.

The Secret Relationship between Blacks and Jews. Vol. 1. Boston, MA: Nation of Islam, 1991.

Sephocle, Marilyn. "Anton Wilhelm Amo." *Journal of Black Studies* 23.2 (Dec. 1992): 182–87.

Shapiro, James. "A Jew at the Globe." *The Chronicle of Higher Education* (June 26, 1998): B 4–5.

Sharpley-Whiting, T. Denean. *Black Venus: Sexualized Savages, Primal Fears, and Primitive Narratives in French.* Durham, NC: Duke UP, 1999.

Shirley, Rodney W. *The Mapping of the World: Early Printed World Maps, 1472–1700.* London: Holland Press Cartographia, 1984.

Shyllon, Folarin. *Black People in Britain, 1555–1833.* London: Oxford UP for Institute of Race Relations, 1977.

Simpson, George Eaton. *Black Religions in the New World.* New York: Columbia UP, 1978.

Skotnes, Pippa, ed. *Miscast: Negotiating the Presence of the Bushmen.* Cape Town: U of Cape Town P, 1996.

Skovmand, Michael, and Steffen Skovmand. *The Angry Young Men: Osborne, Sillitoe, Wain, Braine, Amis.* Copenhagen: Akademisk Forlag, 1975.

Slessarev, Ysevolod. *Prester John: The Letter and the Legend.* Minneapolis: U of Minnesota P, 1959.

Smith, John. *The Complete Works of Captain John Smith (1580–1631)* ed. Philip L. Barbour. 3 vols .Chapel Hill: U of North Carolina P, 1986.

Smitherman, Geneva. *Talkin' and Testifyin': The Language of Black America*. Boston: Houghton Mifflin, 1977.

Soto, Hernando de. *The De Soto Chronicles: The Expedition of Hernando de Soto to North America in 1539–1543*. 2 vols. Ed. Lawrence A. Clayton, Vernon James Knight Jr., and Edward C. Moore. Tuscaloosa, AL: U of Alabama P, 1993.

Soyinka, Wole. *Aké: The Years of Childhood*. London: Rex Collings, 1981.

———. *Collected Plays*. 2 vols. Oxford: Oxford UP, 1974.

Spencer, John, ed. *The English Language in West Africa*. London: Longman, 1971.

Spenser, Edmund. *The Fairie Queene* [1590 and 1596]. New Haven: Yale UP, 1981.

———. *Languages of West Africa*. The Hague: Mouton, 1966.

Spivak, Gayatri Chakravorty. *A Critique of Post-Colonial Reason: Toward a History of the Vanishing Present*. Cambridge, MA: Harvard UP, 1999.

———. *Outside in the Teaching Machine*. New York: Routledge, 1993.

———. "Three Women's Texts and a Critique of Imperialism." *"Race," Writing and Difference*. Ed. Henry Louis Gates Jr. Chicago: U of Chicago P, 1986. 262–80.

Spratlin, Valaurez Burwell. *Juan Latino: Slave and Humanist*. New York: Spinner, 1938.

Stallybrass, Peter. "Shakespeare, the Individual, and the Text." In *Cultural Studies*. Ed. Lawrence Grossberg, Cary Nelson, and Paula A. Treichler. New York: Routledge, 1992. 593–612.

Stanley, Liz, ed. *The Diaries of Hannah Cullwick: Victorian Maidservant*. New Brunswick: Rutgers UP, 1984.

Stefansson, Vilhjalmur, ed. *The Three Voyages of Martin Frobisher*. London: Argonaut, 1938.

Stein, Gertrude. *Three Lives*. 1909. New York: Vintage, 1936.

Suckale-Redlefsen, Gude. *Mauritius: Der helige Mohr/The Black Saint Maurice*. Houston, TX: Menil Foundation, 1987.

Sypher, Wylie. *Guinea's Captive Kings: British Anti-Slavery Literature of the Eighteenth Century*. Chapel Hill: U of North Carolina P, 1942.

Thevet, André. *The New Found Worlde, or Antarctike wherein is Contained Wonderful and Strange Things, as well of Humaine Creatures, as Beastes, Fishes, Foules, and Serpents, Trees, Plants, Mines of Golde and Siluer: Garnished with Many Learned Authorities*. In French 1558. London: Henry Bynneman, 1568.

Thomas, David Hurst, Jay Miller et al., eds. *The Native Americans: An Illustrated History*. Atlanta, GA: Turner, 1993.

Thomas, Lamont D. *Paul Cuffe: Black Entrepreneur and Pan-Africanist*. Urbana, IL: U of Illinois P, 1988.

Tolan, John Victor. *Medieval Christian Perceptions of Islam: A Book of Essays*. New York: Garland, 1996.

Torgovnich, Marianna. *Gone Primitive: Savage Intellect, Modern Lives*. Chicago: U of Chicago P, 1990.

Trennert, Robert. *The Phoenix Indian School: Forced Assimilation in Arizona*. Norman: U of Oklahoma P, 1988.

Triulzi, Allessandro. "African Cities. Historical Memory and Street Buzz." In *The Post-Colonial Question*. Ed. Ian Chambers and Linda Curti. London and New York: Routledge, 1996. 78–91.

Turner, Frederick, ed., *The Portable Native America Reader*. New York: Penguin, 1973.

Turner, Frederick Jackson. "The Significance of the Frontier in American

History." In *America: One Land, One People*. Ed. Robert C. Baron. Golden, CO: Fulcrum, 1987. 245–77.

Turner, Lorenzo. *Africanisms in the Gullah Dialect*. Chicago: U of Chicago P, 1949.

Tutuola, Amos. *The Palm Wine Drinkard*. London: Faber and Faber, 1952.

Utley, Robert M. *The Indian Frontier of the American West, 1846–1890*. Albuquerque: U of New Mexico P, 1984.

Van Sertima, Ivan. *Black Women in Antiquity*. New Brunswick, NJ: Transaction, 1984.

——. *They Came before Columbus*. New York: Random, 1976.

Van Vechten, Carl. *Nigger Heaven*. New York: Knopf, 1926.

Vass, Winifred K. *The Bantu Speaking Heritage of the United States*. Los Angeles: Center for Afro-American Studies, UCLA, 1979.

Vaughan, Alden T., and Virginia Mason Vaughan. "Before *Othello*: Elizabethan Representations of Sub-Saharan Africans." *The William and Mary Quarterly* 3d Series, 54.1 (January 1997): 19–44.

Vespucci, Amerigo. *Letters from a New World*. Ed. Luciano Formisano. New York: Marsilio, 1992.

Walcott, Derek. *Dream on Monkey Mountain and Other Plays*. New York: Farrar, Straus and Giroux, 1970.

——. "Drums and Colours." *Caribbean Quarterly* 38.4 (Dec. 1992): 22–134. Reprint of *Caribbean Quarterly* 7.1–2 (March–June, 1961).

——. *The Gulf and Other Poems*. London: Jonathan Cape, 1969.

——. *In a Green Night*. London: Jonathan Cape, 1962.

——. *Midsummer*. New York: Noonday, 1993. Not paginated.

——. "The Muse of History." In *Is Massa Day Dead?* Ed. Orde Coombs. Garden City, N.Y.:Anchor/Doubleday, 1974. 1–28.

——. *The Odyssey*. New York: Noonday, 1993.

——. *Omeros*. New York: Farrar, Straus and Giroux, 1990.

War against the Indians. The Discovery Channel, 1995.

Waugh, Evelyn. *A Handful of Dust*. 1934. Boston: Little, Brown, 1962.

The Way West. Parts 1 and 2. TV Documentary and accompanying book. Also televised as "The American Experience," Public Broadcasting Service, 1995.

Weatherford, Jack. *Native Roots: How the Indians Enriched America*. NewYork: Fawcett Columbine, 1991.

Weiss, Peter. *The Persecution and Assassination of Jean-Paul Marat as Performed by the Inmates of the Asylum of Charenton under the Direction of the Marquis de Sade*. Performed 1964. New York: Highgate, 1966.

Werbner, Richard, and Terence Ranger, eds. *Postcolonial Identities in Africa*. London: Zed, 1996.

Whiteley, W. H., ed. *A Selection of African Prose*. 2 vols. Oxford: Clarendon, 1964.

Whitten, Norman E. Jr., and Arlene Torres. *Blackness in Latin America and the Caribbean* ed. vols 1 and 2. Bloomington, IN: Indiana UP, 1998

Wiener, Leo. *Africa and the Discovery of America*. 3 vols. Philadelphia: Innes and Sons, 1920, 1923.

The Wild West. Rebroadcast The Discovery Channel, 1995. Parts 1–7.

Winchester, Simon. "After Dire Straits, an Agonising Haul across the Pacific,"*Smithsonian* 22:1, 84–93.

Wroth, Lady Mary. *The First Part of the Countess of Montgomery's Urania (1621)*. Ed. Josephine A. Roberts. Binghamton, NY: Center for Medieval and Early Renaissance Studies, SUNY at Binghamton, 1995.

———. *The Second Part of the Countess of Montgomery's Urania* ed. Josephine Roberts, Suzanne Gossett, and Janet Mueller. Tempe, AZ: Arizona Center for Medieval and Renaissance Studies, 2000.

Wynter, Sylvia. *The Hills of Hebron*. London: Jonathan Cape, 1962.

Young, Robert J. C. *Colonial Desire: Hybridity in Theory, Culture and Race*. London and New York: Routledge, 1995.

———. *White Mythologies: Writing History and the West*. London and New York: Routledge, 1990.

Index

About the Author

O. R. DATHORNE is Professor of English at the University of Kentucky. He directs the Association of Caribbean Studies and has been the editor of the *Journal of Caribbean Studies* for two decades. He is a Fellow of the Royal Society of Arts and a Fellow of the Royal Society of Economics. He is the author of more than one hundred learned articles, short stories, poems, plays, and scholarly works, including *The Black Mind, Dark Ancestor, In Europe's Image: The Need for American Multiculturalism, Imagining the World: Mythical Belief versus Reality in Global Encounters,* and *Asian Voyages: Two Thousand Years of Constructing the Other.*